AF182233

DEMOCRACY AND ONTOLOGY

This book investigates the relationship between liberal democracies and ontology, that is, philosophical claims about the constitution of agents and the social world. Many philosophers argue that ontology needs to be avoided in political and legal philosophy. In fact, political liberalism, a highly influential paradigm founded by the philosopher John Rawls, makes the avoidance of ontology a core ambition of its 'political, non-metaphysical' programme. In contrast to political liberalism, this book argues that attending to ontological disputes is essential to political and legal philosophy. Illuminating, criticising and developing ontological arguments does not only enhance our understanding of justice, but also highlights key features of democratic citizenship. The argument is built up by bringing together three traditions of thought that have so far not been confronted with one another: political liberalism, the work of Michel Foucault, and the psychoanalytic theories of Sigmund Freud and Donald Winnicott. The book also investigates more concrete implications of ontological disputes by drawing on several case studies: a Dutch political-legal debate about greeting rituals; an American conflict about the legalisation of religious freedom; and the struggles for resilience of two American social movement groups.

European Academy of Legal Theory Monograph Series: Volume 13

EUROPEAN ACADEMY OF LEGAL THEORY MONOGRAPH SERIES

General Editors
Professor Mark Van Hoecke
Professor François Ost

Titles in this Series

Moral Conflict and Legal Reasoning
Scott Veitch

The Harmonisation of European Private Law
Edited by Mark Van Hoecke & Francois Ost

On Law and Legal Reasoning
Fernando Atria

Law as Communication
Mark Van Hoecke

Legisprudence
Edited by Luc Wintgens

Epistemology and Methodology of Comparative Law
Edited by Mark van Hoecke

Making the Law Explicit.
The Normativity of Legal Argumentation
Matthias Klatt

The Policy of Law
A Legal Theoretical Framework
Mauro Zamboni

Methodologies of Legal Research
Which Kind of Method for What Kind of Discipline?
Edited by Mark van Hoecke

Objectivity in Law and Legal Reasoning
Edited by Jaakko Husa and Mark van Hoecke

An Introduction to Comparative Law Theory and Method
Geoffrey Samuel

The Tapestry of Reason
An Inquiry into the Nature of Coherence and its Role in Legal Argument
Amalia Amaya

Democracy and Ontology

Agonism between Political Liberalism, Foucault and Psychoanalysis

Irena Rosenthal

•HART•
PUBLISHING
OXFORD AND PORTLAND, OREGON
2018

Hart Publishing
An imprint of Bloomsbury Publishing Plc

Hart Publishing Ltd
Kemp House
Chawley Park
Cumnor Hill
Oxford OX2 9PH
UK

Bloomsbury Publishing Plc
50 Bedford Square
London
WC1B 3DP
UK

www.hartpub.co.uk
www.bloomsbury.com

Published in North America (US and Canada) by
Hart Publishing
c/o International Specialized Book Services
920 NE 58th Avenue, Suite 300
Portland, OR 97213-3786
USA

www.isbs.com

HART PUBLISHING, the Hart/Stag logo, BLOOMSBURY and the Diana logo are trademarks of Bloomsbury Publishing Plc

First published 2018

© Irena Rosenthal 2018

Irena Rosenthal has asserted her right under the Copyright, Designs and Patents Act 1988 to be identified as Author of this work.

All rights reserved. No part of this publication may be reproduced or transmitted in any form or by any means, electronic or mechanical, including photocopying, recording, or any information storage or retrieval system, without prior permission in writing from the publishers.

While every care has been taken to ensure the accuracy of this work, no responsibility for loss or damage occasioned to any person acting or refraining from action as a result of any statement in it can be accepted by the authors, editors or publishers.

All UK Government legislation and other public sector information used in the work is Crown Copyright ©. All House of Lords and House of Commons information used in the work is Parliamentary Copyright ©. This information is reused under the terms of the Open Government Licence v3.0 (http://www.nationalarchives.gov.uk/doc/open-government-licence/version/3) except where otherwise stated.

All Eur-lex material used in the work is © European Union, http://eur-lex.europa.eu/, 1998–2018.

British Library Cataloguing-in-Publication Data
A catalogue record for this book is available from the British Library.

ISBN: HB: 978-1-50991-221-6
ePDF: 978-1-50991-223-0
ePub: 978-1-50991-222-3

Library of Congress Cataloging-in-Publication Data
A catalogue record for this book is available from the Library of Congress.

Typeset by Compuscript Ltd, Shannon

To find out more about our authors and books visit www.hartpublishing.co.uk. Here you will find extracts, author information, details of forthcoming events and the option to sign up for our newsletters.

Acknowledgements

This book was born during my PhD at VU University Amsterdam and could not have been written without the help and support of many people. I would like to thank my two supervisors—Arend Soeteman and Bert van den Brink—for their trust and constructive comments. To Hent de Vries I am indebted for enabling me to do research at the inspiring and intellectually vibrant Humanities Center at Johns Hopkins University. The Fulbright Foundation, the Prins Bernhard Cultuurfonds and the Radboudstichting provided financial support for this wonderful stay. I am also grateful for all the comments on parts of the book that I received from Huub van Baar, Marieke Borren, Govert Buijs, Luigi Corrias, Toni van Gennip, Annemie Halsema, Bonnie Honig, Yolande Jansen, Bart van Klink, Laura Henderson, Hans Lindahl, Gijs van Oenen, Julia van Ooststroom, Nanda Oudejans, David Owen, Roland Pierik, Herman Siemens, Wouter Veraart, Marc de Wilde and Bertjan Wolthuis.

Parts of some chapters have been published earlier as articles. For permission to reprint some of my previously published work, I would like to make the following acknowledgements: part of chapter six appeared as 'Aggression and Play in the Face of Adversity: A Psychoanalytic Reading of Democratic Resilience' (2016) 44 in *Political Theory* 337; parts of chapter two and three appeared in 'Ontology and Political Theory: A critical encounter between Rawls and Foucault', (2016) in *European Journal for Political Theory*, preprint available: DOI: 10.1177/1474885116659633.

I also thank my parents Uri Rosenthal and Dinah Rosenthal-Epstein and my sister Daphne Rosenthal for their support. Above all, I owe gratitude to my partner Haye Koningsveld for helping me disentangle some arguments and for lightening up more than a few difficult writing days. Our two children—Samuel and Dimitri—fill my days with lessons in agonism and tremenduous joy.

Contents

1

Introduction

IN RECENT YEARS, the Netherlands has been confronted with various public debates and legal conflicts about orthodox Muslim citizens who refuse to shake hands with members of the other sex at political meetings, in the civil service, in schools and on the job market. As in many other Western European countries, the handshake is an important aspect of Dutch codes of civility. The shaking of hands establishes a feeling of mutual respect among strangers, colleagues and acquaintances alike, and many citizens consider the ritual essential to their civic identities. Not all citizens, however, want to participate in this greeting ritual. Some Dutch citizens regard it essential to their religious identities to refrain from physical contact with members of the other sex and would rather establish respectful relations with a nod of the head or a friendly smile. In the last decade, Dutch courts had to deliberate upon various disputes between employers—who considered the handshake crucial to job performance—and orthodox Muslim citizens who demanded an exemption from this dominant Dutch greeting ritual.

The conflict concerning the handshake—about which I will say more in chapter two—paves the way for numerous important questions. Some of these inquiries look for normative standards, that is, they focus on values or principles that designate how political life should be structured. Should civic conduct assume a principle of mutual respect? Does the value of mutual respect imply that we ought to respect each other's religious and cultural traditions? Which interests might trump respect for diversity? Such normative questions figure prominently on the agenda of many political philosophers. Current political thought offers a highly divergent supply of normative guidelines, varying from one or two meta-principles of justice to pluralistic accounts of moral capabilities and detailed case studies of issues that are topical in democratic regimes.[1] In doing so, political philosophy

[1] Ronald Dworkin and John Rawls are two prominent political thinkers who aim to settle political dispute by reference to, respectively, one and two principles of justice. R Dworkin, *Sovereign Virtue: The Theory and Practice of Equality* (Cambridge, Harvard University Press, 2000); J Rawls, *A Theory of Justice: Revised Edition* (Cambridge, The Belknap Press of Harvard University Press, 1999). Hereafter, *A Theory of Justice* will be referred to as *TOJ*. For pluralist accounts of moral capabilities or capacities and their application, see M Nussbaum,

contributes to an ongoing argument about the normative aspects of political regimes that could be of help to anyone who seeks to form a judgement about political conflicts, such as the dispute over the handshake.

But there is more at stake in political disputes than normative issues. In this book I draw attention to an aspect of political conflicts that is sometimes overlooked when we become entangled with normative questions, that is, the so-called 'ontological' dimension of disputes. In political philosophy, the term 'ontology' is typically used for presuppositions about the fundamental conditions of political existence and the limits and possibilities that these constituent features open up.[2] For instance, an ontology might indicate that political communities are constituted by individuals that can rise above traditional customs. Or, it may narrate that political communities are essentially conditioned by corporeal social-historical structures, like bodily rituals, that individuals can never completely surmount.

Ontological presuppositions are not identical to normative assumptions: ontology offers a contestable interpretation of what the political world is made of rather than how it should be structured.[3] But ontological assumptions do have a significant impact upon normative inquiries: by indicating which factors of the political world we need to take into account, they structure the normative outlook or proposals that we tend to adopt.[4]

Women and Human Development: The Capabilities Approach (Cambridge, Cambridge University Press, 2000); B Parekh, *Rethinking Multiculturalism: Cultural Diversity and Political Theory* (London, Palgrave, 2000). Joseph Carens argues for a contextual analysis of justice in J Carens, *Culture, Citizenship, and Community: A Contextual Exploration of Justice as Evenhandedness* (Oxford, Oxford University Press, 2000).

[2] Michael Warren offers a helpful, concise division of the subject matter of political philosophy into ontological, epistemological and normative questions, noting that political philosophy is often mistakenly identified with normative theory, see M Warren, 'What is Political Philosophy' (1989) 22 *PS: Political Science and Politics* 606. See also J Bennett, *The Enchantment of Modern Life: Attachments, Crossings, and Ethics* (New Jersey, Princeton University Press, 2001) 160–66; W Connolly, *The Ethos of Pluralization* (Minneapolis, University of Minnesota Press, 1995) 1–40; B Jessop, 'Political Ontology, Political Theory, Political Philosophy, and the Ironic Contingencies of Political Life' in R Schmidinger and C Sedmak (eds), *Der Mensch—ein Zoon Politikon: Gemeinschaft, Őffentlichkeit, Macht* (Darmstadt, Wissenschaftliche Buchgesellschaft, 2005); D Mayhew, 'Political Science and Political Philosophy: Ontological Not Normative' (2000) 33 *PS: Political Science and Politics* 192; C Taylor, *Philosophical Arguments* (Cambridge, Harvard University Press, 1995); S White, *Sustaining Affirmation: The Strengths of Weak Ontology in Political Theory* (New Jersey, Princeton University Press, 2000).

[3] Neither are ontological claims identical to empirical claims about political life: ontology is part of the basic assumptions about the political world that helps to delineate the various domains of empirical research. For instance, when we want to study civic action, an ontological assumption about the role of the body in human identity-formation relations structures the choice to include or exclude bodily conduct in empirical research.

[4] Importantly, normative commitments also affect the ontological thesis that one adopts. I discuss this point in s II.

Consider, for instance, the Dutch conflict about the handshake. One ontological issue that this case opened up was the relation between bodily conduct and human identity-formation. In the media, a Dutch philosopher claimed that the insistence on particular forms of bodily expression, such as exchanging a handshake, was actually an effect of a lack of ideological beliefs:

> [T]he country yearns for new *ideological orientation*, an answer to the question what The Netherlands is, what it wants to be and why. As long as these questions remain unanswered, fear and insecurity take over; newcomers cannot be received in a normal fashion (and characteristic traits are sought for in *trivialities* such as presents on birthdays, headscarves and *shaking hands*).[5]

Another commentator suggested that the refusal by an orthodox Muslim to give a handshake originated in a hidden desire: 'We can also cast some doubts on his motives. Is he really motivated by a deeply felt religious belief, or is he motivated by a deeply felt desire to disrupt Dutch society?'.[6]

These two responses seem to imply that human beings are more fundamentally shaped by inner states of minds, like beliefs and desires, than by bodily acts. That is to say, they suggest that when we try to make sense of an attachment to particular forms of bodily conduct, such as the handshake, we should not so much look at the role of our bodies in constituting identities but focus on mental characteristics. In turn this ontology seems to affect the normative stance one defends. Take, for instance, the proposal by the first commentator to diminish fear in the Netherlands by developing new ideological beliefs about Dutch identity. The strengthening of ideological convictions appears as the natural starting-point for developing normative solutions when you assume that human beings are fundamentally shaped by (ideological) beliefs. But if you treat the physical body as an ontological feature of human identities, this prescription might be less evident: you could find it insufficient to look for solutions in terms of beliefs and aim for practices of civic conduct that take into account the fact that bodies fundamentally shape civic relations.

Addressing the question of whether the body is a fundamental or a rather trivial constituent of civic relations would implicate political philosophers in a difficult ontological investigation. What role do particular forms of bodily conduct play in the enactment of individual and collective identities? Does it make sense to reduce the adherence to bodily rituals to a mental trait? How do bodies and beliefs interact? In comparison to normative topics, however,

[5] G Buijs, 'De Christelijke Traditie Wijst de Weg naar een Nieuw Samenlevingsideaal' (2007) *NRC Handelsblad*, 13 January 15 (emphasis added, translation by the author).

[6] H Mees, 'Moslimemancipatie' (2007) *NRC Handelsblad*, 26 January 7 (translated by the author).

such ontological questions receive relatively little attention in current political thought. In fact, in recent years, one of the most influential paradigms in contemporary political philosophy established the avoidance of ontological issues as a central tenet in its programme. Political liberalism, founded by the American philosopher John Rawls, argues that political philosophers should separate political thought from ontological themes.[7] According to Rawls, ontological issues, such as questions about the 'nature of moral or political agents' or the constituent features of 'personal identity', will distract us from important normative questions, such as the formulation of principles of justice, and will make it impossible to arrive at a consensus on justice in democratic regimes.[8] The strategy to avoid ontology is mirrored in the political liberalist view of democratic debate. In disputes about fundamental issues of justice, such as constitutional rights or a society's basic policies on mutual respect, citizens should limit themselves to political arguments that their fellow citizens will consider uncontroversial, and refrain from introducing ontological arguments about, say, the constitutive role of the body in human identity-formation.

In contrast to political liberalism, this book aims to show the impact of controversial ontological presuppositions upon democratic theory and practice. I seek to show the need for developing an ontology of democracy, and I hope to bring out the need for a critique of ontology in democratic politics. I pursue these goals by critically engaging with political liberalism; the work of the French thinker Michel Foucault; psychoanalytic theory; various case studies such as the Dutch debate on the handshake, an American conflict over the regulation of religious freedom, and the struggles for emotional empowerment of two American social movement groups.

This introduction lays down some thoughts about the need for illuminating ontology in democratic theory and practice, and explains how I will try to evaluate these considerations in this study. I start by saying a bit about my usage of the terms that I bring together here: democracy and ontology. My short terminological exposition, which focuses mainly on current political philosophy, is not by any means intended as a comprehensive overview of the various ways in which these terms are employed by political philosophers, let alone within the philosophical tradition at large. Rather, I want to sketch some preliminary characteristics of these terms so as to get my discussion off the ground—a working definition, one might say, that will be elucidated in this introduction and the chapters that follow.

[7] J Rawls, *Political Liberalism: With a New Introduction and the 'Reply to Habermas'* (New York, Columbia University Press, 1996) 11. Hereafter *Political Liberalism* will be referred to as *PL*.

[8] As I explain in ch 2, Rawls uses the term 'metaphysical' for ontological questions about the nature of human freedom or identity.

I. DEMOCRACY

In the last decades, political philosophers have increasingly affirmed understandings of democracy that express normative ideals.[9] Obviously, the many conflicting normative interpretations of democracy in current political thought are difficult to pin down under one term and are best understood by looking at the ways in which they are used. Nonetheless, for this introductory purpose I will fix the various disagreements over the normative underpinnings of democracy as a dispute about the understanding of 'public autonomy'—a value that I believe to be central to most democratic conceptions. The notion of public autonomy, defined in the most basic terms, suggests that individuals should have a voice in the formation of rules that govern them. In a democratic regime, people are not only subjected to the exercise of power but, to a greater or lesser extent, should also have possibilities to influence the way that power is exercised. In what follows I briefly mention four important interpretations of public autonomy in political philosophy and note how my own understanding of democracy relates to these accounts.

In the minimalist liberal understanding, the value of public autonomy is typically associated with the institutionalisation of individual rights.[10] Basically, citizens are said to be free in virtue of their capacity to pursue a variety of private interests (such as participation in the market or establishing a family) and exercise their rights in order to check whether political representatives adequately safeguard these interests. For instance, by participating in periodic elections, citizens can eject representatives who have abused their power to advance their own interests rather than those of the citizens.

Numerous contemporary political philosophers have argued that this minimalist understanding of public autonomy is inadequate to realise a democratic society. For instance, participatory democrats claim that the periodic exercise of rights is not sufficient to prevent the abuse of power by public officials. A democratic society can only sustain itself through a citizenry that has enough experience in keeping a critical watch on its political representatives by actively taking part in political activities. On this account, public autonomy implies that citizens should regularly participate

[9] That is to say, most contemporary political thinkers no longer aim for a normatively neutral conception of democracy but seek to make democracy intelligible by reference to some kind of moral or ethico-political aspiration. See A Gutmann, 'Democracy' in R Goodin and P Pettit (eds), *A Companion to Contemporary Political Philosophy* (Oxford, Blackwell Publishers, 1993). Gutmann offers a concise overview of current democratic conceptions that has informed my own account here.

[10] Arguments for an interest-based, minimalist understanding of democracy can be found in R Nozick, *Anarchy, State and Utopia* (New York, Basic Books, 1974); R Dahl, *Democracy and its Critics* (New Haven, Yale University Press, 1989).

in political initiatives, such as social movements, representative councils, discussion groups and so on. Furthermore, the claim is that through frequent participation the civic character of citizens will change for the better: democratic participation makes better citizens.[11] Deliberative democrats also consider widespread civic participation integral to public autonomy. They argue that processes of collective decision-making should include public processes of opinion- and will-formation in which citizens engage in arguments for their various positions. In this public dialogue, citizens do not take each other's interests for granted but critically challenge the various traditions that have shaped these interests. The goal of this process is to arrive at a democratic agreement in which the better arguments have been decisive; deliberative democrats oppose agreements that are the aggregate of various interests established prior to democratic deliberation.[12]

Finally, agonic democrats affirm the need for an active citizenry as well as the importance of a vibrant democratic debate that challenges traditions. In opposition to deliberative democracy, however, agonists do not anticipate that democratic processes of opinion- and will-formation can lead to a rational consensus about rules. While democratic debates can enhance our insight into the various traditional backgrounds that shape the citizenry, such a critical learning process remains affected by arbitrary power relations. Moreover, many agonic democrats are wary of conceptions of democracy that reduce democratic participation to public deliberation and argue that public autonomy should also include a set of virtues or habits that helps citizens to live with disagreement.[13]

In the course of this book it will become clear that my own understanding of democracy is closest to agonic democracy. To be sure, I affirm the need for individual rights, a politically active citizenry, and public processes of deliberation. However, I will also argue that democratic regimes cannot transcend arbitrary power relations. In addition, I emphasise the

[11] See B Barber, *Strong Democracy: Participatory Politics for a New Age* (Berkeley, University of California Press, 1984); C Taylor, *The Malaise of Modernity* (Toronto, House of Anansi Press, 1991).

[12] Key authors in the deliberative democratic paradigm include: J Habermas, *Between Facts and Norms: Contributions to a Discourse Theory of Law and Democracy* (Cambridge, MIT Press, 1996); A Gutmann and D Thompson, *Democracy and Disagreement* (Cambridge, The Belknap Press of Harvard University Press, 1996).

[13] For agonic conceptions of democracy, see B van den Brink, 'Liberalism without Agreement: Political Autonomy and Agonistic Citizenship' in J Christman and J Anderson (eds) *Autonomy and the Challenges to Liberalism* (Cambridge, Cambridge University Press, 2005); W Connolly, *Why I am not a Secularist* (Minneapolis, University of Minnesota Press, 1999); B Honig, *Political Theory and the Displacement of Politics* (Ithaca, Cornell University Press, 1993); H Lindahl, 'The Opening: Alegality and Political Agonism' in A Schaap (ed), *Law and Agonist Politics* (Surrey, Ashgate Publishing Limited, 2009); C Mouffe, *The Democratic Paradox* (London, Verso, 2000); D Owen, 'The Expressive Agon: On Political Agency in a Constitutional Democratic Polity' in Schaap (ed), ibid; J Tully, 'The Agonic Freedom of Citizens' (1999) 28 *Economy and Society* 161.

importance of habitual practices that help citizens to participate in and to recover from ongoing political disagreements. Given the fact that I will use the term 'democracy' in various registers, this book will treat democracy as a multi-layered concept, designating three interdependent and partly overlapping phenomena. First, democracy will be used to refer to institutions that enact collective decisions, such as law, the election process and local representative organs. Second, democracy will denote practices that enable the enactment and contestation of these collective decisions, such as the process of public opinion-formation and civic virtues. Third, democracy will refer to a set of ideas that justify and explain these two phenomena. These ideas include, among others, normative intuitions and theories, social theory, traditions of jurisprudence, as well as ontology.

Let us now take a closer look at ontology and address the issue of why it needs to be part of democracy.

II. ONTOLOGY

'Ontology' literally means a theory of being: the etymological roots come from the Greek words for 'being' (*onta*) and 'study' or 'theory' (*logos*). In philosophy, ontology was originally used for investigations that reflect upon the fundamental categories of existence and their relations, such as the claim that all things in the universe have an essence that reason can grasp.[14] Kant is generally considered to be the thinker who has displaced such ontological questions, instigating a shift in Western philosophy away from ontological inquiries (into the essence of being) and toward epistemological questions (concerning the foundations of knowing or understanding being).[15] For instance, Kant's inquiry into the criteria of knowledge famously challenged the idea that human beings can indeed say anything intelligible at all about the characteristics of being as such.

In twentieth century philosophy, the term ontology became primarily associated with the work of the analytic philosopher Willard van Orman Quine and the phenomenologist Martin Heidegger. Quine's usage of ontology was embedded in a scientific worldview: he spoke of an 'ontological commitment' in order to refer to the entities that the acceptance of a scientific theory commits us to.[16] Political philosophers who work in the analytic

[14] The term ontology (in Latin, *ontologia*) was created by seventeenth century scholastics. It was sometimes used in the same sense as metaphysics but also seen as one branch of metaphysical inquiry (the others were cosmology and psychology). See D Borchert (ed), *Encyclopedia of Philosophy* 2nd edn, vol 7 (Detroit, Macmillan Reference USA, 2006) 21–28.

[15] O Marchart, *Post-Foundational Political Thought: Political Difference in Nancy, Lefort, Badiou and Laclau* (Edinburgh, Edinburgh University Press, 2007) 163; Borchert, ibid 28.

[16] W Quine, *Ontological Relativity and Other Essays* (New York, Columbia University Press, 1969) 26–68.

tradition sometimes appeal to Quine's understanding of ontology; for example, Rawls refers to Quine when speaking of general statements about 'what there is'.[17] Heidegger's usage of ontology, in contrast, was closely related to a radical critique of scientific belief-systems. In Heidegger's account, the scientific point of view takes the idea of being for granted without really demonstrating an understanding of what being means. Heidegger considers this neglect of attention towards being itself as problematic because it relegates from view the fact that the scientist's attempt to arrive at knowledge-claims *about* the world is fundamentally dependent upon his existence *in* the world. Since Heidegger has influenced the various political thinkers whose ideas this book draws upon, I will say a bit more about the function of ontology in Heidegger's work. After that I shall sketch how Heidegger's interrogations of being (the *Seinsfrage*) have recently been appropriated by thinkers who have argued for the cultivation of ontology in the context of political thought; I will then outline my own approach.

In his magnum opus *Sein und Zeit*, Heidegger investigates being through an interpretation of the ontological features of human beings. One such feature that Heidegger brings out is that human beings are fundamentally situated or 'thrown' in the world (*Geworfenheit*).[18] That is to say, human beings are, in some sense, always handed over to and concerned with the world, such as by making something, or by taking care of something, discussing or questioning the world, and so on.[19] The things in the world that human beings encounter are bound up with these involvements: we understand and relate to things in light of the worldly practices that we are immersed in.[20]

The scientific point of view seems to contradict this ontological predicament. When the scientist tries to obtain knowledge about the world, he attempts to withdraw from the world. That is, the scientist works with the assumption that the world is no longer entangled with his own particular projects but is present for neutral observation. Heidegger challenges this view by bringing to our attention the possibility that the scientific outlook remains fundamentally conditioned by being thrown into the world.[21] When the scientist tries to arrive at objective knowledge he needs to control the worldly conditions that affect our understanding: he develops specific procedures and experiments so as to ensure that his claims will not be affected by particular biases, he strips things of their everyday meaning with the usage of specialised technical languages, and so on.[22] This suggests that the

17 Rawls, *PL* (n 7) 379.
18 M Heidegger, *Sein und Zeit* (Tübingen, Max Niemeyer Verlag, 1993) 135.
19 ibid, 52–59.
20 ibid, 66–72.
21 ibid, 59–62.
22 *cf* Taylor (n 2) 1–19.

scientist does not just passively observe the world but that he continues to engage himself with it.[23] The scientific outlook, then, is after all not fundamentally different from being situated in the world, but rather, is indeed derivative of this circumstance.

To a greater or lesser extent, Heidegger's move to displace scientific understandings by means of an ontological inquiry has been influential upon various French and Anglo-Saxon political philosophers who have recently come to emphasise that democratic theory needs to elaborate an ontology. This current of thought, that has been dubbed 'weak ontology' or 'post-foundationalism', can be discerned in the work of contemporary thinkers such as Jane Bennett, William Connolly, Ernesto Laclau, Claude Lefort, Oliver Marchart, Chantal Mouffe, Charles Taylor and Stephen White.[24]

One of the central claims in this recent ontological turn is that ontological presuppositions are an intrinsic aspect of political thought. Even when the theorist does not explicitly articulate the ontological background of his argument, political analyses, interpretations and judgements will to some extent invoke ontological claims. As the French political philosopher Claude Lefort puts it: 'The elaboration attested to by any political society … involves an investigation into the world, into Being as such'.[25]

The accentuation of the ontological dimension of political thought was initially prompted by a Heideggerian concern, that is, it was part of a challenge to the predominance of scientific understandings in political thought. For instance, Lefort underscored the investigation into being in order to dispute the idea that political scientists can make value-neutral claims.[26] On Lefort's account, an ontological inquiry reveals that society and the individuals that inhabit it are constituted by a symbolic system, a structure that gives form to society by making value-laden distinctions between true and false, legitimate and illegitimate, and so on. This ontology suggests that the scientist is always conditioned by values, even when he tries to escape a propensity to judge and aspires to value-neutral observations.[27] In the

[23] Consider, for instance, the system of blind peer review that many scientific journals adopt to arrive at objective evaluations about articles. A peer review procedure implicates scientists in an ongoing engagement with the world: the development of protocols, the ongoing testing of whether these protocols have been observed, the establishment of networks with other scientists who can serve as referees, and so on.

[24] For an account of the re-emergence of ontology in the Anglo-American political theory, see White (n 2). For an overview of this development in French post-War political theory, see Marchart (n 15).

[25] C Lefort, *Democracy and Political Theory* (Cambridge, Polity Press, 1988) 219.

[26] I should note that, for Lefort, 'being' is not a direct reference to Heidegger but to Merleau-Ponty who was Lefort's main source of inspiration. Several commentators, though, have noted parallels between Lefort's thinking and Heidegger. See, eg: Marchart (n 15).

[27] Claude Lefort clarified the need for an ontological inquiry with the distinction between 'politics' (*la politique*) and 'the political' (*le politique*). 'Politics', for Lefort, refers to the institutional or functional domain that a society delineates in opposition to law, the social,

Anglo-American context, the Canadian philosopher Charles Taylor also turned to ontology to dispute the prevalence of scientific methodologies in political thought. Drawing on Heidegger, among others, Taylor challenged the idea that subjects can separate themselves from the social world, and brought to the fore the idea that human beings are fundamentally shaped by historically-situated linguistic ways of life.[28] Taylor also argued for the need for an ontological thesis in debates on justice. For example, by calling attention to the dependence of human beings on a historical way of life, Taylor tried to lend strength to his argument that states need to support historical communities.[29]

This brings me to the second feature of the recent ontological turn: that the illumination of ontological assumptions can enrich our understanding of the normative conditions and social effects of democracy. Ontology specifies a range of possibilities that normative reflection can intelligibly pursue. As Taylor puts it:

> [T]he ontological [view] help[s] to define the options it is meaningful to support by advocacy. Your ontological proposition, if true, can show that your neighbor's favorite social order is an impossibility or carries a price he or she did not count on.[30]

For example, when your ontology considers a plurality of conflicting bodily habits constitutive of social practices, you will most likely consider it senseless to aspire to a democratic regime which remains unaffected by conflicts about forms of bodily conduct.

I should stress, however, that the linkage between ontology and normativity should not be mistaken for the assertion that ontological claims are a more privileged entry-point for thinking about democracy than normative claims. Ontology offers an important *supplement* to normative assumptions but is not a *substitute* for ethico-political values. For a start, ontological assumptions need to be connected to substantive normative intuitions in order to arrive at satisfactory judgements. For instance, when I assume that conflicting bodily habits are an ontological feature of social life, this thesis is not attempting to clarify, let alone prescribe, how citizens should respond to

economics, religion, etc. Lefort allocates this viewpoint to the social (ie political) scientist: it is the task of empirical research to delineate particular facts and to discern (causal) relations between these facts. The 'political' on the other hand concerns an inquiry into the constitutive principles of a society that allows articulations of politics (vis-a-vis, for instance, civil society, religion or law) to emerge. Interpretations of the political, according to Lefort, are the task for political philosophers and are similar to what I qualify as an ontological interpretation. Marchart (n 15) 35–59 offers an instructive genealogy of the distinction between politics and the political.

[28] Taylor (n 2).
[29] See ch 2 s IV.A.i.
[30] Taylor (n 2) 183.

a particular bodily custom, such as an unfamiliar greeting ritual. We need to invoke normative ideas to form such an opinion, such as the aim to respect cultural differences, or the goal to enact a pluralist or, for that matter, a homogeneous culture.[31] Furthermore, ontological investigations do not proceed from a normatively neutral position, but will to some extent express the values of one's social-historical context. For example, the attribution of the body with an ontological status will be more likely in a religious culture that specifies multiple norms for bodily conduct (such as Catholicism, Islam or Judaism) than in a religious practice which prescribes very few bodily rituals (such as Protestantism).

Ontology also helps to illuminate the unintended effects of democratic aspirations. Each normative vision needs to encounter the fact that it generates social consequences that it deems undesirable. For instance, an ideal of active citizenship might in practice turn out to be so demanding and exhausting that many citizens will turn their back on civic engagement. Reflections about democratic politics become more intelligible when democratic theory sheds light on such counterproductive effects. An ontological investigation can contribute to this diagnosis by indicating which factors of social life we need to take into account when scrutinising the consequences of democratic politics.

Third, the recent ontological turn, to a greater or lesser extent, acknowledges that ontological accounts are contestable, and generally affirms a plurality of possible ontological interpretations. That is to say, it distances itself from perspectives that consider ontological grounds immune to revision as well as those approaches which claim that the various ontological positions can be reduced to one ultimate ground. In his overview of the re-emergence of ontology in Anglo-American political theory, Stephen White explains this point by distinguishing 'strong' from 'weak' ontologies:

> Strong ontologies are those ontologies that claim to show us 'the way the world is' ... this foundation's validity is unchanging and of universal reach. ... Weak ontologies respond ... to the idea that all fundamental conceptualisations of self, other, and world are contestable.[32]

Oliver Marchart makes a similar point in his account of ontological investigations in French post-War political theory: '[W]hat is still accepted by post-foundationalism is the necessity of some grounds. What becomes problematic as a result is not the existence of foundations (in the plural) but their ontological status—which is seen now as necessarily contingent'.[33]

[31] Obviously, there is no necessary link between ontological investigations and democratic aims: ontological inquiries might be appropriated for democratic purposes but can also be put to work for dictatorial or totalitarian projects.

[32] White (n 2) 8.

[33] Marchart (n 15) 14.

Finally, the fourth characteristic of the ontological turn that I should mention pertains to the content of ontology. Political thinkers who have contributed to this train of thought typically agree with Heidegger that human beings are, in one way or another, fundamentally thrown or situated in the world. Among others, they draw attention to the way in which the human self is fundamentally conditioned by history, language and intersubjective relations, and thereby seek to displace overly individualist and rationalist conceptions of the human being.

In short, what emerges from the recent ontological turn is that ethico-political arguments gain strength when supported by a contestable ontology. While ontology cannot discharge the theorist from developing normative claims, political thinkers should not limit their focus to normative theory either. By actively cultivating ontological claims political theory offers a better incentive for the understanding of political disputes than it does when treating ontology as a latent or irrelevant set of background assumptions.

III. POLITICAL LIBERALISM, FOUCAULT AND PSYCHOANALYSIS

This book seeks to contribute to the renewed interest in ontology in current political thought through a critical engagement with political liberalism, the work of Michel Foucault, and psychoanalysis. Political liberalism offers an excellent starting-point from which to evaluate the claims and concerns raised by the ontological turn. If the political liberalist arguments about the separation of ontology from democratic theory and practice can be maintained, the case for illuminating ontological issues becomes much less plausible. For this reason, I believe that the political liberalist arguments for separating ontology and democracy warrant much more critical scrutiny than they have received thus far.[34]

[34] Several critiques of *A Theory of Justice*, Rawls' initial account of justice, focused on ontological issues—eg, Honig (n 13) 126–61; Taylor (n 2); M Sandel, *Liberalism and the Limits of Justice* (Cambridge, Cambridge University Press, 1982). The debate about *Political Liberalism*, however, focused mainly on normative issues, such as the question of whether political liberalism amounts to a perfectionist or comprehensive ethical doctrine. In a five volume collection of influential articles about Rawls in H Richardson and P Weithman (eds), *The Philosophy of Rawls: A Collection of Essays, Volume 1–5* (New York, Garland, 1999) only one article critically interrogates the adequacy of a 'non-metaphysical' conception of justice: J Hampton, 'Should Political Philosophy Be Done Without Metaphysics?' in H Richardson, vol 5, ibid, 177. Connolly and Honig, do challenge the plausibility of a 'non-metaphysical' conception of justice in their critical readings of Rawls (Connolly (n 2) 3–4; Honig (n 13) 196–99). But they do not discuss how much the strategy of avoidance is at odds with commitments that are central to political liberalism itself, namely, the need for providing orientation on the normative possibilities of democratic regimes and the ongoing democratic politicisation of political philosophy (I discuss these two political liberalist commitments below and in ch 2). I believe that the case against political liberalism becomes more persuasive when we can show that the separation between ontology and democracy runs counter to important political liberalist commitments.

At the centre of my challenge to political liberalism will be the staging of an encounter between Rawls and Foucault. Like many recent French philosophers, Foucault has been influenced by Heidegger and, in a very general sense, one might say too that Foucault considers human beings to be fundamentally thrown into the world.[35] Foucault, however, sketched a very different picture of worldly background conditions than Heidegger did: he approached being as an ongoing power struggle, a 'warlike clash between forces' that enacts various hierarchical norms.[36] By critically exposing the exclusionary effects that power relations enact, Foucault aspired to an ongoing transformation of these worldly constituents of human thought and action. For example, Foucault has become well-known for his challenge to the social contract tradition, unmasking the universal normative theories central to this tradition as partisan competitors in the quest for power.

Now, clearly, Foucault's project is in many respects radically opposed to that of Rawls which attempts to strengthen the social contract tradition with a systematic theory of justice.[37] However, the gap between Foucault and Rawls is not so wide as to make no sense in critically comparing these two thinkers. In fact, I will highlight an important point of convergence between Foucault and Rawls which allows for a productive engagement between these two thinkers that has not so far been articulated by authors working in the Rawlsian and Foucaultian traditions: both Rawls and Foucault believe that political philosophical ideas need to be subjected to an ongoing vibrant process of democratic contestation.[38]

The first benefit of this comparative approach is that it helps to bring into view the contentious ontological claims that political liberalism draws upon. Foucault's critique of the social contract tradition strengthens my case that political liberalism is not ontologically impartial. Second, Foucault's project helps me show that ontological accounts need not, as Rawls suggests,

[35] Foucault mentioned his indebtedness to Heidegger in his final interview: 'My entire philosophical development was determined by my reading of Heidegger.' (M Foucault, 'Final Interview' (1985) 5 *Raritan* 1). Hubert Dreyfus offers a succinct comparison of Heidegger and Foucault. (HL Dreyfus, 'Being and Power: Heidegger and Foucault' (1996) 4 *International Journal of Philosophical Studies*).

[36] M Foucault, in M Bertani and A Fontana (eds), *'Society Must Be Defended': Lectures at the Collège de France, 1975-1976* (New York, Picador, 2003) 16.

[37] For Foucault, philosophy consists of various attempts ('essays') to problematise self-evident truth claims—the results of which could and should not be united into one normative systematic scheme of thought (M Foucault, *The Use of Pleasure: The History of Sexuality, Volume 2* (London, Penguin Books, 1992) 9).

[38] See, for instance, J Moss, 'Foucault, Rawls and Public Reason' in J Moss (ed), *The Later Foucault: Politics and Philosophy* (London, SAGE Publications, 1998). Moss does not note that Rawls and Foucault share a commitment to the democratic contestation of political philosophy. See ch 3, n 114 for my critique on Moss' account of Rawls.

lead to a stifling of democratic debates. By fleshing out the ontology that informs Foucault's project, I will demonstrate that ontological accounts can stimulate processes of democratic politicisation, and go on to argue that Foucault's ontology of freedom offers a much needed corrective to Rawls' account of freedom. Third, this undertaking contributes towards evaluating the merits of politicising ontological claims. In opposition to political liberalism, Foucault includes ontological frameworks in his practice of critique and opens up space for democratic debates that include a critical interrogation of ontology.

Finally, the last tradition of thought that this book seeks critical assistance from is psychoanalytic theory. By means of a critical investigation of the work of Sigmund Freud and Donald Winnicott, I develop an ontology of the affective consequences of losing a democratic contest: feelings of embarrassment, failure, anger and sadness when one is unsuccessful in implementing an ideal or dissenting practice. With this ontology, I hope to strengthen my ontology of democratic politics and try to repair a lacuna in current democratic thought: that most democratic thinkers who are committed to a vibrant democratic process, including Rawls and Foucault, have too little to say about the affective burdens of democratic politics.

A. An Ontology of Democracy

One of my disagreements with Rawls concerns the question of whether ontology can offer fruitful insights into democratic politics.

Rawls' definition of democracy has increasingly moved towards a deliberative democratic understanding of public autonomy, emphasising, among other things, that democratic regimes need to be sustained by vibrant civic debates on justice. Political philosophers can contribute to such ongoing debates by developing conceptual frameworks that offer citizens orientation within the various normative possibilities—or 'possible ends'—of a democratic regime.[39]

On Rawls' account, political philosophy can pursue this task without articulating an account of the ontological conditions of democratic politics. For sure, Rawls affirms that most citizens see an intrinsic connection between ideas of democratic justice and contestable ontological worldviews. He argues, however, that the political theorist is able to transcend these circumstances when formulating a theory of democratic justice: political liberalism claims to offer a normative framework that is ontologically so

[39] J Rawls, *Justice as Fairness: A Restatement* (Cambridge, The Belknap Press of Harvard University Press, 2001) 2.

latent and impartial that it can serve as a relatively unproblematic grid or 'coat-rack' for a plurality of ontological positions. In fact, Rawls believes that a political-theoretical illumination of ontology will only distract attention from much needed democratic debates on normative issues.

In the course of this book I will try to unsettle these claims. For instance, in chapter two, I will show that Rawls' conception of individual autonomy is premised upon a deeply controversial ontology of human agency. That is to say, it articulates freedom in terms of individualist characteristics and disregards the situatedness of the self in practices, such as language, tradition and bodily discipline. I also emphasise that this contentious ontological commitment has a significant impact upon Rawls' normative framework: that political liberalism cannot provide adequate orientation for citizens who—unlike Rawls—understand freedom in more situated terms. I will defend this claim, among other things, by returning to the discussion about the handshake that I mentioned at the beginning of this introduction.

In the remaining part of the book I turn to the work of Michel Foucault and psychoanalytic theory to develop a contrasting alternative ontology of individual freedom. I will show that Foucault's thesis about the ubiquity of power reveals that power relations are essentially two-faced. On the one hand, they endow the human body with capacities for thinking and action and thereby offer crucial conditions for public autonomy or civic empowerment. But, on the other hand, power works by issuing exclusionary effects, by barring certain possibilities of reflection and types of behaviour. Power produces these effects by means of various intersubjective forms, such as language and practices of bodily discipline. We shall see that Foucault's ontology of power offers an important challenge to several political liberalist aspirations. For instance, Foucault's account disputes the ideal of a normative consensus. Rawls wagers that participants in democratic debates can freely consent to a particular proposal and thereby arrive at a consensus that is unaffected by social hierarchies. For Foucault, participants can only agree with a particular proposal because they are subjected to hierarchies that, to a greater or lesser extent, escape consciousness. But Foucault's ontology does not only temper democratic ambitions. Indeed, I go on to show that Foucault's theory of power can provide an impetus to democratic life by helping us see new possibilities for democratic empowerment. For instance, one of the promising insights of Foucault's later work is that the subjection to certain kinds of power relations can strengthen the capacity to contest oppression. By submitting ourselves to social forms that offer possibilities for resisting and experimenting with power, we can become more capable of contesting domination. This aspect of freedom—empowerment of the democratic subject through the subjection to power—is often missed in liberal individualism, including political liberalism.

To investigate the affective parameters of democratic politics, I turn to the psychoanalytic ontologies of Freud and Winnicott. In order to persist in democratic struggles, citizens need to be resilient enough to face the emotional pain of political disappointment. The psychoanalytic tradition offers crucial insights into some of the obstacles to democratic resilience. Like Foucault, psychoanalytic ontologies assume a situated notion of the human being. But psychoanalytic conceptions of man typically look at the influence of socially constituted (partly) unconscious desires and feelings on thought and action, an aspect of subjectivity that neither Foucault nor Rawls address much. For example, psychoanalytic theory helps us see that the fear of authority often thwarts attempts to critically confront either norms or people invested with power. That is to say, we may aspire to be watchdogs of authority and make an effort to learn the necessary critical skills, but when the possibility actually arises to contest power relations many of us are not always courageous enough to do so. Furthermore, when we do make an effort to challenge power, we could be confronted with the painful fact of losing a contest, that is, that our critiques are unsuccessful or are met with ridicule. Such experiences could become so overwhelming that they eventually undermine civic motivation to participate in democratic struggles.

At the same time, I will try to show that a diagnosis of this affective dimension of democratic politics may help us develop new approaches to stimulate democratic participation. For instance, psychoanalytic ontologies teach us that we should not devote all our intellectual and political energies to ethical initiatives that increase the critical skills of citizens, but that we should also look for ways to empower citizens emotionally. Winnicott's insights about creative agency, in particular, will offer crucial help in conceptualising democratic forms of emotional empowerment.

In short then, throughout this book I hope to establish that ontological illumination does important theoretical work in orienting citizens towards the normative possibilities and social effects of democratic regimes. *Pace* Rawls, I find that ontology does have an effect on our ethico-political deliberations and I argue that political philosophers should include ontology as a crucial element in their democratic theory.

B. The Democratic Politicisation of Ontology

This book does not only aim to show that ontology might illuminate important aspects of democratic politics, it also hopes to bring out the need to subject ontology to a critique by democratic politics. My argument picks up on an important development in recent political thought that I will characterise as the 'democratic politicisation of political philosophy'. In what follows I offer a brief account of this tendency and explain why that ontology needs to be part of an ongoing process of democratic contestation. I will also outline some of the implications of a democratic politicisation of ontology for the task of political philosophy and democratic practice.

In recent years, political philosophers have increasingly come to question the authority of political philosophy in democratic regimes. Instead of assuming that political philosophers have exceptional insight into the conditions of democratic politics, political philosophy has put more and more emphasis on the fact that no political philosopher, as trained or talented as he might be, can adequately represent the plurality of interests and perspectives that constitute a democratic polity. For this reason, political philosophy needs to be submitted to an ongoing process of democratic politicisation: political philosophers should challenge their claims to expertise by confronting their concepts with the various struggles and plurality of concerns raised by the citizenry.

The democratic politicisation of political philosophy can be discerned in several competing modes of political thought, including political liberalism (such as the later Rawls), deliberative democracy and agonic democracy.[40] In chapters two and three, we shall look more closely at the distinct and conflicting ways in which Rawls and Foucault have articulated the democratic politicisation of political philosophy. At this point, I simply want to address some of the more general implications of this tendency for the self-understanding of political philosophy and its relation to democratic practice.

When the political philosopher presents his theory to others, one might say that he adopts an educational role in relation to his fellow citizens: he tries to teach his public an account of the conditions of the democratic association and hopes that they will adopt this perspective when reflecting and deciding upon the values or principles that need to be implemented.[41] In this

[40] The democratic politicisation of political philosophy was a central topic in the ongoing exchange between Jürgen Habermas and Rawls. According to Habermas, Rawls' justificatory procedures arrogate too much reasoning potential to the individual: 'Rawls views the substantive parts of his study ... not as contribution of a participant in argumentation of a process of discursive will formation ... but as the outcome of a "theory of justice", which he as an expert is qualified to construct'. (J Habermas, 'Discourse Ethics: Notes on a Program of Philosophical Justification' in *Moral Consciousness and Communicative Action* (Cambridge, Polity Press, 1990) 66)); *cf* J Habermas, 'Reconciliation through the Public Use of Reason' in C Cronin and P De Greiff (eds), *The Inclusion of the Other: Studies in Political Theory* (Cambridge, The MIT Press, 1998). In ch 2, we shall see that the later Rawls mitigated his reliance on individual reason. For an interesting contribution to the democratic politicisation of political philosophy from a political liberal perspective, see A Laden, 'Taking the Distinction between Persons Seriously' (2004) 1 *Journal of Moral Philosophy* 277. The comprehensive liberal Wibren van der Burg presents an 'open and dialogical model' for moral theory (W van der Burg, 'Dynamic Ethics' (2003) 37 *The Journal of Value Inquiry* 13). For an agonic democratic contribution, see J Tully, 'Political Philosophy as a Critical Activity' (2002) 30 *Political Theory* 533.

[41] See H Pitkin, *Fortune is a Woman: Gender and Politics in the Thought of Niccolo Machiavelli* (Berkeley, University of California Press, 1984) 108: 'The political theorist is not merely an observer, but also a teacher, a bridge builder offering a new vision of the familiar world and trying to make it accessible to people through and despite of their old ways of seeing.' In ch 2, we shall see that Rawls also attributes political philosophy with an educational task.

capacity as educator, the political philosopher situates himself in a position of authority with respect to other citizens: he assumes that he has a particular insight or expertise that has not yet been sufficiently understood or acted upon by his fellow citizens when they participate in democratic politics. Seen in this light, the political philosopher suggests that he is in some sense 'ahead' of democratic politics: he believes himself to be entitled to give guidance to the various institutions and civic practices in democratic regimes and to be able to criticise the mainstream opinions in these practices.

The democratic politicisation of political philosophy has led to a significant revision of this educational task, moving away from depicting political philosophers as 'ahead of' democratic politics towards imagining political philosophers as 'taking part in' democratic politics. To be sure, political philosophers continue to use their particular skills and insights to improve the understandings of the conditions of a democratic association and thereby hope to offer guidance to democratic politics. But this educational ambition is no longer seen as a solitary enterprise but understood as a contestatory collective practice in which the political philosopher is seen as presenting an opinion that has to compete with others. James Tully offers an eloquent formulation of this ongoing democratic challenge to political-philosophical articulations in his defence of political philosophy as a 'critical activity':

> The experiments of the participants in negotiating, implementing, and reviewing concrete changes in practice provide a pragmatic, concrete test of the studies and their limitations. By studying the unanticipated blockages, difficulties, and new problems that arise in the cycle of practices of freedom—of negotiation, implementation, and review—political philosophers can detect the limitations and faults of their own account, make improvements, and exercise again, on the basis of new problems, this permanent critical ethos of testing the practices in which we are governed.[42]

It is important to stress that while this confrontation between theory and practice can encourage political philosophers to diminish the exclusionary effects in their account, such critical interventions cannot entirely displace the limitations of a political-philosophical point of view. To keep up with the multiple struggles in democratic practice, the democratic politicisation of political philosophy considers it vital that democratic politics is nourished by a plurality of competing political-philosophical notions. This implies that the ineradicable disagreement within political philosophy is no longer regarded as a problem that the political philosopher can or needs to surmount, but rather that this ongoing conflict is seen as an essential and positive feature of democratic politics.

[42] Tully (n 40) 551.

Up to now, the democratisation of political philosophy has focused mainly on the need to subject normative theory to democratic contestation. In the course of this book, however, I will show that the democratic politicisation of political philosophy needs to apply to ontology as well. That is to say, the ontological conditions of democratic politics need to be conditioned by an ongoing democratic process of contestation, just as is now increasingly argued for in the context of normative theory.

In chapters three and four I turn to Foucault on behalf of a democratic politicisation of ontology. What appeals to me in Foucault's work is his treatment of ontology as an inherently political construction. For Foucault, ontologies are constituted by power struggles: they are stamped by a conflict between forces that try to effect influence in the social world, and therefore political philosophers who defend particular ontological claims cannot transcend these conflicts. In turn, ontology gives rise to new power relations and thereby contributes to patterns of subordination: by singling out some features of the social and political world and some capacities of agents as more fundamental than others, ontologies help us decide what will or will not constitute a legitimate or good democratic action and thereby contributes to a particular stratification of this world. Foucault, then, will help us see that ontology is never ahead *of* politics but that it instead takes part *in* a political struggle.

We shall also see that Foucault develops an important methodology that stimulates the democratic politicisation of ontology. His practice of critique—the 'critical ontology of ourselves'—underscores the need for a historical investigation of the ontological regimes that constitute subjectivity.[43] The political philosopher, revealing the social-historical contingencies and exclusions in an ontological account, presents his critique to the democratic public and thereby seeks to disturb ontological regimes that are taken for granted.

I should emphasise, however, that while my understanding of the democratic politicisation of ontology draws much upon Foucault it is not identical to his approach. For Foucault, the democratic politicisation of ontology often seems to imply that political theorists should give up their ambition to develop an ontology of democratic politics altogether. In my account, the cultivation of an ontology remains an important part of political thinking and might even help to displace hegemonic ontological accounts. For example, the confrontation between Rawls' (implicit) ontology of autonomy

[43] Foucault also refers to this practice as a 'historical ontology of ourselves' (M Foucault, 'What is Enlightenment?' in P Rabinow (ed), *Ethics: Subjectivity and Truth* (New York, The New Press 1997) 315, 319).

and Foucault's ontology of freedom is crucial in my attempt to sketch an alternative to the influential political liberalist ontology. What implications for the task of political philosophy follow therefore from my understanding of the democratic politicisation of ontology?

A first, much needed step, is that political philosophers make ontological commitments explicit. In this way, political philosophers and other citizens who turn to political philosophy to develop democratically efficacious actions can include ontological considerations in their reflections on democratic politics, and evaluate the relevance of these ontological accounts by confronting them with their own struggles.

My second suggestion is that political philosophers strengthen their own ontological proposals by taking a close look at the concrete struggles in democratic politics. Such a confrontation presents the political philosopher with very different struggles from those that have shaped his own ontology and might thereby help to expose the blind spots in his account. Throughout this book I offer several examples of the way in which a confrontation between concrete democratic struggles and ontology can help to interrogate and ameliorate the ontological assumptions of political philosophers. I have already mentioned that I will criticise Rawls' (implicit) ontology by means of a case study on Dutch democratic codes of civility. In chapter four, I stage another confrontation between actual struggles and ontology when I investigate the political liberalist thinker John Tomasi, who sets out to develop an impartial ontology of tradition and its relation to law. One of the strategies that I mobilise to question Tomasi's account is that of confronting his ontology with the actual struggles of American citizens with regard to the implementation of religious freedom.

A third strategy is to submit ontologies to the historical critiques as developed by Foucault. In chapters three and six, I try to show the relevance of this approach by turning to the historical critiques that Foucault himself has made of the social contract tradition and psychoanalysis. In chapter four, I conduct my own application of Foucault's historical methodology in the context of individual rights, by showing the effect of social-historical power relations on the conceptualisation of the essential features of religious freedom.

A fourth strategy aimed at stimulating the democratic politicisation of ontology is to stage a critical comparison between competing ontological accounts. When political philosophers include in their account of democracy a critical confrontation between various conflicting ontologies, such a comparison could help make the public mindful of the fact that democratic politics cannot draw on one ontology alone, but that it takes its cue from a variety of contentious ontological accounts. The confrontation with various, conflicting ontologies in a democratic theory can also help to make implicit ontological convictions more explicit. This in turn can contribute to the evaluation and revision of the various answers that are currently available.[44]

Fifth, the critical interrogation of ontology can benefit by explicitly confronting ontology with normative purposes. As noted earlier, I assume that ontological investigations are normative-laden: they are influenced by the values that the political philosopher either tacitly or explicitly adopts. By fleshing out these normative commitments and by reading ontological accounts through a normative lens, we can become attentive to potential flaws or weak spots in an ontological regime. For example, in chapter three I criticise Foucault's initial ontology of the body and power by holding it up to his own normative perspective that strives for pluralism and a critically concerted experiment with inherited identities. This confrontation between ontological and normative premises helps us to see how Foucault initially underestimated the need for an ontology of critical agency and self- discipline. I pursue a similar strategy in chapter six where I critically confront Freud's ontology of mourning with my normative commitment to agonic freedom.

And finally, the sixth contribution to the democratic politicisation of ontology is the development of a democratic ethics of discussion. In chapter three, I draw upon and augment Foucaultian ethics to make democratic debates more hospitable to a critique of ontology than Rawls' account of public reason, which seeks to displace such critiques from fundamental democratic discussions.

IV. RESEARCH QUESTIONS

These considerations of ontology and democracy suggest a very different task for political theory than the one construed by political liberalism. Rather than avoiding an engagement with ontology, the theorist seeks to illuminate ontological assumptions, to submit them to a critique and, if necessary, to cultivate an alternative that is more suited to democratic politics.

Having introduced my approach to democracy and ontology, and the two most prominent thinkers that this thesis discusses, let me now sum up the central questions that the following chapters will investigate. Since these questions cut across the next chapters, the final section of this introduction will offer a sketch of the chronology of the book so that the reader can get a sense of how the argument will unfold over its course.

[44] As we shall see in ch 2, Rawls makes this point in the context of moral theory but fails to see that it might also apply to ontology.

My first question is: how plausible is the political liberalist attempt to separate contentious ontological claims from an account of democracy? I address this question by looking at two political liberalist thinkers: John Rawls and John Tomasi (chapters two and four). Whereas my critical reading of Rawls will focus on the normative ideals of political liberalism, my critique of Tomasi will focus on the social consequences of political liberalism. I will argue that the separation between, on the one hand, normative and social theorising about democracy and, on the other hand, contentious ontology, is inconsistent because political liberals mobilise various controversial ontological claims that have profound disorienting effects.

My second question follows from the answer to the first question: which ontological conditions should we take into account when we seek to nourish democratic politics? I will illuminate my ontology through a critical reconstruction of Foucault's account of social-historical power/knowledge relations, the body and agonic freedom (chapters three and four), and by means of a psychoanalytic account of the affective underpinnings of agonic freedom (chapter six). With this ontology of agonic democratic politics, I want to show that the illumination of ontological themes helps us to see social effects, as well as normative possibilities, of democratic politics that remain invisible in the political liberalist view.

The third and final question that I raise is methodological: which practice of critique—the democratic politicisation of ontology or the political liberalist strategy of avoidance—is more plausible in light of the commitment to a democratic politicisation of political philosophy as well as the orienting task of political philosophy? The potential of a critical interrogation of ontology will be addressed most explicitly in chapter three where I compare Foucault's contribution to the democratic politicisation of ontology—his model of critique and his ethics of discussion—with Rawls' reflective equilibrium and public reason. The other chapters continuously mobilise the various strategies of the democratic politicisation of ontology where I work towards a critique of, and an alternative to, political liberalism. For example, by making explicit Rawls' latent ontological premises and by confronting these with a competing ontological account (as developed by Taylor and Foucault) as well as a case study on democratic codes of civility, I try to bring into view the disorienting effects of political liberalism. And to strengthen my own ontological alternative, I submit Foucault's own ontology to a democratic politicisation by confronting it with the psychoanalytic ontology of affect. This will help to remedy Foucault's relative lack of attention to the emotional challenge of democratic politics and thereby increase the orienting strength of my ontology of democratic agency. In turn, Foucault's methodology of critique and his ontology of power are crucial to repairing some flaws in the psychoanalytic approaches that I draw upon. By implementing the democratic politicisation of ontology and critically comparing it with political liberalist strategies of critique, I will show that the critical interrogation of ontology is more conducive to the need for orientation and democratic contestation of political philosophy than the political liberalist strategy of avoidance.

V. OVERVIEW OF CHAPTERS

Chapter two starts my critical analysis of political liberalism by looking at the work of John Rawls. I flesh out Rawls' commitment to a democratic politicisation of political philosophy, a tendency in Rawls' later work to which many of his readers have attended all too little.

To challenge Rawls' strategy of avoidance, I critically investigate his ideal of individual autonomy and the principle of mutual respect, and show that these conceptions are based upon contentious ontological premises that hamper the orientation towards democratic politics. I also critically interrogate public reason (the political liberalist criterion for fundamental democratic debates) and show that the restrictions within public reason upon critical usage of ontological arguments work against Rawls' commitment to a democratic politicisation of political philosophy. My analysis of Rawls paves the way for my discussion of Foucault who does aim to include a critique of ontology in democratic debates.

Chapter three is the central chapter of this book, because here I turn to Foucault to introduce the basic tenets of the ontology of democratic politics that I defend as an alternative to the political liberalist conception of freedom. In addition, this chapter introduces Foucault's critical methodology ('a historical ontology of ourselves') and his ethics of discussion ('game of reciprocal elucidation') that offer help in politicising ontological claims. As in my interpretation of Rawls, I highlight in Foucault's work a commitment to a democratic politicisation of political philosophy. For Foucault, however, critiques of ontology are an integral feature of democratic debates. I will illustrate the usefulness of the Foucaultian critique by confronting Foucault's critique of the social contract tradition with Rawls' conception of freedom. Moreover, I critically reconstruct Foucault's ontology of power, body and agonic freedom and show that this normative-laden ontology opens up an agonic alternative for the political liberalist understanding of democracy.

Chapter four enlists both Foucault's practice of critique and his ontology of power and freedom by addressing a concern which is much more central to political liberalism than to Foucault: the institutionalisation of state law. I develop an argument that is structured analogously to that of chapter two: I show the partiality of the ontology that informs political liberalism—in this case: Tomasi's political liberalist analysis of individual rights—and reveal how this account's terms hamper the orientation of citizens (within legal regimes). Foucault's concept of 'governmentality' offers critical assistance here: this framework applies the methodology of a historical ontology of ourselves to statehood and thereby helps us to investigate the relation between ontological regimes and state action, such as law.

A short transit (chapter five) asks to what extent my perspective of agonic democracy allows for concerted actions with political liberalism. I argue that my perspective is philosophically incompatible with political liberalism and does not allow for an overlapping consensus but that it does not preclude an *instable* coalition with political liberals. I conclude by formulating a drawback to my agonic perspective: the participation in democratic struggles confronts citizens with various painful emotions that could eventually jeopardise the willingness of citizens to engage in agonic democracy. This problem of the democratic 'burn-out' provides the stepping-stone for the last chapter where I turn to psychoanalysis to strengthen my ontology of democratic politics.

Chapter six presents the final step in developing my alternative ontology of agonic freedom. Here I present an ontology of democratic resilience by means of a critical engagement with the psychoanalytic thinkers Sigmund Freud and Donald Winnicott. I introduce three capacities that empower disempowered citizens who suffer from political disappointments: a capacity to mourn, a capacity for dissent and a capacity to invent new techniques for interaction.

In concluding chapter seven, I sum up my main findings and suggest some directions for future research.

2

Politicising Political Liberalism

[J]ustification is argument addressed to those who disagree with us, or to ourselves when we are of two minds. It presumes a clash of views between persons or within one person, and seeks to convince others, or ourselves of the reasonableness of the principles upon which our claims and judgments are founded. Being designed to reconcile by reason, justification proceeds from what all parties to the discussion hold in common.[1]

In this discussion I shall make some general remarks about how I now understand the conception of justice that I have called 'justice as fairness' (presented in my book *A Theory of Justice*). I do this because it may seem that this conception depends on philosophical claims I should like to avoid, for example, claims to universal truth, or claims about the essential nature and identity of persons. My aim is to explain why it does not.[2]

I. INTRODUCTION

DOES THE POLITICAL liberalist strategy to avoid ontological disputes succeed in developing an overlapping consensus on justice? And what are the effects of bracketing inquiries into ontological disputes? This chapter provides the first step in answering these key questions of this book: it aims to evaluate the conceptual coherence and consequences of political liberalism through an analysis of Rawls' understanding of individual freedom, distributive politics of mutual respect, and his conception of democratic debate. I reconstruct Rawls' justificatory methodology, and argue that his strategy to separate ontological disputes from democratic thought and practice is incoherent, that it provides insufficient orientation towards the normative possibilities in democratic regimes and undermines his commitment to a democratic politicisation of political philosophy. This chapter also explores the merits of the methodology that his book evaluates: the democratic politicisation of ontology. We shall see that my argument

[1] J Rawls, *A Theory of Justice: Revised Edition* (Cambridge, The Belknap Press of Harvard University Press, 1999) 508. Hereafter, *A Theory of Justice* will be referred to as *TOJ*.

[2] J Rawls, 'Justice as Fairness: Political not Metaphysical' (1985) 14 *Philosophy and Public Affairs* 223.

employs three methodological devices that are central to this politicisation: I make Rawls' implicit ontology explicit; I oppose it to a competing ontological theory; and I confront it with a case study on the Dutch dispute about the handshake that I alluded to in the introduction.

In 1985, John Rawls published an essay which urged political philosophers to cease the search for metaphysical and moral truth and to 'stay on the surface, philosophically speaking.'[3] Rawls observed that ontological and moral disputes did not admit of a solution and suggested that a consensus on justice could be formulated independently of contentious philosophical and religious views. By limiting himself to ideas that are widely shared in the political tradition of liberal-democratic societies the political philosopher could arrive at an agreement that is 'political, not metaphysical.'

The strategy to separate political thought from ontology (or, as Rawls puts it, metaphysics)[4] was further developed in Rawls' second book *Political Liberalism.* It is a highly innovative justificatory methodology in light of the tradition of political philosophy. Most leading political philosophers, such as Plato, Aristotle, Hobbes, Locke, Kant and Hegel, located their account of justice within an elaborate account of human nature.[5] For instance, Kant's defence of individual freedom was linked with a complex argument that human beings are not completely determined by history and biological drives but that they possess free will. Rawls, in contrast, says that it is not necessary for political philosophers to get involved in such difficult debates. A theory of justice can be built around a notion of political freedom, such as the idea that human beings need a set of rights and economic opportunities, and can remain agnostic about the philosophical status of freedom.

Political liberalism has found a large following among academic liberal political philosophers, both in the United States and in Europe.[6] It is not difficult to see why. In the last decades, liberal philosophers have often been confronted with various critiques of the central categories of liberalism: it was argued that important liberal notions, such as autonomy, equality and citizenship, were highly parochial because they were premised upon an

[3] ibid, 223–51.

[4] Rawls mostly uses the term metaphysics for what I have in the previous chapter defined as ontology (see s II). I will continue to use the term ontology in this chapter, except for the citations.

[5] *cf* J Rawls, *Political Liberalism: With a New Introduction and the 'Reply to Habermas'* (New York, Columbia University Press, 1996) xxix. Hereafter *Political Liberalism* will be referred to as *PL*.

[6] In the United States political liberalism has found a warm response among political philosophers such as Martha Nussbaum, Richard Rorty, Joshua Cohen, John Tomasi, William Galston, Stephen Macedo and Anthony Laden. In the Netherlands and Belgium, political liberalism has also been adopted by a number of political and legal philosophers such as Veit Bader, Cees Maris, Serge Gutwirth, Paul De Hert.

individualist worldview that is deeply contested in most liberal-democracies.[7] Political liberalism does not shy away from such disagreements but appears to take the contestability of individualism seriously: it acknowledges that individualist ways of life, such as those propagated by Kant, cannot be taken for granted in pluralist societies. At the same time however, political liberalism maintains that liberals need not abandon their hope of developing a just agreement for profoundly divided polities. Its proposal for a 'political, non metaphysical'—or, as Rawls later came to call it, 'free-standing'—consensus is so modest that it can provide an uncontroversial moral framework for solving political disputes. And, what is more, political liberalism provides an impetus to a much-needed democratic debate on justice by offering citizens insight into the various normative ideals in pluralist societies and by seeking to stimulate the democratic politicisation of political philosophy.

This chapter examines whether or not Rawls lives up to these promises. I will start by looking at some of Rawls' more general ideas about justification in political philosophy. We shall see that Rawls designed a sophisticated justificatory methodology to stimulate a democratic politicisation of political-philosophical accounts of justice, the so-called 'reflective equilibrium'. I will then piece together Rawls' reasons for excluding ontological argument from the reflective equilibrium and reconstruct his idea of a 'free-standing' consensus. *Political Liberalism* and some of Rawls' early articles such as the 'Independence of Moral Theory' provide important leads for assisting in this task.

The reconstruction of the concept of a 'free-standing' justification provides an important stepping-stone for the evaluation of the conceptual possibility and practical implications of a consensus that is 'political, not metaphysical'. This analysis first addresses Rawls' defence of political freedom in political liberalism. Does Rawls' concept of freedom succeed in avoiding taking sides in ontological dispute? Is it true that ontology has no orienting potential on matters of justice? To answer these questions I start by explicating Rawls' implicit ontology and confront his account with a competing ontology in democratic thought that has been developed by Charles Taylor. My evaluation of Rawls' strategy of avoidance then addresses the

[7] For communitarian critiques on *A Theory of Justice*, see M Sandel, *Liberalism and the Limits of Justice* (Cambridge, Cambridge University Press, 1982); C Taylor, *Philosophy and the Human Sciences: Philosophical Papers 2* (Cambridge, Cambridge University Press, 1985). Seyla Benhabib criticised the individualist presuppositions in the early Rawls from a feminist perspective, see S Benhabib, *Situating the Self: Gender, Community and Postmodernism in Contemporary Ethics* (Cambridge, Polity Press, 1992). A perceptive multicultural and postcolonial critique of liberalism in general and Rawls—including Rawls, *PL* (n 5)—can be found in the work of Bikhu Parekh (B Parekh, 'Superior People: The Narrowness of Liberalism from Mill to Rawls' (25 February 1994) *Times Literary Supplement*; B Parekh, *Rethinking Multiculturalism: Cultural Diversity and Political Theory* (London, Palgrave, 2000).

distributive principle of mutual respect in political liberalism. Next, I ask whether this principle is 'freestanding' and evaluate its orienting strength by confronting Rawls' account of justice with the case study from the Netherlands about the handshake. I conclude with an evaluation of the effects of separating ontology and political reflection in public reason: the guidelines for democratic discussions that citizens need to honour when they deliberate upon matters of basic justice. What are the implications of the restrictions on ontology in such democratic debates for Rawls' commitment to the democratic politicisation of political philosophy?

II. THE DEMOCRATIC POLITICISATION OF POLITICAL PHILOSOPHY

A. The Democratic Turn

The quest for a stable society is a central and classic concern in the tradition of Western political philosophy. Western political thought has, since its inception in ancient Greece, been preoccupied, as Sheldon Wolin puts it, with 'factors conducive to, or militating against, the maintenance of order'.[8] Rawls is no exception to this rule: he identifies the search for a consensus that can establish a just order in profoundly divided societies as the first task of political philosophy. Crucial to Rawls' political philosophy is the idea that political philosophers need to *justify* such an agreement or 'conception of justice': political philosophers must offer reasons that explain why they propose a particular consensus or, for that matter, why they think that such a consensus cannot be realised.[9] As the epigraph to this chapter suggests, the political philosopher offers such reasons to people with whom he *disagrees*: justification ought not to be mistaken for an exchange of viewpoints among those who are already of one mind in matters of justice. But, at the same time, justification must assume some common ground. For Rawls, this shared basis consists in the expectation that reason can reconcile our profound disagreements.

The function of reason in Rawls' justificatory approach has been interpreted in various conflicting ways. Rawls is often cast as a thinker who believes that political-philosophical reason can transcend historical contingencies and provide us with definite, unquestionable answers on matters of justice that need not be submitted to democratic contestation. As Chantal Mouffe puts it:

> By bringing to light the potential consequences of Rawls' project, my aim was to reveal the danger of postulating that there could be a rational definite solution to

[8] S Wolin, *Politics and Vision: Continuity and Innovation in Western Political Thought* (London, George Allen & Unwin Ltd, 1961) 8.

[9] A 'conception of justice' specifies principles and values that explain fair terms of cooperation for a society's main political, social and economic institutions (Rawls, *PL* (n 5) 11).

> the question of justice in a democratic society. ... To present the institutions of liberal democracy as the outcome of a purely deliberative rationality is to reify them and make them impossible to transform.[10]

Others have understood Rawls' justificatory methodology in a more historical vein. On this reading, Rawls does not so much assume that reason can transcend socio-historical practice, but rather that it helps the theorist to develop a coherent defence of historical practices. In the words of Richard Rorty:

> Rawls is not attempting a transcendental deduction of American liberalism or supplying philosophical foundations for democratic institutions, but [is] simply trying to systematize the principles and intuitions typical of American liberals.[11]

These readings are not unwarranted. For example, Rawls' ahistorical rationalism can be discerned in his infamous remark in *A Theory of Justice* that moral reasoning can be compared with adopting an eternal perspective ('sub specie aeternitatis'): a viewpoint that allows us to 'regard the human situation not only from all social but also from all temporal points of view'.[12] The historical Rawls is typically aligned with *Political Liberalism* wherein Rawls compares moral reasoning with the description of a culturally established consensus, or currently held moral intuitions ('we start by looking to the public culture itself as the shared fund of implicitly recognised basic ideas and principles').[13] But while both rationalist and historical interpretations find some support in Rawls' text they also tend to downplay another important commitment within Rawls' project, that is, of the need for democratic politicisation of political-philosophical reason. This 'democratic voice' is already present in earlier writings such as *A Theory of Justice*, but is most clearly audible in subsequent writings such as 'Reply to Habermas', *Public Reason Revisited*, *Justice as Fairness Revisited* and his *Lectures on the History of Political Philosophy*.[14] In these texts, Rawls explains that he does not intend to depoliticise justice with an appeal to either ahistorical reason or the authority of historical traditions but that he wants to submit competing understandings of justice to the critical scrutiny of the democratic public.

[10] C Mouffe, *The Democratic Paradox* (London, Verso, 2000) 32.

[11] R Rorty, 'Priority of Democracy to Philosophy', in H Richardson and P Weithman (eds), *The Philosophy of Rawls: A Collection of Essays, Volume 5* (New York, Garland, 1999) 215.

[12] Rawls, *TOJ* (n 1) 514. Or take the comparison that Rawls makes between formulating a set of moral principles and the attempt to unveil a universal grammar that foregrounds the capacity of native speakers to recognise well-formed sentences. This analogy comes close to identifying moral reflection with an intimation of an ahistorical moral order or structure (Rawls, *TOJ* (n 1) 41).

[13] Rawls, *PL* (n 5) 8.

[14] 'Reply to Habermas' was included as the ninth lecture in the revised edition of *Political Liberalism*.

For instance, in the introduction to the *Lectures on the History of Political Philosophy* Rawls distinguishes between two viewpoints on the relations between political philosophy and democratic practice.[15] In the so-called 'Platonic view' political philosophers are assumed to have a privileged access to truth that allows them to shape and determine the outcome of politics.[16] The 'democratic view', in contrast, does not consider the political philosopher to be in charge of the truth in political regimes but sees him as a *participant* in democratic processes of opinion-formation and decision-making. On this reading, philosophers offer concepts and ideals that may persuade and inspire political officials and other citizens but cannot command a privileged position in virtue of their expertise.

Rawls endorses the second, democratic, of these two portrayals of the political philosopher. To be sure, he notes that political philosophers will to some extent aspire to be *ahead* of politics. That is to say, in his role as educator, the political philosopher tries to influence the public culture that shapes everyday political reflection and decision-making:

> Political philosophy has an educational role as part of the background culture ... It plays this role in strengthening the roots of democratic thought and attitudes. This role it performs not so much in day-to-day politics as in educating citizens to certain ideal conceptions of person and political society before they come to politics, and in their reflective moments throughout life.[17]

But when political philosophy enacts this educational ambition it remains *part of* politics, that is, it is subjected to the consent of the democratic public:

> It is writers *and readers* together who produce and cherish works of political philosophy over time and it is always up to the voters to decide whether to embody their ideas in basic institutions. Thus, in a democracy, writers in political philosophy have no more authority than any other citizen, and should claim no more.[18]

The democratic turn in the later Rawls is also discernible in his suggestion that political philosophers should offer citizens *orientation* in a range of normative possibilities in a democratic regime. In addition to defending a just, stable agreement for collective decision-making, the second task of political philosophy consists in providing citizens with a conceptual framework through which they can reflectively orient themselves within the various ideals of a democratic society and their status as citizens:

> [P]olitical philosophy may contribute to how a people think of their political and social institutions as a whole, and their basic aims and purposes as a society with

[15] J Rawls in S Freeman (ed), *Lectures of the History of Political Philosophy* (Cambridge, The Belknap Press of Harvard University Press, 2007).

[16] Rawls considers Plato's philosopher king and Lenin's revolutionary vanguard exemplary role models for this mode of thought.

[17] Rawls (n 15) 5–7.

[18] ibid, 2 (emphasis added).

> a history—a nation—as opposed to their aims and purposes as individuals, or as members of families and associations. ... the idea is that it belongs to reason and reflection (both theoretical and practical) to orient us in the (conceptual) space, say, of all possible ends, individual and associational, political and social.[19]

The task of orientation seems to be much more attuned to the quality of the process of arriving at an agreement than focused on the result or outcome of democratic reason. For instance, it may stimulate political philosophers to deepen our understanding of the arguments that we draw upon in democratic deliberations and make us aware of normative possibilities ('all possible ends') in liberal democracies that we have so far not been particularly mindful about. Or, it might encourage political philosophers to clarify the various political-philosophical ideals that vie for hegemony in democratic culture instead of merely defending one version as the best. In this way, political philosophy actively encourages the democratic contestation of various political-philosophical projects and situates itself as being inherently part of democratic politics.[20]

B. The Reflective Equilibrium

Rawls' democratic view is powerfully illustrated by the methodological approach of the 'reflective equilibrium.' This figure specifies the criteria for the justification of a conception of justice and thus helps us to evaluate whether a particular conception conforms to Rawls' standard of a plausible judgement or 'reasonableness'.[21] Essentially, the reflective equilibrium says that one develops a conception of justice by confronting and mutually adjusting moral theory, intuitions and particular cases.

[19] J Rawls, *Justice as Fairness: A Restatement* (Cambridge, The Belknap Press of Harvard University Press, 2001) 2. Rawls adopts the term orientation from Kant (I Kant, 'What is Orientation in Thinking' in H Reiss (ed), *Kant: Political Writings* 2nd edn (Cambridge, Cambridge University Press, 1991). Rawls also identifies a third and fourth aim of political philosophy, that is, respectively, the encouragement of the reconciliation with, or the positive affirmation of, a society's institutions and the realisation of an agreement that is realisable in light of social and historical conditions.

[20] Rawls does not explicitly say that the task of orientation applies to political philosophy itself. Given his commitment to the democratic politicisation of political philosophy and his account of the reflective equilibrium (see next section), I assume that orientation includes the illumination of the various normative ends as specified by political philosophy as well as the application of these ends in fundamental law and policy-making (as discussed in public reason).

[21] In *Political Liberalism* Rawls makes a distinction between the 'reasonableness' and the 'truth' of moral and political judgements. The standard of reasonableness proposes a criterion of validity that only applies to the defence of a conception of justice for the political sphere and does not, like a theory of truth, offer a general philosophical account of the validity of all moral claims. So, in contradistinction to *A Theory of Justice*, where the reflective equilibrium was presented as an account of justification for all moral judgements, *Political Liberalism* limits the applicability of the reflective equilibrium to the political domain. As shall become clear in the next section, *Political Liberalism* needs to restrict the reach of its validity criterion to make it acceptable for citizens who subscribe to various competing theories of truth.

This section will reconstruct the reflective equilibrium and flesh out how this justificatory figure exemplifies Rawls' commitment to a democratic politicisation of political philosophy. Before presenting this account, however, I want to enter a caveat. By developing a democratic reading of Rawls I do not want to rescue him from his critics. Rawls' work contains what I consider problematic rationalist and uncritical historical trends and I will criticise some of these in this chapter. The point of attending to Rawls' 'democratic voice' is rather to bring into view a problematic tension in political liberalism that Rawls himself did not sufficiently acknowledge: as we shall see, the commitment to a democratic debate on political philosophy works against the strategy that attempts to avoid ontological disputes.

The reflective equilibrium specifies three justificatory conditions that citizens, including political philosophers, have to take into account when they defend or accept a fixed conception of justice. It holds that the justification of a conception of justice: (1) should include a critical learning process concerning moral intuitions and theory; (2) is inductive and leads to a contingent outcome; (3) needs the input of an ongoing, actual, democratic debate.[22]

First, the reflective equilibrium considers the critical evaluation of convictions and the tradition of philosophy essential to justificatory deliberations. Rawls assumes that our moral judgements are based in historical practices. A judge who tries to decide a legal case, a political philosopher who develops a theory of justice, and a citizen who evaluates such moral judgements, draw upon intuitions or what Rawls calls 'considered judgments.' A 'considered judgment' is a historically constituted conviction held with some confidence over a certain period of time. It is more thought-out than an instinctive response or an opinion formed under deep emotional distress but still 'pre-reflective' in the sense of not having been tested by a systematic

[22] I should mention that Rawls' scheme includes several other justificatory concepts, such as the method of political constructivism, the original position and public reason. I focus on the reflective equilibrium because it is Rawls' most general concept of justification and is systematically prior to the other justificatory notions: it elucidates the choice for these figures and, so to speak, serves as a criterion through which these other justificatory figures can claim to be reasonable. The last section will apply the insights of the reflective equilibrium that I reconstruct here in order to criticise the account of public reason and Rawls' justificatory appeal to the public culture of liberal-democracies. I do not, however, discuss political constructivism and the original position. The reason for this is that these figures explain the choice for a set of principles in light of the idea of political autonomy but do not offer a methodology to evaluate the reasonableness of political autonomy itself. Since my discussion questions the presupposition of political autonomy, I will evaluate the reasonableness of Rawls' idea of political autonomy in light of the reflective equilibrium. For an overview and discussion of Rawls' justificatory concepts, see S Freeman, *Rawls* (London, Routledge, 2007). For a discussion of the reflective equilibrium in the work of Rawls and moral theory, see, W van der Burg and T van Willigenburg (eds), *Reflective Equilibrium: Essays in Honour of Robert Heeger* (Dordrecht, Kluwer Academic Publishers, 1998).

set of principles.[23] For instance, when someone believes that gay marriage is unacceptable without having confronted this opinion with a moral principle, such as the right to sexual freedom or Mill's harm principle, Rawls would qualify this belief as a considered judgement.

While considered judgements are indispensable in developing a conception of justice, they are far from sufficient. Rawls considers it crucial that we critically examine our intuitions by confronting them with leading conceptions of justice in the philosophical tradition. And although we may in the end affirm our initial convictions, we have only reached a reflective equilibrium on justice when we allow for the possibility of a radical change of view. The reflective equilibrium should thus not be mistaken for the attempt to arrive at a coherent account of existing historical practices: *pace* Rorty, we do not only use philosophical thought to systematise our intuitions, we also consider such reflection as an aid to revise our convictions. As Rawls puts it in *A Theory of Justice*:

> There are, however, several interpretations of reflective equilibrium. For the notion varies depending upon whether one is to be presented with only those descriptions [conceptions of justice] which more or less match one's existing judgments except for minor discrepancies, or whether one is to be presented with all possible descriptions to which one might plausibly conform one's judgments together with all relevant philosophical arguments for them. In the first case we should be describing a person's sense of justice more or less as it is although allowing for the smoothing out of certain irregularities; in the second case a person' sense of justice may or may not undergo a radical shift. Clearly, it is the second kind of reflective equilibrium that one is concerned with in moral philosophy.[24]

I should note that the study of theory in the reflective equilibrium not only follows after an evaluation of intuitions but intends to stimulate a critique of the philosophical tradition as well. Rawls assumes that every theory of justice is biased to some extent: 'all theories are presumably mistaken in places'. Such flaws can be brought to light by confronting theoretical notions with intuitions, competing theoretical conceptions, as well as particular cases. Ideally, each citizen will reach a 'wide reflective equilibrium': he has considered 'the leading conceptions of political justice found in our philosophical tradition (including views critical of the concept of justice itself) and has weighed the force of the different philosophical and other reasons for them'.[25]

[23] J Rawls, 'Outline of a Decision Procedure for Ethics' in S Freeman (ed), *Collected Papers* (Cambridge, Harvard University Press, 2001) 6.

[24] Rawls, *TOJ* (n 1) 43.

[25] Rawls, *PL* (n 5) 384. The distinction between a narrow and a wide reflective equilibrium is identical with the distinction between the first and second equilibrium in the quote above from *A Theory of Justice*, see n 24. It is worth mentioning that *A Theory* recommends a somewhat more conservative reading list than *Political Liberalism*: whereas the first suggests that

The second characteristic of the reflective equilibrium is its emphasis on the contingent and inductive nature of moral claims. Rawls rejects justificatory criteria that model standards of reasonableness in terms of deductive logic, that is, a mode of reasoning which derives a conception of justice as a necessary conclusion from a few axiomatic premises.[26] Justificatory argument is inductive: it is 'a matter of mutual support of *many* considerations, of everything fitting together into one coherent view'.[27] While such a web of assumptions can convince us that one outcome is more probable or likely than others, it cannot ensure that its conclusions are compulsory or unavoidable. Both the 'input' of justificatory processes, that is, the convictions, cases and theories that we base our conception upon, as well as the 'output', namely, the conception of justice, are contingent.[28] Reaching a reflective equilibrium is hence not identical with setting up a logical proof, but is much closer to what Wittgenstein called our tendency to think in 'pictures' or holistic systems of judgement: 'It is not single axioms that strike me as obvious, it is a system in which consequences and premises give one another *mutual* support'.[29]

These considerations shed a somewhat different light on the ahistorical features in Rawls' project. As I noted at the beginning of this section, Rawls compares the justification of a conception of justice with the attempt to embrace a perspective of eternity. However, he also notes that this is a 'form of thought and feeling that rational persons can adopt *within the world*'.[30] The reflective equilibrium reveals that the ambition to transcend the current social and historical context remains constituted in a holistic network of contingent theoretical texts and (historical) intuitions.

The holistic nature of justificatory argument does not imply, however, that a conception of justice cannot draw support from key notions, or present certain ideas as central or first premises of a certain theory. Rawls' own conception of justice revolves around several such intuitions, such as an idea

the study of moral and political philosophy ought to be limited to those theories that make up 'the historical consensus about what so far seem to be the more reasonable and practicable moral conceptions', *Political Liberalism* underscores the need to study theories that are critical of justice as well (Rawls, *TOJ* (n 5) 509).

[26] During the process of the reflective equilibrium there is 'no point at which an appeal is made to self-evidence in the traditional sense either of general conceptions or particular convictions' (Rawls, *TOJ* (n 1) 19).

[27] ibid, 507 (emphasis added). For an account of moral reasoning as an inductive practice, see Rawls (n 23) 12.

[28] Rawls, *TOJ* (n 1) 506.

[29] L Wittgenstein, *On Certainty* (Oxford, Blackwell Publishing, 1969) para 142 (emphasis added). For a wonderful exploration of the relevance of Wittgenstein's notion of picture for political philosophy and its relation to the genealogical method of Foucault (which I discuss in the next chapter), see D Owen, 'Wittgenstein and Genealogy' (2001) 2 *Nordic Journal of Philosophy* 5.

[30] Rawls, *TOJ* (n 1) 514 (emphasis added).

of freedom, an account of material justice, and a central role for individual rights. But these notions—'fixed points' as Rawls qualifies them—will never do all the justificatory work. For example, an economic theorist who discerns an inconsistency in Rawls' defence of material justice will not reject Rawls' conception of justice for this reason alone. He might still come to accept Rawls' conception of justice because, say, he shares its insight that distribution is crucial for the realisation of freedom and believes that the general outlines of Rawls' proposal for distribution provide a good moral yardstick to evaluate current welfare states.

Finally, the reflective equilibrium demands that the justification of a conception of justice must include a deliberative process of the democratic citizenry. In *A Theory of Justice* Rawls envisaged the reflective equilibrium as a reasoning process of one individual. He assumed that one person could carry out the justificatory reasoning process on behalf of all her fellow citizens: 'We may suppose that everyone has in himself the whole form of a moral conception. ... The opinions of others are used only to clear our own heads'.[31] The later Rawls mitigates this position: from *Political Liberalism* on he conceptualises the justification of a conception of justice as the outcome of a collective, democratic reasoning process rather than an exercise in individual introspection. He now divides the justification process in three stages. In the first 'pro tanto' stage of justification, the political philosopher (or, for that matter, anyone interested in developing a conception of justice) presents a conception of justice. In this stage, a conception is justified when it is so complete that it can provide answers to questions of fundamental political justice.[32] Yet, justification is only prima facie here, because it can be superseded by the beliefs of citizens in the second, 'full justification' stage. During this stage, citizens evaluate whether the various conceptions of justice can be reconciled with their own moral convictions and other philosophical commitments, and each arrives at her own reflective equilibrium. The point of this stage is not just to critically evaluate *one* conception of justice, but to engage in a thorough politicisation of *several* conceptions of justice and reach wide reflective equilibrium. Finally, the third stage involves public justification by the political society. Here citizens deliberate with others to determine whether the conception of justice endorsed by them individually is also supported by other citizens and thus truly part of an overlapping consensus. In other words, a conception of justice can only claim to be fully justified or 'reasonable' when it has been critically examined in a collective reasoning process.[33]

[31] Rawls, *TOJ* (n 1) 44.

[32] For the definition of 'fundamental political justice', see below, text to n 92.

[33] In a nuanced, sympathetic reading of Rawls, Anthony Laden also highlights the more democratic aspects in Rawls' work as an alternative to more rationalist interpretations of Rawls (A Laden, 'The House that Jack Built: Thirty Years of Reading Rawls' (2003) 113 *Ethics* 367.

The reflective equilibrium permits no end to discussions on justice. While Rawls expects that the reflective equilibrium will result in a just, stable agreement he underscores that this consensus is tentative: 'the struggle for reflective equilibrium continues indefinitely'.[34] Furthermore, no conception of justice—including his own particular version of political justice, 'justice as fairness'—will suffice to give voice to groups and interests that arise from social change. This is why a well-ordered society needs to be governed by a 'family of reasonable political conceptions' rather than just one, and why democratic debate needs to welcome new proposals on justice that challenge the current hegemony.[35]

III. A 'FREESTANDING' JUSTIFICATION OF JUSTICE

We have seen that the democratic politicisation of political philosophy is integral to political liberalism. A reasonable conception of justice is not understood as an a priori truth that is found by the philosopher who is ahead of politics, but is seen as the product of historical practices that need to be submitted to a democratic learning process. Ideally, democratic cultures include a vibrant debate on political philosophy—a discussion that is not just carried out by professional political philosophers but by each and every citizen.

A distinct feature of political liberalism is its acknowledgement that citizens in liberal democracies support a variety of ontological worldviews. Rawls explicitly distinguishes his perspective from secular or rationalist thinkers who assume that human history will culminate in one rationalist

I agree with Laden that many readings of Rawls' work have paid insufficient attention to the role of democratic deliberation in Rawls' project and that it is somewhat misleading to suggest that Rawls sees himself as an expert whose principles of justice can claim an uncontestable authority over the citizenry. But I think that Laden's alternative reading of Rawls models Rawls' ambitions too much on the narrow reflective equilibrium and fails to address that, for Rawls, political philosophy should not just establish the coherence of our intuitions but must also stimulate a critique of our considered judgements. For Laden, Rawls' project is 'limited, as it involves defending the coherence of democratic thought and practice' and aims for 'a greater appreciation of the structure and content of our considered judgments' (Laden, ibid 384). In my view, once you take seriously Rawls' commitment to a critique of considered judgements the possibility of a coherent, just, stable agreement, that Laden seems to endorse, becomes much harder to defend.

[34] Rawls, *PL* (n 5) 97; *cf* Rawls, *TOJ* (n 1) 18: 'But this equilibrium is not necessarily stable. It is liable to be upset by further examination of the conditions which should be imposed on the contractual situation and by particular cases which may lead to revise our judgments.'

[35] J Rawls, 'The Idea of Public Reason Revisited' in *The Law of Peoples with 'The Idea of Public Reason Revisited'* (Cambridge, Harvard University Press, 1999) 140–43. For Rawls, reasonable conceptions depart from an idea of a free and equal person and a society as a fair system of cooperation over time, and include an account of basic rights, assume the priority of rights over the common good and perfectionist values and, finally, endorse an idea of material justice.

outlook, and who treat ontology and religion as temporary, irrational, aspects of human existence.[36] Political liberalism, in contrast, considers these phenomena as permanent features of human life in a liberal democracy; they are part of the so-called 'fact of pluralism'. The fact of pluralism means that public cultures of liberal democracies are characterised by a permanent plurality of incompatible, reasonable worldviews or 'comprehensive doctrines'.[37] Rawls regards this plurality as permanent because it arises naturally when citizens exercise their reason and judgement within a framework of free institutions.[38]

How does the plurality of ontological worldviews affect the justificatory deliberations on a conception of justice?

Political liberalism assumes that most citizens will want to give their conception a 'metaphysical foundation', and it allows ordinary citizens to investigate the compatibility of such a foundation with various conceptions of justice during the process of public justification.[39] So when a Catholic citizen tries to choose between Rawls' justice of fairness or, say, a Catholic type of communitarianism, she can make ample room in her reflective to examine how these views of justice relate to her own ontological commitment that human beings are equal creatures of god. But when someone participates in these debates as a *political philosopher*, that is, when she presents and defends her own *pro tanto* conception of justice, Rawls requires that she withholds ontological claims. A political philosopher needs to limit her defence of a conception of justice to moral theory, cases and moral intuitions and should not touch upon ontological issues.

[36] Rawls attributes this tendency to the neo-Kantian philosopher Jürgen Habermas: 'Habermas often criticizes religion and metaphysical views without taking much time to argue against them in detail; rather, he lays them aside … in light of his philosophical analysis of the presuppositions of rational discourse and communicative action.'(Rawls, *PL* (n 5) 376–77). I should mention that Habermas has developed a more sympathetic view of the merit of religious and metaphysical doctrines in the writings published subsequent to *Political Liberalism*: 'Even today, religious traditions … rescue from oblivion the dimensions of social and personal relations in which advances in cultural and social rationalization have caused utter devastation.' (J Habermas, *Between Naturalism and Religion: Philosophical Essays* (Cambridge, Polity Press, 2008) 6.

[37] A 'comprehensive doctrine' is a worldview that organises the moral, epistemological, metaphysical and religious in a relatively consistent theory. A 'reasonable' comprehensive doctrine is a doctrine that is developed through the exercise of reason and draws upon a tradition of thought (Rawls, *PL* (n 5) 19, 59).

[38] Rawls explains the fact that reason cannot transcend moral, ontological and epistemological disagreement in light of the so-called 'burdens of judgments': the multi-interpretability of empirical and scientific evidence, the vagueness of concepts, the differences in social backgrounds and experience, make it impossible for our capacities of reason and judgement to arrive at similar conclusions (Rawls, *PL* (n 5) 54–58). The distinction, then, between the 'fact of reasonable pluralism' and the 'fact of pluralism' is that the first is (at least partly) an effect of the exercise of reason whereas the latter is the result of 'self- and class interests' and the 'understandable tendency to view the political world from a limited standpoint.' (Rawls, *PL* (n 5) 37, 59).

[39] Rawls, *PL* (n 5) 126.

This strategy of avoidance for political philosophers seems a somewhat surprising step when one assumes, as Rawls does, that many citizens see a strong connection between ontology and political justice. For example, it appears quite at odds with the justificatory interest that these citizens could have in the ontological background theories of conceptions of justice. Imagine a Catholic citizen who believes that human beings are equal because they are made in the image of god and who tries to bring her considered judgement in reflective equilibrium with a conception of justice. Let us also assume that the principles she consults are presented in political liberalist fashion: they affirm her intuition that human beings ought to be treated equally but they do not explain why they attribute human beings with an equal status. This silence on ontological premises of equality could render our citizen dissatisfied. For instance, in discussions on bio-ethics, she has often noted that ontological beliefs tend to play an important role in deciding which human beings are worthy of equal respect. And she is very concerned about some of these beliefs: in her view, the claim that human beings are equal in light of their capacity for rational choice is dangerous because it makes it possible to exclude those who cannot make rational choices, such as the mentally handicapped or brain-dead citizens, from the principle of equal respect. So for this citizen the strategy of avoidance in political liberalism creates a justificatory deficit: given the effect of ontological beliefs on matters of fundamental justice, she finds it is crucial that political philosophers elucidate the ontological premises that foreground their conception of justice.[40]

Why, then, is it so crucial for Rawls to exclude ontological theories from political philosophy? How does he explain to citizens, who may find it intuitively implausible to separate ontology from justice, that the strategy of avoidance is in fact the best conception of political philosophy available? And what exactly *is* a 'political, non-metaphysical' justification?

[40] In their interesting articles on the role of fundamental worldviews in moral reasoning Ton van den Beld and Carl Reinhold Bråkenhielm have also pointed out the relevance of ontological and religious worldviews in the wide reflective equilibrium of individual moral enquirers (T van den Beld, 'Background Theories and Religious Beliefs: Their Role and Relation in Reflective Equilibrium' in W van der Burg and T van Willigenburg (eds), *Reflective Equilibrium: Essays in Honour of Robert Heeger* (Dordrecht, Kluwer Academic Publishers, 1998) 73; C Bråkenhielm, 'Reflective Equilibrium and Cosmological Claims' in van der Burg and van Willigenburg (eds), ibid 157. They do not, however, discuss the implications of this point for the *pro tanto* justification that is carried out by the political philosopher. Van den Beld appears to endorse Rawls' strategy of avoidance in the context of reaching a political agreement: he agrees with Rawls' exclusion of ontology from public reason while pointing out that individual citizens must retain the possibility of bringing political agreement in reflective equilibrium to their own comprehensive beliefs. This position is similar to Rawls' argument for an 'overlapping consensus', see next section.

A. Stability and Ontology

Rawls gives no straightforward definition of 'metaphysics', but his understanding of the term comes close to what, in the introductory chapter, I have qualified as an ontology: presuppositions about the fundamental conditions of political existence and the limits and possibilities that these constituent features open up.[41] For example, Rawls says that 'metaphysical' claims may involve a thesis about the 'nature of persons as moral or political agents'.[42] And, elsewhere, he defines metaphysics as 'a general account of what there is, including fundamental, fully general statements—for example, the statements "every event has a cause" and "all events occur in time and space."'[43]

It is easy to assume that when Rawls speaks of a 'political, not metaphysical' justification he has in mind a political philosophy that does not appeal to ontological claims whatsoever. But Rawls' picture of the relation between ontology and political philosophy is more nuanced than that. In light of the fact of pluralism the claim that a conception of justice can be strictly separated from ontology is difficult to maintain: since there is no agreement on the meaning of 'metaphysical' in the philosophical tradition citizens will most likely disagree as to whether a particular assumption is 'metaphysical' or 'purely political'. So Rawls rather suggests that a political philosopher ought not to show any affiliation with a particular ontological tradition and limit herself to the usage of ontological notions that do not discriminate between competing conceptions of justice:

> If metaphysical presuppositions are involved, perhaps they are so general that they would not distinguish between the metaphysical views—Cartesian, Leibnizian, or Kantian; realist, idealist, or materialist—with which philosophy has traditionally been concerned. In this case they would not appear to be relevant for the structure and content of a political conception of justice one way or the other.[44]

Rawls' most familiar argument for the need of a 'free-standing' justification comes from *Political Liberalism*. Here Rawls considers the separation between political philosophy and ontology as an essential condition of possibility for realising stability in pluralist societies. To explain this point I must first briefly address the problem of the account of stability in *A Theory of Justice*.

Rawls advances a *moral* understanding of stability. Unlike a social contract thinker, such as Hobbes, Rawls is not satisfied with a modus vivendi,

[41] See ch 1.
[42] Rawls, *PL* (n 5) 29.
[43] ibid, 379. Rawls presents this definition in a discussion with Habermas where he qualifies Habermas' social ontology of communicative action as a metaphysical perspective.
[44] ibid, 29.

that is, a society where justice provides order due to a balance of forces. Rawls envisages citizens subscribing to a conception of justice for *moral* reasons: they ought to support it because it converges with their own moral outlook and not act upon it for mere prudential reasons. The possibility of realising stability became increasingly troublesome for Rawls. In *A Theory of Justice* Rawls assumed that most citizens subscribed to his so-called 'Kantian interpretation' of freedom. Like Kant, Rawls identified individual autonomy with self-legislation, that is, the capacity of human beings to be directed by principles that reason imposes upon oneself, rather than being led by heteronomous inclinations such as historical customs, social pressure or emotional impulses.[45] Rawls expected that individuals would want to realise this capacity in all domains of life: both in public matters (such as when accepting a conception of justice), and in private issues (say, when joining a church or marrying someone), human beings were seen as trying to overcome heteronomy through the exercise of reason. This account of stability was construed in light of this Kantian notion of autonomy. For instance, Rawls said that human beings desire to act upon principles of justice because they 'express their nature as rational and equal members of the intelligible realm with precisely this liberty to choose'.[46] He also argued that we would never compromise our sense of justice, that is, the innate capacity to formulate and act upon moral principles, because this 'sentiment reveals what the person is and to compromise it is not to achieve for the self free reign but to give way to the contingencies and accidents of the world'.[47] Stability was further secured by the premise that all individual life-plans are part of 'the larger comprehensive plan that regulates the community', one that encompassed 'ideals and forms of life … developed and tested … sometimes for generations'.[48]

Political Liberalism departs from this somewhat homogenous conception of human society. Rawls came to see that his Kantian-inspired account of stability misrecognises the fact of reasonable pluralism: in light of the ineradicable disagreements between moral, philosophical and religious worldviews, it is unrealistic to expect that all citizens will eventually understand themselves as essentially free and equal individuals or, for that matter, that they will come to agree on another comprehensive doctrine in support of justice. Rawls hence revises his account of a stable society. He now envisions

[45] If the will seeks the law that is to determine it *anywhere* else than in the fitness of its maxims for its own giving of universal law—consequently if, in going beyond itself, it seeks this law in a property of any of its objects—*heteronomy* always results. The will in that case does not give itself the law; instead the object, by means of its relation to the will, gives the law to it (I Kant, 'Groundwork of the Metaphysics of Morals' in *Immanuel Kant: Practical Philosophy* (Cambridge, Cambridge University Press, 1996) 89).

[46] Rawls, *TOJ* (n 1) 225.

[47] ibid, 503.

[48] ibid, 493–94.

that a conception of justice will be supported by an overlapping consensus of various comprehensive doctrines instead of one comprehensive set of reasons. This implies, for instance, that the equal status of citizens—a central value in political liberalism—can be justified in different ways. A Kantian might support this idea with an appeal to the essentially autonomous nature of human beings, whereas our Catholic citizen may draw upon the insight that all human beings are creatures of god.

The reconceptualisation of stability as an overlapping consensus has important consequences for the justificatory methodology of the political philosopher. An account of justice that wants to yield support from the various incompatible reasonable comprehensive doctrines cannot appeal to reasons that contradict or offend one of those worldviews. Therefore Rawls suggests that a conception of justice should not draw on moral, epistemological or ontological comprehensive doctrines, but appeal to ideas implicit in the political tradition of democratic societies or, more specifically, 'its traditions of interpretation of the constitution and basic laws, as well as of its leading historical documents and widely known political writings'.[49] By presenting itself in such 'purely political' terms, a *pro tanto* conception of justice will be able to forge an overlapping consensus:

> The central idea is that political liberalism moves within the category of the political and leaves philosophy as it is. It leaves untouched all kinds of doctrines—religious, metaphysical, and moral—with their long traditions of development and interpretation. ... For in presenting a freestanding political conception and not going beyond that, it is left entirely open to citizens and associations in civil society to formulate their own ways of going beyond, or of going deeper, so as to make that political conception congruent with their comprehensive doctrines.[50]

In other words, Rawls suggests that the strategy of avoidance does *not* lead to a justificatory deficit for citizens who see a strong link between ontology and justice but rather leaves them ample space to make the conception of justice compatible with their own ontological doctrines. Even though he expects that citizens will come to agree on a conception of justice, he assumes that they will continue to *disagree* on the reasons for why they support this conception.

B. The Disorienting and Depoliticising Effects of Ontology

Rawls presents another set of considerations for the strategy of avoidance in the article 'Independence of Moral Theory'—an essay that was published

[49] Rawls, *PL* (n 5) 376.
[50] ibid, 375–78.

between *A Theory of Justice* and *Political Liberalism*.[51] While these arguments are not as fully developed as his later stability-argument, I will briefly address some of the points in this essay because they appear to be a forerunner of his later commitment to the orienting task of practical philosophy, and the need for a democratic politicisation of dominant political philosophical ideas.

One of the central claims in this essay is that ontological arguments provide no insight into debates of justice but rather draw our attention away from such disputes. In Rawls' view, ontological claims are so underdetermined that they only become intelligible in light of a substantive moral ideal: 'the variations among the [ontological] criteria are not antecedent to moral theory but explained by it'.[52] For example, when I compare a utilitarian or Kantian conception of justice in my reflective equilibrium this investigation might reveal that these moral ideals appeal to a very different ontology of personal identity. Utilitarianism typically sees the human person as a sequence of agreeable feelings, whereas Kantian ideals assume that the human self does not only have a capacity for agreeable consciousness but can also take responsibility for goals and desires over a lifetime. To explain the differences between these ideals, however, Rawls suggests that it is much more important to understand the *moral* argument for an account of personhood than to analyse the ontological claims. For instance, utilitarians typically do not adopt a theory of personal identity because they think that this account is the most convincing outcome of difficult ontological debates. Rather, they choose a particular ontological account for distinctly *moral* reasons, namely, because they strive for a society that maximises the net amount of happiness. Likewise, Kantians aim for a regime where individuals take responsibility for their interests and desires and therefore use an ontological criterion that fits this moral requirement.

Rawls does not only believe that ontological argument teaches us very little about justice, he also claims that a theorist who engages with ontological disputes runs the risk of relegating more urgent moral issues, such as a conception of a just society, to the reserve bench. As in his later work, Rawls wagers that ontological questions will most likely not admit of definitive resolution and suggests that the best way to deepen our understanding of justice is to bracket ontological questions and to focus on the study of moral conceptions themselves. In this way the theorist does not waste reflective energies on issues that might become superfluous in reaching a satisfactory account of justice.

[51] J Rawls, 'The Independence of Moral Theory' in Freeman (ed) (n 23). During the early phase Rawls did not distinguish between comprehensive moral conceptions and political moral conceptions. Since I concentrate here on the early argument this section uses the term 'moral' for both political and comprehensive moral claims.

[52] ibid, 296.

The second reason for the strategy of avoidance that I need to address is Rawls' claim that ontological inquiries provide an obstacle for a critique of dominant ideas of personhood. Rawls seems to worry that an engagement with ontology blinds us to the profound influence of socio-historical practices on realising a particular ideal of the person. For example, he observes that focusing the dispute between utilitarian and Kantian ideals on ontological issues could easily convince us that a utilitarian notion of the person ought to be preferred over a Kantian one. After all, the Kantian idea that human beings can take responsibility over their lifetime appears to be much more difficult to substantiate than the utilitarian notion of agreeable consciousness. But Rawls emphasises that the possibilities of personhood are not just an effect of theoretical debates but are also deeply shaped by the dominant ethico-political order in a particular society:

> What persons we are is shaped by how we think of ourselves and this is turn is influenced by the social forms we live under. ... There is no degree of connectedness that is natural or fixed; the actual continuities and sense of purpose in people's lives is relative to the socially-achieved moral conception.[53]

So even if utilitarian self-understandings would have become predominant in a particular context, we should not take this as a natural state of affairs. As long as a Kantian concept of the person is not impossible given our theoretical insights, we can develop and defend this viewpoint and use it as a critical counterpoint to the practices that constitute the current hegemonic self-understanding and its intuitions. In other words, Rawls suggests that an engagement with ontology moves us closer to views that situate philosophical notions ahead of political practice and jeopardises a more democratic account in which dominant assumptions ought to be challenged in a democratic debate.

IV. POLITICISING POLITICAL LIBERALISM

So far I have developed a reconstruction of Rawls' concept of a democratic, 'freestanding' justification. Why and how does Rawls exclude ontological argument from political philosophy? By now, I hope that the answers to these questions have become clear. In Rawls' view, an engagement with ontological disputes provides an obstacle for arriving at an overlapping consensus, gives no insight into debates on justice, and discourages the democratic politicisation of dominant political-philosophical notions of the self. As an alternative, Rawls proposes the idea of a 'political, not metaphysical' justification. This notion should not be mistaken for the claim that ontological claims play no role in political philosophy but rather holds that any

[53] ibid, 300.

(latent) ontological premises are, first of all, not partisan and, second, that these claims have no discriminatory effect on the principles of justice.

In this section I shall evaluate Rawls' plea for a strategy of avoidance. Is Rawls right that a 'freestanding' justification can provide a just, stable agreement? And is it true that ontological assumptions provide no orientation in debates on justice and hamper the democratic contestation of philosophical notions of personhood? The analysis will start by turning to Rawls' ideas of individual freedom. Rawls considers his notion of autonomy central to all reasonable conceptions of democratic justice. That is to say, he assumes that each of the 'family of reasonable conceptions' that are part of political liberalism will endorse his account of freedom (even though they may disagree on the best interpretation of this ideal).[54] It therefore does not come as a surprise that Rawls defends the possibility of a freestanding justification most ardently in his argument for freedom or, as he later came to call it, political autonomy. I challenge the 'freestanding' and orienting quality of Rawls' understanding of freedom by confronting his defence with a competing ontologically-grounded concept of freedom in current democratic thought that has been developed by Charles Taylor.

The second part of my analysis concentrates on an essential condition for realising political autonomy and establishing allegiance to a just liberal-democratic regime: a fair distribution of mutual respect. At this point, I will no longer evaluate Rawls in light of disagreements in contemporary democratic thought but analyse his position in relation to a democratic struggle in the Netherlands: the conflict about orthodox Muslims who refuse to shake hands with members of the other sex. I argue that Rawls' framework is not impartial enough, and offers too little orientation for citizens who do not affirm an individualist, rights-based account of freedom.

I end my discussion by taking a critical look at the separation between ontology and political argument in public reason. Political liberalism claims that citizens need to conduct their democratic debates on basic justice in light of purely political reasons specified by public reason and should not appeal to controversial ontological arguments. I argue that this restriction on ontology in public reason undermines Rawls' commitment to the democratic politicisation of political philosophy.

A. Ontological Remnants in the Notion of Political Freedom

Political Liberalism confronts Rawls with the difficult task of developing a concept of freedom that does not rest upon a contentious ontological worldview. Earlier, I explained that Rawls initially assumed that we saw

[54] 'Each of these liberalisms endorses the underlying ideas of citizens as free and equal persons and of society as a fair system of cooperation over time' (Rawls (n 35) 141).

ourselves 'as essentially free and equal rational beings' and that each one of us would strive for a critical examination of ends in both public and private life. *Political liberalism* reconceptualises this ideal of freedom into a *political* principle: it limits the pursuit of freedom to the political sphere and sees freedom as a status that we adopt as citizens rather than as an expression of our human nature. In fact, Rawls now assumes that many citizens do *not* aspire to an autonomous way of life in their personal or associational life but pursue heteronomous ideals in these spheres:

> They may have, and often do have at any given time, affections, devotions, and loyalties that they believe they would not, indeed could and should not, stand apart from and evaluate objectively. They may regard it as simply unthinkable to view themselves apart from certain religious, philosophical, and moral convictions, or from certain enduring attachments and loyalties.[55]

The task for citizens in political liberalism is to reconcile their heteronomous collective attachments with the demands of political autonomy. This implies that citizens come to appreciate that individual rights are prior to collective attachments: citizens are allowed to change their faith or end their participation in a cultural practice such as a religiously sanctioned marriage. It also entails that citizens accept that the state recognises citizens as bearers of individual rights rather than as members of cultural or linguistic groups, classes or religious affiliations, and that it cannot enforce citizens to practice a particular conception of the good.

Rawls realises that these demands are sometimes painful and difficult given the strong sense of belonging that many citizens experience. Yet he wagers that this ideal is 'free-standing' enough to forge an overlapping consensus in a profoundly pluralised polity. Central to this claim is a reference to the political tradition of democratic society. Rawls does not appeal to a contentious ontological doctrine but is merely giving an account of the self-understanding of citizens in a democratic culture: 'we *describe* how citizens think of themselves in a democratic society when questions of justice arise'.[56]

i. The Democratic Culture-Argument for Political Autonomy

To what extent does the appeal to the democratic culture of liberal democracies provide a sound defence for a 'free-standing' notion of political autonomy?

An answer to this question must first address a methodological point. *Political Liberalism* seems burdened by a tension between, on the one hand, the way that Rawls carries out the justification with regard to democratic

[55] Rawls, *PL* (n 5) 31.
[56] ibid, 33 (emphasis added).

culture and, on the other hand, the critical learning process central to the wide reflective equilibrium. The plea for political autonomy in terms of public culture represents this notion as an empirically verifiable, considered judgement: it is an intuition that is said to rest upon a coherent reconstruction of the ruling moral and political ideas in the public culture of liberal democracies.[57] Now, we have seen in the account of the wide reflective equilibrium that Rawls does not want to take such considered judgements for granted but instead aims to submit them to a learning process. His democratic culture-defence of individual freedom, however, does not live up to this commitment to a democratic politicisation of political philosophy. For instance, *Political Liberalism* does not critically examine the contestability of the intuition of political autonomy in the light of competing conceptions of justice in democratic culture. Quite the contrary: it assumes, rather than argues for, the claim that the intellectual sources of liberal-democratic culture converge in a coherent commitment to political autonomy. How convincing, then, would Rawls' idea of freedom be if we *do* apply the insights of the wide reflective equilibrium and confront political autonomy with some 'widely known political writings' in the tradition of liberal democracies that consider this idea deeply controversial?

Such a critique would, I believe, most likely provide a powerful challenge to Rawls' claim that his ideal is only a coherent reconstruction of democratic thought. For instance, many influential modes of thought that are part of the tradition of liberal democracies reject the primacy of individual rights central to the social contract tradition. Marxism, utilitarianism and communitarianism, to a greater or lesser extent, allow for the possibility that rights can be overruled by collective or perfectionist aims and thus reject a basic tenet of Rawls' concept of freedom.

Let me explain this point by taking an example from contemporary democratic thought: the work of Charles Taylor, a communitarian thinker who has become well-known for his support of collective rights for cultural communities and who is one of the most influential critics of current social contract theorists, such as Rawls.[58] Taylor agrees with Rawls that a concept of freedom needs to be supported by liberal-democratic theory and practices. However, Taylor offers a very different and conflicting reconstruction of the democratic tradition: on his reading, the self-understanding of democratic

[57] *cf* Rawls (n 15) 335: 'It is a conception of the person that is based in empirical facts about social cooperation and how we actually conceive of ourselves in one important area of our lives, in our capacity as citizens.' Rawls himself qualifies the basic ideas of political liberalism as 'convictions' or 'provisional fixed points' (Rawls, *PL* (n 5) 8).

[58] It is unfortunately not possible in the context of one chapter to confront Rawls' notion of freedom with more than one position and to really bring his notion into a wide reflective equilibrium. Nonetheless, even a comparison with one competing position already challenges Rawls' understanding of political autonomy. The next chapter will introduce another competing position, namely, Foucault's notion of freedom, into the reflective equilibrium.

citizens is implicitly bound up with the good of 'cultural recognition', that is, with the idea that the positive affirmation of one's cultural background is a vital human need.[59] In Taylor's view, any sensible conception of political freedom must take into account this good: misrecognising the cultural distinctness of people can 'inflict a grievous wound, saddling its victims with a crippling self-hatred'.[60] And he argues that this value should, in some cases, trump the individual rights central to liberal interpretations of public culture: when individual rights do not suffice to protect vulnerable cultural communities, the constitution should open up a space for the recognition of such groups even if this violates the exercise of certain individual rights.[61]

Taylor's critique of the social contract tradition suggests that Rawls' defence of political autonomy is not merely describing 'the' self-understanding of democratic citizens but that political liberalism is rather arguing for *one* contentious interpretation of the democratic tradition over the other. How can Rawls, then, sustain his claim that his concept of freedom is the most plausible one? If the democratic tradition yields competing conceptions of freedom, why should we opt for Rawls' account?

Contrary to what some of his readers have claimed, I want to suggest that Rawls' defence of freedom is not limited to the description of a 'social fact' about democratic culture but that Rawls supplements this empirical justification of freedom with an ontological argument.[62] For instance, *Political Liberalism* grounds the assumption that we consider ourselves rights-bearing individuals in an account of moral personality and a theory

[59] C Taylor, 'The Politics of Recognition' in A Gutmann (ed), *Multiculturalism: Examining the Politics of Recognition* (New Jersey, Princeton University Press, 1994). Taylor refers to nationalist, minority and multicultural movements that have demanded public recognition as members of cultural groups rather than rights-bearing individuals and draws on thinkers such as Hegel.

[60] ibid, 26.

[61] Taylor's defence of cultural group rights concentrates on the French-Canadian province Quebec. At issue here was a dispute pertaining to the constitution which, according to Rawls, ought to depart from the primacy of individual rights. The Quebeckers wanted to make the flourishing and public recognition of the distinctness of French culture a leading principle for the judicial interpretation of constitutional rights (ibid, 53).

[62] For instance, Samuel Freeman suggests that Rawls does not make any ontological claims but is limiting himself to an empirical defence of freedom: 'The suggestion is that *it is simply a social fact* that in practical contexts we regard ourselves as free agents who can be held responsible for our actions; and that in matters of justice we regard one another as equals. … This less ambitious account of persons does not make any metaphysical claims regarding our nature. But notice that it also does not rule out one either. For one can always ask, "*Why* do we conceive of ourselves as free and equal persons?" And the answer may well be that our self-conception stems from our "nature" as such beings.' (emphasis added) Rawls (n 15) 301. On the reading that I develop in this section, Rawls proposes an *ontological* thesis himself: he is justifying his notion of political autonomy with a historical claim—showing us *where* to find his belief in political autonomy—and an ontological argument—showing us *why* we conceive ourselves as free and equal. My reading finds support in Rawls' acknowledgement that his account could presuppose a thesis about the constitutive features of human agency, though I disagree, of course, with Rawls' claim that his ontology is uncontroversial.

of personal identity. Are these ontological arguments so general that they do not discriminate between ontological traditions and conceptions of justice?

ii. The Ontological Defence

As in *A Theory of Justice,* Rawls argues that moral agency consists of two moral powers (a sense of justice and a capacity for the conception of the good). This conception of moral personhood constitutes the ground for our political autonomy and our public recognition as rights-bearing individuals:

> The basic idea is that *in virtue of* their two moral powers (a capacity for a sense of justice and for a conception of the good) and the powers of reason (of judgment, thought, and inference connected with these powers), persons are free.[63]

> *Given their* moral power to form, revise and rationally pursue a conception of the good, their public identity is not affected by changes over time in their determinate conception of it.[64]

These assumptions, brief as they may be, are not as general or uncontroversial as they need to be for a 'freestanding' justification. Like Kant, Rawls presents a distinctly mentalist account of moral personhood: it conceptualises moral agency as a mental disposition rather than as a characteristic of intersubjective practices. For instance, Rawls sees our moral powers as interior mental acts: they are understood as an 'exercise of thought', 'willingness' or 'desire' (in the case of a sense of justice) or 'deliberative rationality' that is expressed in a plan of life (with regard to the capacity for a conception of the good).[65] Moreover, Rawls considers these moral capacities as innate characteristics that individuals *possess*: they are understood as 'natural attributes' and we are seen as '*having* these two moral powers'.[66]

[63] Rawls, *PL* (n 5) 19 (emphasis added).

[64] ibid, 30 (emphasis added).

[65] '[W]e regard the sense of justice as a *mental capacity, as involving the exercise of thought*' (emphasis added) (Rawls, *TOJ* (n 1) 42); 'A sense of justice is the capacity to understand, to apply, and to act from the public conception of justice (Rawls, *PL* (n 5) 19). While acting is part of a sense of justice, Rawls considers mental states such as will and desire prior to action: 'a sense of justice also expresses a *willingness, if not the desire, to act* in relation to others on terms that they can also publicly endorse' (emphasis added) (Rawls, *PL* (n 5) 19). For the capacity for a conception of the good, see Rawls, *TOJ* (n 1) 49: 'a rational plan is one that would be chosen with *deliberative rationality*' (emphasis added); Rawls, *PL* (n 5) 19: 'The capacity for a conception of the good is the capacity to form, to revise, and rationally pursue a conception of one's rational advantage or good'. I should stress that *Political Liberalism* does no longer assume that all citizens will develop their plan of life by using their capacity for deliberative rationality and acknowledges that heteronomous attachments may become more decisive in the pursuit of a life-plan. Nonetheless, Rawls maintains his assumption that each individual maintains the capacity to submit historical practices to the test of critical reason and it is in virtue of this capacity that he assumes that citizens will want to be recognised as rights-bearing individuals in public life.

[66] Rawls, *PL* (n 5) 19 (emphasis added). The argument that the moral powers rely on a natural basis is developed in *A Theory of Justice* (Rawls, *TOJ* (n 1) 444) and is taken on in *Political Liberalism* (Rawls, *PL* (n 5) 19 (fn 21)).

This individualist, mentalist account of freedom has been fiercely criticised in much of twentieth century philosophy. Pragmatists, hermeneutic philosophers and post-structuralists have all rejected the identification of freedom with an individual mental capacity and have argued that thought and moral agency are constituted by intersubjective linguistic practices.[67] To explain this point let me briefly return to Charles Taylor who offers an elaborate example of such an alternative ontology. Central to Taylor's account of personhood is a critique of Kant's understanding of individual freedom. For Taylor, moral agency cannot be reduced to individual mental acts but is essentially dependent upon linguistic practices that offer moral standards or 'qualitative distinctions' that render 'some action, or mode of life, or mode of feeling ... incomparably higher than the others'.[68] Human beings cannot submit these practices to autonomous choice because we can never transcend these practices or make them fully transparent:

> [T]he words we use now only have sense though their place in a whole web, we can never in principle have a clear oversight of the implication of what we are saying at any moment. Our language is always more than we can encompass; it is in a sense inexhaustible.[69]

And, Taylor underscores the point that these linguistic practices are inherently historical: they become available to us through an ethnic, national or religious way of life that is shared and practised by a group of people over time. In other words, Taylor's ontology reveals that Rawls' account of moral personality is ontologically much more controversial than Rawls claims it to be. Taylor sees agency as a historically situated intersubjective linguistic practice and this account is deeply at odds with Rawls' understanding of agency in terms of a mental capacity that can be attributed to the individual subject.

Rawls' second argument for the primacy of individual rights appeals to a notion of personal identity and has similar difficulties in maintaining its ontological impartiality. In an oblique response to his communitarian critics, Rawls emphasises the profound influence of non-public affections and loyalties on human identity. Robbing people of such commitments could lead to an identity crisis: 'we would be disoriented and unable to carry on'.[70] Rawls even notes that sudden changes in fundamental commitments often give the impression that we are no longer the same person. However, Rawls

[67] For a brief but clear discussion of the pragmatist and hermeneutic critique of the mentalist notion of subjectivity, see J Habermas, 'Philosophy as Stand-In and Interpreter' in *Moral Consciousness and Communicative Action* (Cambridge, Polity Press, 1990) 1–20. The next chapter will elaborate on the post-structuralist critique of Michel Foucault.

[68] C Taylor, *Sources of the Self: The Making of the Modern Identity* (London, Cambridge University Press, 1989) 19.

[69] C Taylor, *Human Agency and Language: Philosophical Papers I* (Cambridge, Cambridge University Press, 1985) 231.

[70] Rawls, *PL* (n 5) 31.

claims that such existential *Angst* has no effect on the primacy of individual freedom in public life because individuals can never be reduced to fundamental commitments and loyalties:

> On the road to Damascus Saul of Tarsus becomes Paul the Apostle. Yet such a conversion implies no change in our public or institutional *nor in our personal identity* as this concept is understood in the philosophy of the mind.[71]

Rawls mentions several possibilities that explain why our personal identity remains intact irrespective of the particular changes in loyalties and affections. He alludes to a sense of continuity in terms of memory, the body, the Kantian ego, or fundamental moral aims, but he does not pursue this point any further: the question of personal identity is obviously too contentious to be explored extensively in the defence of a 'free-standing' concept of freedom. Yet, scarce as the references may be, the few mentioned possibilities are ontologically controversial: they foreground our capacity for personal identity in individual characteristics (one's body, capacity for memory, or reason) and, like his account of moral personality, exclude the constitutive role of linguistic and historical practices in the formation of personal identity.[72] So Rawls' attempt to ground the primacy of individual rights in a free-standing notion of personal identity is unsuccessful.

Let us take stock of the discussion so far. My analysis of Rawls' defence of political autonomy suggests that political liberalism cannot sustain the claim that its concept of freedom stays out of ontological disputes. Rawls' notion of freedom rests upon a controversial individualist-mentalist ontology that misrecognises the function of heteronomous historically-situated linguistic practices in the constitution of moral agency and personal identity. Moreover, we have seen that the ontological partiality of political liberalism has significant consequences for its conception of justice and the orientation that it provides in the normative possibilities of liberal-democratic regimes. The assumption that moral agency is rooted in an individual mental capacity is an important step in Rawls' defence of the primacy of individual rights and is thus not indiscriminate with respect to the content of justice. That is to say, when one sees freedom as inevitably constituted by historical linguistic frameworks rather than located in the individual, Rawls' prima facie rejection of collective recognition becomes less intelligible and convincing: in that case one might opt, as Taylor does, for a conception of justice that allows for the protection of cultural groups through public recognition, such as constitutional law.

[71] ibid (emphasis added).

[72] The communitarian thinker MacIntyre makes a similar point with regard to the conceptualisation of personal identity in the analytic tradition in general, see A MacIntyre, *After Virtue: a Study in Moral Theory* 2nd (corrected) edition (London, Duckworth, 1985) 217. I address MacIntyre's theory of tradition in ch 4.

So, in sum, the ontological partisanship of political liberalism makes it much less plausible than Rawls claims it to be for his conception of justice to realise an overlapping consensus. During public justification many citizens will most likely not come to see political liberalism as 'free-standing', but rather will consider it representative of citizens who affirm an individualist, mentalist understanding of autonomy.

B. The Principle of Mutual Respect and Public Reason

I have argued that political liberalism has a disorienting effect on debates about justice and is not freestanding enough to forge a just, stable agreement. But perhaps putting it that way is a little hasty because Rawls would most likely raise the following objection to this conclusion: even if the account of freedom includes some contested ontological premises, it is unfair to dispute the reasonableness of political liberalism in light of one contentious assumption alone. As I explained earlier, Rawls underscores the point that the justification of a conception of justice ought not to be reduced to the defence of one premise, arguing that it is dependent upon a wide range of concerns. This section will therefore evaluate political liberalism through the perspective of two additional concepts that Rawls considers crucial for the plausibility of the conception of justice: the principle of mutual respect, and public reason. I analyse these concepts with reference to the dispute that I already touched upon in the introductory chapter: the conflict concerning orthodox Muslims seeking exemption from the dominant basic greeting rituals in Dutch institutions, such as political consultation meetings, the civil service, public schools and the job market. I begin by providing some more information about the Dutch dispute over the handshake. After that, I first unpack and evaluate the idea of mutual respect and then turn to the idea of public reason.[73]

i. Political Liberalism, a Fair Distribution of Mutual Respect and the Dutch Debate on Greeting Rituals

In 2004, the Dutch imam Ahmad Salam declined the hand of the Secretary of Immigration Affairs and Integration at that time, Rita Verdonk. The imam said that he respected Verdonk but that his religion prohibited him from shaking the hands of women. Some pious Muslims refrain from physical

[73] Rawls, *PL* (n 5) 212–30. Rawls prefers to speak of self-respect rather than mutual respect or respectful relations. However, as I will explain below, Rawls assumes that self-respect is premised upon social practices which include a principle of mutuality. So, even for Rawls, respect does not simply concern the 'self' but is essentially social. To emphasise the relational aspect of respect, I will use the words mutual respect here, except when I cite Rawls.

contact with members of the other sex, (except for spouses and family members), because they consider such contact a potential stimulus of sexual desire which could, in turn, increase the chance of adultery.[74] Verdonk, in turn, tried to convince the imam to shake her hand by emphasising that they were equals. The incident gave rise to much discussion. Several left- and right-wing politicians insisted that the shaking of hands was an expression of mutual respect and civility that should be observed by all citizens. Others claimed that Verdonk's emphasis on equality testified to a lack of empathy with, and respect for, other cultures.[75] In 2008, another incident occurred which centred around male civil servants of the city of Amsterdam who refused to shake hands with women. The mayor of Amsterdam at that time, Job Cohen, defended the civil servants and held that their refusal provided no obstacle for their job performance as long as they treated others in a respectful manner. In addition, Cohen challenged the Dutch custom of identifying mutual respect with the handshake and underlined the multi-interpretability of respect: 'I do not consider refusing the handshake disrespectful. It might rather be a sign of respect when, on religious grounds, a muslim refuses to offer his hand to women'.[76]

The Netherlands Institute for Human Rights—a paralegal committee that oversees compliance with the constitutional prohibition on discrimination and other equal treatment laws—issued several decisions on conflicts between employers and citizens who demanded an exemption from

[74] In their overview of current theological debates on the handshake the Dutch scholars Herman Beck and Gerard Wiegers point out that Islamic theologians worldwide disagree as to whether authoritative sources such as the Koran and the Hadith (the traditions on the life of Mohammed) permit Muslims to shake hands with members of the other sex. For instance, the influential scholar Al-Qaradawi says that a man should not shake hands with a woman when he suspects that either one of them could become sexually aroused, but he argues that such a prohibition does not apply when the woman in question is no longer of child-bearing age. Kutty, an Islamic scholar from the Islamic institute in Toronto, in contrast, claims that the shaking of hands is a matter of one's individual conscience (H Beck and G Wiegers, *Moslims in een westerse samenleving: Islam en ethiek* (Zoetermeer, Meinema, 2008) 146.

[75] There is no consensus about the origin of the handshake. The handshake appeared to be customary in the Roman army from the 1st to 4th centuries AD where it was part of the initiation rite of the popular mystery cult of the god Mithras. During the Middle Ages kings and knights shook each other's hands to demonstrate that they did not carry weapons and did not intend to hurt the other. The sociologist Herbert Spencer, however, speculates that the handshake has an Arab origin. Among Arab men it was considered respectful to kiss the other's hand but this gesture was not always successful: quite often both men tried to kiss the other hand simultaneously which had the effect of each man trying to raise the other's hand to his lips while the other was pushing it down. Eventually this problem became widely acknowledged and the confusable motions gave rise to the regular and rhythmical movement of the handshake (H Spencer, *The Principles of Sociology, Volume II* (Oxford, Williams and Norgate, 1902) 135–36.

[76] Job Cohen during a council meeting (B Peters, *Cohen heeft gelijk, handen schudden hoeft niet* (Elsevier, 22 February 2008). (In Dutch: 'Ik vind een hand weigeren niet respectloos. Het kan juist een teken van respect zijn, als een moslim vanuit zijn geloof een vrouw geen hand wil geven.').(translated by author).

the dominant Dutch greeting ritual.[77] In its decisions the Institute took a similar stance to Cohen and stressed that civility and gender equality could be practised in plural ways. For instance, in 2006 the Institute ruled that a public school could not fire a female teacher because she refused to shake hands with members of the other sex, and said it was sufficient for employees to convey mutual respect by means of a friendly nod (accompanied by an explanation as to why she did not shake hands.)[78] In 2009 a Dutch court, however, overruled this decision of the Institute. The court argued that the implementation of a uniform greeting ritual could be a legitimate instrument in preventing social conflicts in a multicultural school community, and agreed with the management of the school that a uniform greeting ritual was necessary to prepare the students for their tasks as citizens and their participation in the labour market. Such uniformity would give students a clear indication of what was generally regarded as a respectful custom in Dutch society:

> The refusal to offer a hand and the motivation that the person concerned advances for that—in light of her religion, she experiences the shaking of hands with adult men as sexual intimidation—might be experienced by the other person concerned as confronting and unpleasant and puts pressure upon cordial relations. ... the Council is of the opinion that a much greater weight should come to bear on the interest of the school to give priority to uniformity over diversity in light of the aim to prevent segregation and to promote clarity in a multicultural school, and considers uniformity in greeting rituals appropriate and necessary.[79]

In 2012, in another case, a higher Dutch court argued that a government official in a representative function could also not be exempted from shaking hands.[80]

In the introduction to this book, I mentioned that some commentators in the Dutch debate considered the handshake dispute somewhat trivial and

[77] The Institute was formerly known as The Commission of Equal Treatment.

[78] Commissie Gelijke Behandeling, 7 November 2006 (2006-220).

[79] Centrale Raad van Beroep, 7 May 2009, (LJN: BI2440). ('De weigering om in voorkomende gevallen een hand te geven en de redengeving die betrokkene daarvoor geeft—zij ervaart het schudden van handen met volwassen mannen vanuit haar geloofsovertuiging als seksuele intimidatie—kan door de ander als confronterend en onaangenaam worden ervaren en de onderlinge relaties onder druk zetten. ...In de gegeven omstandigheden is de Raad van oordeel dat een zo veel groter gewicht toekomt aan het belang van de school om ter voorkoming van segregatie en ter bevordering van de duidelijkheid in een multiculturele schoolgemeenschap uniformiteit op de wijze, zoals dat is gebeurd, te stellen boven diversiteit, dat de uniformiteit in begroetingswijze passend en noodzakelijk is te achten.') (translated by the author).

[80] In this ruling, the court claimed that the shaking of hands was necessary, because the other person could experience the refusal of a handshake as insulting, hurtful and disrespectful. Gerechtshof 's-Gravenhage, 10 April 2012 (ECLI:NL:GHSGR:2012:BW1270). And, during the election campaign in 2017, Dutch Prime Minister Mark Rutte explicitly mentioned the handshake as a key element of Dutch civic conduct in an open letter to the Dutch public. M Rutte, *Lees hier de Brief van Mark* (22 January 2017), https://vvd.nl/nieuws/lees-hier-de-brief-van-mark/.

argued that Dutch debates had to focus on other, more important, issues. Rawls would probably not agree with this line of argument. The conflict over Dutch citizens seeking an exemption from the dominant greeting rituals occurs within some of the most basic political, social and economic institutions of the Netherlands. Rawls identifies this set of arrangements—which he qualifies as the 'basic structure'—as the primary focus of political liberalism.[81] Moreover, the issue at the heart of this dispute—the regulation of mutual respect—is deeply significant for Rawls.[82] On Rawls' account, a fair distribution of mutual respect is of utmost importance towards establishing legitimacy for liberal-democratic regimes. For instance, mutual respect is a vital condition for realising moral agency:

> The importance of self-respect is that it provides a secure sense of our own value, a firm conviction that our determinate conception of the good is worth carrying out. Without self-respect nothing may seem worth doing, and if some things have value for us, we lack the will to pursue them.[83]

Moreover, a proper distribution of mutual respect is crucial for sustaining allegiance to liberal-democratic regimes. In his social theory of motivation, Rawls explains that the motivational support for a just regime is essentially dependent upon the fact that such a regime secures the need for mutual respect. When a democratic regime fails to provide citizens some degree of mutual respect, citizens become unwilling to act on behalf of principles of justice.[84]

How then does Rawls conceptualise a fair distribution of mutual respect? Do the implicit ontological assumptions in this criterion provide a 'free-standing' framework? And do these tacit ontological claims have any impact on the orienting strength of his principle?

To begin with, I should stress that Rawls treats mutual respect as an inherently social practice. Even though he mostly speaks of '*self*-respect', Rawls realises that a sense of self-worth cannot be realised individually but is dependent upon the positive affirmation of others: 'For our sense of our

[81] Rawls, *PL* (n 5) 11.

[82] Though I should note that political liberalism does not intend to settle disputes on such a detailed level as my case study but only intends to specify the normative principles in light of which the participants in democratic debates, and judges, carry out their deliberations.

[83] Rawls, *PL* (n 5) 318. The institutional or social conditions of self-respect are 'among the most essential primary goods' (ibid, 319).

[84] It is not entirely clear whether Rawls considers his formulation of respect inherent to all the conceptions of political liberalism or whether it is only part of his own interpretation of this doctrine, 'justice as fairness'. Rawls does not explicitly mention respect in his enumeration of the essential features of a political liberalist conception (Rawls (n 35) 141, 143) but elsewhere he treats respect as a value that every reasonable liberal-democratic regime needs to realise (Rawls (n 35) 50; Rawls, *PL* (n 5) 157). In light of the fact that Rawls puts so much emphasis on mutual respect in realising liberal-democratic regimes, I believe that it is most plausible that this idea forms part of all the conceptions of political liberalism.

own value, as well as our self-confidence, depends upon the respect and mutuality shown us by others.'[85] Political liberalism specifies several 'social bases' that ought to realise 'self-respect'. The first criterion calls for the institutionalisation of basic liberties, such as freedom of thought and conscience, freedom of association and integrity of person.[86] These rights are important for realising mutual respect because they guarantee the exercise of the earlier-mentioned two moral powers (a sense of justice and a capacity for a conception of the good). The development and exercise of these powers, in turn, provide the ground for our 'self-confidence as a cooperating member of society'. The second basis of 'self-respect' consists of the public recognition of our basic liberties. Rawls wagers that the realisation of this condition will stimulate the belief that we are able to fulfil a worthwhile life-plan: 'By publicly affirming the basic liberties citizens in a well-ordered society express their mutual respect for one another as reasonable and trustworthy, as well as their recognition of the worth all citizens attach to their way of life.'[87] Finally, 'self-respect' demands redistributive measures that provide each citizen with sufficient material goods and equal opportunities for political participation ('the fair value of political liberties').[88]

Rawls' framework for promoting mutual respect provides some important normative points by which to measure the current Dutch discussion on mutual respect. For instance, in recent years it has become much more acceptable for politicians to argue for abolishing the constitutional provisions on religious freedom and anti-discrimination prohibition on which some of the demands for an exemption of dominant greeting rituals are based.[89] Rawls' account highlights a potential injustice within this tendency: when politicians and ordinary citizens no longer publicly affirm the basic rights of their fellow citizens, the moral agency of citizens could be seriously undermined. But is his account indeed so 'free-standing' that it can forge an overlapping consensus? To some extent, Rawls' account of mutual respect is much more responsive to the concerns and self-understandings of citizens who do not affirm an individualist way of life than is his defence of freedom. Indeed: in his discussion of mutual respect Rawls comes close to affirming an intersubjective ontology of moral agency. And this increases the plausibility of his framework for citizens who believe that their potential for moral

[85] Rawls, *PL* (n 5) 319.

[86] In *Political Liberalism* the list of basic liberties includes freedom of thought and conscience but does not mention religious freedom (Rawls, *PL* (n 5) 291). In 'The Idea of Public Reason Revisited' Rawls says that a reasonable conception of justice must also specify religious liberty (Rawls (n 35) 141).

[87] Rawls, *PL* (n 5) 319.

[88] The 'fair value' of political freedoms implies that everyone has a fair opportunity to hold public office and to influence the outcome of political decisions (ibid, 327).

[89] For example, Geert Wilders, the leader of the biggest populist party in the Netherlands, has argued for the abolishment of the constitutional prohibition on discrimination.

agency is inherently bound up with the recognition of others. Still, even this implicit appeal to a more intersubjective ontology remains contentious. One of the aspects that the handshake dispute highlights is that culturally-sanctioned bodily practices might play a constitutive role in developing and sustaining mutual respect. Notwithstanding their disagreement, both the proponents of a uniform greeting-ritual claim and the orthodox Muslims who challenge this practice converge in their emphasis of the crucial role of bodily customs in realising mutual respect. Political liberalism, however, does not confront the relation between the body and mutual respect. While Rawls' ontology acknowledges the relationality of mutual respect, it ignores the effect of bodily habits in realising respectful relations.

This omission is reflected in Rawls' normative proposal. Like his ontology, Rawls' criterion for a fair distribution of mutual respect makes no mention of the relation between bodily practices and the realisation of mutual respect but rather leads us away from struggles involving the bodily conditions of the basic structure. That is to say, while the social bases of mutual respect include the public recognition of rights and the fair distribution of economic and political opportunities, the impact of bodily customs on realising mutual respect carries no normative weight. My case study, however, suggests that struggles concerning the bodily conditions of mutual respect might be just as central to democratic regimes as conflicts about rights and economic and political opportunities. For instance, some proponents of a uniform greeting ritual claim that it is not enough that orthodox Muslims and the state acknowledge their *rights*: their sense of self-worth is inextricably bound up with the public recognition of a *cultural bodily custom in the basic structure,* that is, the traditional ritual of shaking hands. Some orthodox Muslims also call for a public affirmation of a bodily practice, albeit that they claim the basic structure needs to open up a space for religious citizens to practice bodily customs that dissent from a society's mainstream practices. These conflicts are in need of a vocabulary which takes into account that civic relations are also structured by historically-situated bodily practices, and that offers orientation in the struggles of bodily conditions in liberal-democratic regimes.

To be sure, the absence of the body in Rawls' normative framework does not imply that the relation between bodily practices and mutual respect could not be given normative weight in the *implementation* of the social bases of mutual respect. For instance, political liberalism does not prohibit judges from giving weight to bodily customs in the interpretation of rights.[90]

[90] As stated, Rawls only specifies the basic normative principles that are in need of implementation in order to solve this case. But the centrality of the body to this dispute does not merely raise questions about the way in which political liberalism would need to be implemented, but contests the very way that Rawls construes the normative principle of mutual respect in the first place.

Still, when a democratic regime adopts political liberalism, the fair distribution of rights and economic opportunities will be much more secured than a fair distribution of the bodily conditions of mutual respect. That is, whereas a fair distribution of rights, and economic and political opportunities, will provide a relatively stable starting-point for legislators and the judiciary, a fair distribution of the bodily conditions of mutual respect will be dependent upon many more contingencies, such as the way in which a judge uses her discretionary powers and the possibilities within democratic discourse of mobilising citizens for a fair distribution of the bodily conditions of mutual respect. The relatively weak position of the bodily conditions of respectful relations renders the political-liberalist proposal for realising mutual respect much less 'free-standing' than Rawls claims: it structurally excludes the ontological understandings and ethico-political concerns of citizens who affirm that mutual respect is inevitably bound up with historically-sanctioned bodily practices.

ii. Public Reason and the Democratic Politicisation of Political Liberalism

I argued that citizens who conceive of mutual respect as an inherently bodily practice might find that Rawls' conception of justice lacks conceptual resources to voice their concerns. I said earlier that the later Rawls came to appreciate the need for a democratic politicisation of political liberalist conceptions of justice. To recall, he says that it is crucial that a society is sustained by multiple political liberalist conceptions of justice and that democratic deliberations need to welcome the input of citizens who challenge the biases in principles of justice. To end my discussion, I will look at the possibilities that Rawls' conception of public reason opens up which could stimulate such a democratic politicisation of conceptions of justice. I first explain the concept of public reason and then evaluate its restrictions in allowing for the introduction of ontological arguments.

Political liberalism assumes that a democratic citizenry will remain deeply divided about the constitution and other fundamental issues of justice:

> The political relationship we characterize as having at least two significant distinctive features. First, it is a relationship of persons within the basic structure of society. ... Second, political power is, of course, always coercive power backed by the state's machinery for enforcing its laws. But in a constitutional regime political power is also the power of equal citizens as a collective body: it is regularly imposed on citizens as individuals, *some of whom may not accept the reasons widely believed to justify the general structure of political authority (the constitution); or when they do accept that structure, they may not regard as well grounded many of the laws enacted by the legislature to which they are subject.*[91]

[91] Rawls (n 19) 182 (emphasis added).

To ensure that citizens will abide by the forms of political authority that they do not endorse, Rawls introduces the idea of public reason. Although a representative democracy will inevitably enact laws that remain unacceptable to some citizens, these laws are considered legitimate when government officials and citizens follow public reason in their democratic deliberations about fundamental issues of political justice. These issues include discussions about 'constitutional essentials' (such as the content of rights that are specified by the constitution) and 'basic justice' (the regulation of social and economic inequalities, such as the distribution of mutual respect in the basic structure).

A central requirement in public reason is that participants in democratic deliberations about fundamental issues of justice exchange reasons for their position that are most likely reasonable. Rawls qualifies this requirement as the criterion of 'reciprocity':

> When those terms are proposed as the most reasonable terms of fair cooperation, those proposing them must also think it at least reasonable for others to accept them, as free and equal citizens, and not as dominated or manipulated or under pressure of an inferior political or social position.[92]

For Rawls, reciprocity implies, among other things, that citizens should conduct their debates in terms of purely political values rather than by reference to comprehensive doctrines; it is, one might say, an application of the strategy of avoidance of the democratic deliberations in which a conception of justice is translated into constitutional laws and fundamental policy-making. These political values are proposed by the family of reasonable political liberalist conceptions, such as the principle of mutual respect in justice as fairness. In addition, public reason includes norms of public inquiry, that is, beliefs and forms of reasoning that are found in common sense and uncontroversial scientific knowledge claims.[93] Moreover, the later, more democratic, Rawls has opened up some space for ontological arguments within political deliberation. As he points out in *Justice as Fairness: A Restatement*, the introduction of comprehensive doctrines into public reason has an orienting or hermeneutic potential:

> [It] has the advantage of citizens informing one another where they come from, so to speak, and on what basis they support the public political conception of justice. … [It] gives citizens a deeper understanding of their several points of view.[94]

Still, it is important to note that this 'wide' view of public reason specifies a crucial condition for the participation of ontology: Rawls considers it a

[92] ibid, 136–37.

[93] These insights cannot appeal to grand scientific theories or contested views but must be limited to 'the plain truths now widely accepted, or available, to citizens in general' (Rawls, *PL* (n 5) 225).

[94] Rawls (n 19) 90.

'duty of civility' that citizens will eventually defend their position in terms of political liberalist values.[95]

To ward off criticisms that public reason tends to stifle democratic discourse, Rawls emphasises that public reason only applies in a rather limited domain of a liberal-democratic regime, the so-called 'public political forum'.[96] This forum is constituted by the discourse of judges, government officials and citizens who are campaigning for public office. In other arenas of collective opinion and will-formation, such as the media, universities and religious associations, the requirements of public reason do not apply: in these debates, citizens could have much more space to deliberate comprehensive doctrines, such as ontological accounts. But this does not mean that citizens who do not aspire to become part of the public political forum can always put aside the requirements of public reason within their discussions. For instance, when citizens make up their mind about fundamental questions of justice and deliberate whether or not government officials enact satisfactory laws and policies on these questions, or ponder whether candidates in political campaigns propose plausible solutions, they need to evaluate these proposals in light of public reason. That is to say, they have to imagine themselves to be 'ideal legislators' and carry out their deliberations as much as possible in terms of purely political values.[97] And, crucially, this capacity to bracket comprehensive doctrines is not an incidental thought-experiment that one only needs to undertake when, say, exercising a vote, but amounts to a habit of discussion that political liberalism considers essential for its success:

> When firm and widespread, the disposition of citizens to view themselves as ideal legislators, and to repudiate government officials and candidates for public office who violate public reason, is one of the political and social roots of democracy, and is vital to its enduring strength and vigor.[98]

The restrictions on comprehensive doctrines also appear to apply when public reason touches upon issues of political philosophy. Rawls emphasises that public reason makes room for the democratic politicisation of political philosophy. In fact, public reason needs to reflect the disagreement within political philosophy and allow citizens to challenge dominant conceptions of justice. But, like his appeal to political philosophers, Rawls urges every citizen who debates political philosophy within public reason to stay on the 'surface, philosophically speaking':

> Political liberalism, then, does not try to fix public reason once and for all in the form of one favored political conception of justice. … For instance, political

[95] ibid, Rawls calls this requirement the 'proviso.'
[96] Rawls (n 35) 133.
[97] ibid, 135.
[98] ibid.

> liberalism also admits Habermas' discourse conception of legitimacy ... as well as Catholic views of the common good and solidarity *when they are expressed in terms of political values.* ... new variations may be proposed from time to time and older ones may cease to be represented. It is important that this be so; otherwise the claims of groups or interests arising from social change might be repressed and fail to gain their appropriate political voice.[99]

So how successful, then, is public reason in stimulating an ongoing debate about political philosophy, such as Rawls' own variety of political liberalism?[100]

Let us imagine that the Dutch handshake dispute has brought together a group of citizens who are critical of the way in which the Dutch state realises the mutual respect of its citizens. Since their intention is to deliberate about the fundamental laws and policies that the legislators would need to enact in order to realise a fair distribution of mutual respect, they are submitted to the requirements of public reason. Let us also assume that some of these citizens are familiar with political philosophy conceptions of justice, such as political liberalism. In fact, a few citizens might find the political liberalist outlook on mutual respect so persuasive that their judgements of state policies are primarily affected by political liberalism. Others would rather approach issues of mutual respect through ontological angles, such as an Islamic notion of human dignity and respectful relations. One of the debatable issues that arises is that political liberalism might not be attentive enough to the effect of bodily conduct on establishing mutual respect. One of the participants wants to introduce her Islamic faith to explain that pious bodily practices—and not just rights—are crucial for realising mutual respect. She is accustomed to doing so because in the various participatory debates within associations (universities, mosques) discussions are typically carried out in the light of comprehensive ideals.

Public reason would give this citizen some space to introduce her religious ontology to the debate on mutual respect. For instance, when she wants to persuade the others that the implementation of political liberalism needs to take into account the role of the body, she will be given scope to advance her religious ontology. But public reason does not appear to appreciate contributions of ontology in democratic discourse that criticise the central assumptions of political liberalism. I mentioned that, for the later Rawls, the function of ontology in democratic deliberations is to elucidate to the others

[99] ibid, 142 (emphasis added).

[100] I will not engage with the question about the legitimacy of the political values that public reason draws upon. As I have shown with regard to the political liberalist principles of freedom and mutual respect, these values are not purely political but structured by contestable ontological claims. So since political liberalism is so much more contested than Rawls assumes, I don't think that public reason will realise its aim of legitimacy. Still, public reason might, as Rawls seems to suggest, also support a second goal: the democratic politicisation of justice, including political liberalism. This is the aim that I will look at here with which to evaluate public reason.

'on what basis they support the public conception of justice'. This suggests that, for Rawls, the point of introducing ontological commitments is essentially to *strengthen* the stability of (a version of) political liberalism rather than to *criticise* some of its basic tenets. So a citizen who challenges policies of mutual respect within the domain of public reason is not permitted to use ontological arguments, such as an appeal to an embodied conception of religion, to render up for democratic contestation central elements of political liberalism that she considers contentious.

This restriction upon the functioning of ontological arguments in public reason has two problematic consequences. First, it reduces political liberalism to an uncontestable parameter that is ahead, rather than part of, democratic politics. As we have seen, Rawls' more general ruminations on justification in the wide reflective equilibrium claim that the 'reasonableness' of any conception of justice is an *effect* of an ongoing democratic debate. That is to say, the reflective equilibrium considers political liberalism as a historically contingent, contestable set of claims that need to be made accessible to democratic politicisation. But Rawls' account of public reason works against this commitment to democratically politicise biases in political liberalist conceptions of justice: by assuming as unreasonable, and excluding from democratic deliberations, all citizens who appeal to ontological arguments that dispute political liberalist tenets, it treats 'reasonableness' as a criterion that is settled *prior to* democratic contestation. Public reason thereby hampers the democratic politicisation of political-philosophical notions and may, in effect, encourage citizens to take contentious political- philosophical claims for granted. Second, within democratic discourse, the barriers to ontology that Rawls erects could alienate many citizens from the democratic process. Citizens who are not immediately taken in by political liberalism and who subscribe to a competing ontology could feel dissatisfied with a democratic discourse that does not permit them to use their ontological commitments to highlight its possible flaws. It is thus very doubtful whether political liberalism can stimulate, let alone sustain, that vibrant democratic debate on justice that Rawls hopes for.

V. CONCLUSION

This chapter investigated the conceptual coherence and consequences of political liberalism, through an analysis of Rawls' understanding of individual freedom, politics of mutual respect and his conception of democratic debate. We have seen that Rawls' attempt to develop a 'freestanding' consensus is unsuccessful: political liberalism does not provide an uncontroversial ontological framework to settle political disputes. His argument for the primacy of individual rights is partly premised upon a contentious individualist ontology that reduces moral agency to mental traits. These ontological presuppositions in Rawls' concept of political autonomy have important implications for the way in which he construes his conception of justice because they orient us away from the normative possibility of public recognition of cultures in democratic regimes. In addition, I brought into view the ontological partiality of the political liberalist principle of mutual respect, highlighting the point that this principle blinds us to the bodily dimension of democratic politics.

This chapter also investigated the merits of the democratic politicisation of ontology in comparison to the political strategy of avoidance. I adopted three strategies of the democratic politicisation of ontology: I made Rawls' ontological assumptions explicit; I staged a confrontation between his ontology and a competing ontology taken from democratic thought; and investigated his ontology in the light of the Dutch handshake debate. We have seen that these methodological devices gave an important impetus to the democratic politicisation of political philosophy. For instance, juxtaposing Rawls' ontology of freedom with Taylor's ontology was crucial in exposing the mentalist bias in Rawls' account of justice. And, the Dutch handshake debate made us mindful of Rawls' blindness to the role of bodily practices in constituting mutual respect. In opposition to my proposal for a democratic politicisation of ontology, Rawls' strategy of avoidance has no critical methodology that could render available for debate his contentious ontological claims. For a start, his reflective equilibrium excludes ontology from critical scrutiny. And, in the public reason domain, citizens can only introduce ontological arguments to express their support for political liberalism, but are not allowed to use these claims in a more critical vein, that is, as a means to politicise the contentious ontological framework that structures political liberalism. So, in contrast to the democratic politicisation of ontology, the strategy of avoidance works against Rawls' own commitment to the democratic politicisation of political philosophy.

In the chapter that follows, I turn to another political theorist who identifies himself with the Kantian tradition but who is deeply committed to a critique of the Kantian ontology that structures the liberal social contract tradition: Michel Foucault. Foucault is not a canonical democratic theorist and generally not considered part of those 'widely known political writings' that, according to Rawls, will provide us with a set of familiar ideas in support of a consensus. Quite the contrary: Foucault is highly sceptical of the possibility of arriving at a just, stable agreement and is often seen as rejecting any normative position whatsoever. But, as Rawls rightly observes, there is merit in engaging with a critic of liberal justice:

> Wide reflective equilibrium (in the case of one citizen) is the reflective equilibrium reached when that citizen has carefully considered alternative conceptions of justice and the force of various arguments for them. More specifically, the citizen has considered the leading conceptions of political justice found in our philosophical

> tradition (*including views critical of the concept of justice itself*) and has weighed the force of the different philosophical and other reasons for them.[101]

Taking to heart Rawls' suggestion, the next chapter will add Foucault's project to the reflective equilibrium and thus help to evaluate its critical methodology, concept of freedom and ethics of democratic discussion in comparison to political liberalism.

[101] Rawls, *PL* (n 5) 384 (emphasis added).

3

The Stimulation of Enlightened Contest

We are all neo-Kantians.[1]

That which is susceptible of introducing a significant difference in the field of knowledge, at the cost of a certain difficulty for the author and the reader, with, however, the eventual recompense of a certain pleasure, that is to say of access to another figure of truth.[2]

I. INTRODUCTION

CHAPTER TWO HAS shown that Rawls' account of democracy is premised upon a contentious ontology: it frames freedom in terms of a controversial individualist-mentalist ontology and disregards the role of bodily practices in conceptualising the social bases of respect. We also saw that Rawls lacks a critical methodology to politicise these contentious ontological claims. Both his account of philosophical justification and democratic debate do not include ontology in their critical investigations. This chapter seeks to develop an alternative to the political liberalist ontology of democratic politics. By turning to Foucault's normatively-laden ontology of agonic freedom, I present the first step of my investigation into the ontological conditions of democratic politics. I will argue that this ontology opens up two normative possibilities for democratic regimes that are missing in political liberalism: it shows that citizens need to develop contestatory skills and reveals that democratic debates need to encourage an ongoing critical experiment with 'settled' normative and ontological convictions in public culture. In addition, I pursue further my investigation into the relevance of a democratic politicisation of ontology in comparison to the political liberalist strategy of avoidance. By confronting political liberalism

[1] M Foucault, 'Une Histoire Restée Muette' in D Defert and F Ewald (eds), *Dits et Ecrits I* (Paris, Gallimard, 2001) 546.
[2] Foucault's definition of work. M Foucault, 'Des Traveaux' in D Defert and F Ewald (eds), *Dits et Ecrits IV* (Paris, Gallimard, 2001) 367.

with the practice of critique and ethics of discussion that have been developed by Michel Foucault, and by means of my own critical reconstruction of Foucault's contentious ontology, I will show that a critique of ontology encourages the democratic politicisation of political philosophy. Such a critique also stimulates the development of alternative concepts that increase the orienting potential of democratic theory.

The political thinker Foucault agrees with Rawls that the plurality of worldviews cannot be represented in one theoretical outlook. And, like Rawls, he is suspicious of ontological truth-claims within political reflection, and considers it crucial to make political thought more hospitable to plurality. In addition, Foucault's thought converges with that of Rawls in his assumption that political philosophy needs to be submitted to an ongoing democratic process of contestation. Foucault's democratic politicisation of philosophy does not, however, call for a separation between political reflection and ontology, but develops a methodology to *politicise* ontological truth-claims. Unlike Rawls, his practice of critique underscores the need to challenge the ontological truth regimes that underpin conceptions of liberal democracies and highlights their exclusionary effects.

Foucault's critique of ontology is part of a larger political-theoretical project that I characterise as 'The Stimulation of Enlightened Contest'. This undertaking consists of three features.

First, we will see that Foucault attributes political thought with the task of *illuminating* the conceptual disputes, such as ontological ones, in liberal democratic regimes. The theorist examines the assumptions that underpin liberal democratic practices and clarifies which conflicting conceptual alternatives are currently available. This goal bears some resemblance to Rawls' suggestion that political theorists ought to orient citizens in the conceptual possibilities within liberal democratic regimes: both theorists point out that political disputes cannot only be reduced to clashes of interest, they are also shaped by competing modes of thought that reason can reflect upon.[3] However, in contrast to Rawls, Foucault's acute awareness of reason's indebtedness to historical power relations challenges the possibility of transcending these disputes. While philosophers can provide insight into conceptual disputes, Foucault departs from Rawls in his assumption that political reflection cannot end political contest by developing a just and stable agreement.

The second characteristic of 'The Stimulation of Enlightened Contest' refers to an important contribution that Foucault has himself made to such contests. Foucault develops a disturbing critique of the social contract tradition and shows that this tradition lacks conceptual resources to analyse

[3] M Foucault, 'So Is It Important to Think' in J Faubion (ed), *Power* (New York, The New Press, 2000) 457.

oppression that has arisen in the modern Western disciplinary societies. Foucault's reconceptualisation of juridical notions of power offers an innovative framework in which to bring this new form of oppression into view.

The third feature of 'The Stimulation of Enlightened Contest' explains the *telos* of stimulating such contests: by circulating a critique in democratic debates the political theorist can contribute to the struggle for 'agonic freedom'. This ideal is committed to an ongoing challenge of historical exclusions but emphasises that individuals cannot *transcend* but, at best, *creatively transform* and *pluralise* power relations.

This chapter introduces these three features of Foucault's project into Rawls' reflective equilibrium. The confrontation between political liberalism and Foucault's 'Stimulation of Enlightened Contest' will disrupt the commitments of both these thinkers. First of all, we shall see how an engagement with ontology can stimulate a critical learning-process on key notions in political thought. I briefly address how Foucault positions himself vis-a-vis Kant, and then turn to his critique of the social contract tradition which includes a critique of the Kantian mentalist idea of subjectivity. Next, I revisit political liberalism to analyse the current usefulness of Foucault's critique of the social contract tradition. However, I also confront Foucault with a concern Rawls would most likely raise: to what extent is Foucault's critique useful for democratic politics? Does Foucault's critique of liberal individualism not undermine our commitment to democratic regimes?

In the remaining part of the chapter, I shift the focus from Foucault's *critique* of democracy to Foucault's *affirmation* of democracy and individualism and, *pace* Foucault's own intentions, reconstruct the ontologically grounded, normative position that Foucault defends. I first flesh out Foucault's ontology of historical power relations and bodily forces. With this reconstruction, I challenge Foucault's claim that his critical project does not rest upon an ontological worldview. This reconstruction will also help us see that the affirmation of an ontology in political theory need not, as Rawls suggests, become a byword for an aversion to a critique of philosophy, or a reification of the conceptual status quo. I then proceed with a reconstruction of Foucault's normative position and confront his normative commitments with his ontological assumptions. Reading Foucault through a normative lens encourages the democratic politicisation of Foucault's ontology: it helps us see that Foucault initially underestimated the role of critical agency and the need for discipline in political struggles. Foucault corrects this flaw in his later work where he stresses the need for disciplinary restraint in training the bodily forces, and presents a heteronomous account of individual freedom: the agonic struggle for (self-) creation. We will see that Foucault's concept of agonic freedom is of a very different kind than Rawls' notion of political autonomy: whereas Rawls tries to refrain from conceptualising freedom as a fully-fledged way of life, Foucault sees freedom as a rather comprehensive ethos that needs to be cultivated in everyday ethical practices. In light of these differences some readers may object that it makes little sense to put these two accounts side by side. I wish to unsettle that conviction. Rawls and Foucault are both committed to the democratic contestation of justice and from this shared normative perspective it becomes clear that Foucault's agonic freedom orients us in two normative possibilities for democratic regimes that are relevant to political liberalism which Rawls fails to see.[4]

II. 'A HISTORICAL ONTOLOGY OF OURSELVES'

Foucault offers a brief and eloquent presentation of his philosophical ethos in the essay 'What is Enlightenment?'—a text which takes up a question that was addressed by Kant two centuries earlier in the essay 'An Answer to the Question: What is Enlightenment?'.[5] In this text Kant famously characterises the Enlightenment as a process in which people release themselves from their 'immaturity' (*Unmündigkeit*), that is, the inability to think for oneself ('without the guidance of others').[6]

Kant's essay discusses several institutional conditions for overcoming immaturity. He explains that free thinking requires specific rights, such as

[4] My reading of Foucault focuses on the texts and developments in his thinking that are most directly relevant to my aim of developing an alternative methodological approach for political liberalism, as well as a contrasting ontology of democratic agency. These texts include work from the early and mid-1970s—a period that I will refer to as Foucault's 'middle period'—as well as some of Foucault's latest writings from the late 1970s until his death in 1984. Foucault's middle period—which includes texts such as *'Society Must Be Defended'* and *History of Sexuality 1*—is important for my discussion because during this phase Foucault explicitly criticises political philosophy, and, in particular, the social contract tradition to which Rawls belongs. See M Foucault, in M Bertani and A Fontana (eds), *'Society Must Be Defended': Lectures at the Collège de France, 1975–1976* (New York, Picador, 2003) and M Foucault, *The History of Sexuality, Volume 1: An Introduction* (New York, Random House, 1978) Hereafter *The History of Sexuality, Volume 1: An Introduction* will be referred to as *HS1*. The alternative view of power that Foucault develops in this period, and his genealogical methodology with which to criticise power, will be central to this chapter and the ones that follow. Foucault's later writings—such as 'What is Enlightenment?', 'The Subject and Power', *The Use of Pleasure*—merit attention because they connect his theory and critique of power to an account of individual freedom that was only tacitly assumed in the earlier writings. The texts from Foucault's later period will also be important for the discussion in the next chapter, where I use Foucault's analytics of the state to challenge a political liberalist understanding of statehood. See M Foucault, 'What is Enlightenment' in P Rabinow (ed), *Ethics: Subjectivity and Truth* (New York, The New Press, 1997), M Foucault, 'The Subject and Power' in Faubion (ed) (n 3) and M Foucault, *The Use of Pleasure: The History of Sexuality, Volume 2* (London, Penguin Books, 1992).

[5] Foucault, 'What is Enlightenment' (n 4) 303–19. This text was originally delivered as a lecture in 1978. The text of Immanuel Kant originally appeared in 1784: I Kant, 'Beantwortung der Frage: Was ist Aufklärung?' (1784) 4 *Berlinische Monatschrift* 481. For an English translation of 'Was ist Aufklärung?' and excellent commentaries on the historical context and philosophical implications of this text, see J Schmidt (ed), *What is Enlightenment? Eighteenth-Century Answers and Twentieth-Century Questions* (Los Angeles, University of California Press, 1996).

[6] Elsewhere Kant defined this state as 'heteronomy'. See ch 2, n 45.

freedom of religion and freedom of free speech, that enable men to follow their conscience, express their own judgements and, if necessary, criticise religious and political authorities. Kant is optimistic about the possibility to achieve these institutional prerequisites. In his view, they have been largely realised in the, then, contemporary political regime and he praises the Prussian leader Frederick the Great (a 'shining example')[7] for being the first leader in history to allow men to make use of their free thinking. But Kant is much more sombre with regard to the effort that people have made themselves to overcome their immaturity. He observes that most people are satisfied with their dependence upon the judgements of others, and lack the will to think for themselves:

> Laziness and cowardice are the reasons why such a great part of mankind ... still gladly remains immature for life and why it is so easy for others to set themselves up as guardians. It is so easy to be immature. If I have a book that has understanding for me, a pastor who has a conscience for me, a doctor who judges my diet for me, and so forth, surely I do not need to trouble myself. I have no need to think, if only I can pay; others will take over the tedious business for me.[8]

Ultimately, Kant suggests, the process of Enlightenment is man's own responsibility or, as he puts it in the opening sentence of this essay, immaturity is 'self-incurred' (*selbstverschuldet*).[9] And to encourage people to strengthen their will Kant introduces the following motto for the Enlightenment: '*Sapere Aude*! Have the courage to use your own understanding!'

Foucault's essay 'What is Enlightenment?' builds upon Kant's suggestion of looking at the Enlightenment as an attitude or ethos rather than a historical epoch or institutional achievement. In particular, Foucault is interested in the implications of this ethos for philosophy, and he compares his own philosophical project with that of Kant. For Kant, philosophy needs to support men's attempts to overcome immaturity by submitting the capacity for reason to a 'critique': it has to examine the validity and boundaries of reason so that people will acquire insight into what they can justifiably know, do and hope for. By disclosing universal criteria for knowledge, morality and faith, philosophy would help people to use their reason in such a way that they would no longer become subjected to unwarranted beliefs, dogmas and historical prejudice.[10] Foucault agrees with Kant that the thinker needs to adopt a critical relation vis-a-vis the convictions

[7] I Kant, 'An Answer to the Question: What is Enlightenment?' in Schmidt (ed) (n 5) 62.
[8] ibid, 58.
[9] ibid.
[10] Foucault takes this point from Kant's famous three critiques: I Kant in M Gregor (ed), *Critique of Practical Reason* (Cambridge, Cambridge University Press, 1997); I Kant in P Guyer and A Wood (eds), *Critique of Pure Reason* (Cambridge, Cambridge University Press, 1999); I Kant in P Guyer and E Matthes (eds), *Critique of Judgment* (Cambridge, Cambridge University Press, 2000).

that constitute her historical predicament by means of an investigation into the boundaries of human subjectivity. However, the methodology and aim of his critique are diametrically opposed to that of Kant. For Foucault, philosophical critique needs to pursue an 'historical ontology of ourselves', that is, it should analyse the historical practices in which we have come to recognise ourselves as subjects.[11] But these historical studies do not aim to specify necessary universal criteria: like many other twentieth century philosophers such as Heidegger and Taylor, Foucault considers the subject an effect of contingent social and historical practices. In opposition to Kant, who claims that critique ought to reveal the *universal and necessary* conditions of our current subjectivity, Foucault's critique rather tries to disclose these conditions as *contingent* historical practices and wants to show us '[i]n what is universal, necessary, obligatory, what place is occupied by whatever is singular, contingent, and the product of arbitrary constraints'.[12]

Why does Foucault believe that the task of philosophy is to make us aware of the contingency of our current self? What exactly is the purpose of his critique? Like Kant, Foucault links his critique to an ideal of autonomy and says that his historical ontologies support 'the constitution of ourselves as autonomous subjects'.[13] Yet we shall see that Foucault's interpretation of this ideal is very different from Kant's understanding of autonomy. Whereas Kant considers us free, and hence autonomous, to the extent that we act in accordance with the transcendental conditions of our freedom, Foucault believes that our freedom consists of the possibility to think and act differently from what was mistakenly considered a necessary condition. Critique 'will separate out, from the contingency that has made us what we are, the possibility of no longer being, doing, or thinking what we are, do, or think' and in this way philosophy 'is seeking to give a new impetus, as far and wide as possible, to the undefined work of freedom'.[14]

[11] More precisely, a historical ontology consists of a historical investigation of the following three domains that constitute subjectivity: the knowledge relations that structure our consciousness by opening up possibilities of thought; the power relations through which we guide others by opening up possibilities of actions; and the ethical relations or the ethical ideals that constitute the ways in which we govern ourselves. The first axis applies to the construction of consciousness and thought, the second and third apply to the will or the domain of action. For an excellent discussion of Foucault's concept of 'historical ontology', see D Owen, *Maturity and Modernity: Nietzsche, Weber, Foucault and the Ambivalence of Reason* (London, Routledge, 1994) and J Tully 'To Think and Act Differently: Foucault's Four Reciprocal Objections to Habermas' Theory' in S Ashenden and D Owen (eds), *Foucault contra Habermas: Recasting the Dialogue between Genealogy and Critical Theory* (London, Sage Publications, 1999).

[12] Foucault, 'What is Enlightenment' (n 4) 315.

[13] ibid, 313.

[14] ibid, 316.

III. A HISTORICAL ONTOLOGY OF POLITICAL PHILOSOPHY

Foucault's critique has also looked into political philosophy or, more exactly, the juridical or social contract tradition within political thought. According to Foucault, this type of reflection fails to reveal non-sovereign forms of oppression that have become such an important threat to our freedom since the eighteenth century. This section will first take up Foucault's historical ontology of the social contract tradition—a critique which, as we shall see, centres on the conceptualisation of power. I will then sketch how his own alternative notion of power wants to problematise some of the main tenets in the liberal social contract tradition and confront this critique with political liberalism.[15]

A. Two Views on Power

Foucault's critique of political philosophy is succinctly expressed in his remark that '[i]n political thought and analysis, we still have not cut off the head of the king'.[16] With this metaphor Foucault wants to demonstrate that political philosophy has remained too much indebted to the so-called 'juridical' or 'contract-oppression'-schema: it models power on the juridical monarchy that became the predominant form of government in Western societies in the Middle Ages.[17]

Foucault explains that the reactivation of Roman law during the Middle Ages allowed monarchies to establish themselves through a legal apparatus. Law enabled the construction of an administration necessary for a centralised state and was a crucial instrument in the ensuring of obedience. The monarch exercised power primarily through legal prohibitions, even though he could—in the case of disobedience—resort to violence, such as torture and the death penalty. The aim of power was appropriative: the monarch extracted wealth, land and goods from its subjects and, in the case of war, took their lives.

In social contract theory, the law obtains a very different function than that of the Middle Ages. Thinkers such as Locke and Rousseau developed theories of legitimate state sovereignty that had to provide an alternative to absolute monarchical rule, and that considered law a necessary

[15] Foucault's criticism of juridical and liberal concepts of power and their distinctions from disciplinary power are elaborated in Foucault, *'Society'* (n 4), especially in the first two lectures, and in Foucault, *HS1* (n 4).

[16] Foucault, *HS1* (n 4) 88–89.

[17] Foucault, *'Society'* (n 4) 17.

restriction on sovereign power rather than an *instrument* to increase such power. In liberal juridical theory, the central idea is that citizens can exercise their individual freedom in virtue of a set of inalienable individual rights that are protected by the sovereign state.

Foucault acknowledges the differences between liberal and monarchical rule but he also points out an important resemblance between them: on closer investigation liberal social contract theory employs a similarly appropriative and sovereign model of power to that which was used in the earlier theories of sovereignty. For instance, the social contract considers power as a commodity that is appropriated by the sovereign through the consent of the individuals. Furthermore, it treats power as centralised: it flows or is exercised from a centre so as to ensure the freedom of the members of the political community.

Foucault argues that this model of power is not equipped to analyse the non-sovereign forms of domination that become prevalent in modern liberal democracies. He observes that seventeenth and eighteenth century Western societies are increasingly infiltrated by 'disciplinary power': power relations that are not so much tied to the state but dispersed throughout institutional sites such as the prison, the hospital, the factory and the school. These power relations are very different from earlier forms of power. For instance, Foucault notes that disciplinary power has a very different object than does sovereign power: its aim is not to appropriate and repress but rather to *produce* 'subjected and practised bodies, "docile" bodies'.[18] Moreover, disciplinary power uses a variety of techniques that were not so much employed by the sovereign: it resorts to continuous surveillance, diagnosis, training and scientific norms, rather than making use of legal prohibitions. To illustrate the mechanisms of these new power relations let me briefly turn to Foucault's famous account of 'panopticism'. The panopticon is a roundly-built prison where each of the cells has a window facing a central tower. The guard in this tower can quickly check upon each prisoner and put the prisoners under permanent supervision to ensure their obedience. The prisoners, however, cannot see if there is really someone present in the tower: they are never sure that they are indeed checked upon, but only know that they could be kept under surveillance. The suggestion of permanent visibility has the effect that the prisoner starts to monitor himself and 'becomes the principle of his own subjection'.[19] In this way the panopticon can exercise power with minimal effort.

To analyse the predominance of the new disciplinary techniques, such as the panopticon, Foucault develops a new approach to power. He calls his

[18] M Foucault, *Discipline and Punish* (London, Penguin Books, 1977) 138.
[19] ibid, 203.

perspective 'Nietzsche's hypothesis' or 'war-repression schema' which pictures society as an ongoing battlefield or 'warlike clash between forces'.[20] Unlike juridical notions of power, Foucault does not conceptualise power as something that can be possessed, or that originates centrally, but uses the term power for the 'multiple subjugations' that arise from, circulate through and constitute social life.[21] Various modes of social interaction such as the economy, the family or knowledge relations, give rise to inequalities that effectuate force and, in turn, depend upon power to construct and establish non-egalitarian distinctions. Consider, for instance, the traditional nuclear family. This institution attributes a very different status to parents and children and to that extent establishes an unequal relationship. But the family is also dependent upon power: for instance, it sustains itself through moral and religious distinctions that consider the family a 'natural' institution which is more admirable than, say, a commune.

Foucault's understanding of power also departs from the juridical assumption that sees power as an essentially repressive or negative relation or a mere limit on behaviour. For Foucault, power is both constraining and enabling. On the one hand, disciplinary techniques diminish bodily forces: it 'dissociates' the energies in the body and 'the power that might result from it' and establishes a relation of obedience. On the other hand, disciplinary power increases bodily forces by redirecting the energies into an 'aptitude' or a 'capacity' that makes the body useful.[22] Here one might think of the physical training of children in schools and families. It is generally considered a norm of proper conduct that children sit up straight during meals and study. The practice of such obedient behaviour limits the possibilities of bodily force: at some point children will no longer continuously move around. At the same time such training increases bodily potentials: I can only write a text because I have been taught to sit at a desk for some time.

B. Foucault's Challenge to Liberal Social Contract Theory

Foucault's alternative view of power challenges three key assumptions of the liberal tradition of juridical thought. First, he disagrees with the liberal view on democracy which holds that the law constitutes a limitation of power. The analysis of the disciplinary society accentuates the point that the capacities to reflect and act are shaped by a variety of disciplinary practices in schools, workplaces, court systems, and so on. This in turn suggests that the establishment of liberal popular sovereignty—a citizenry that has the

[20] Foucault, '*Society*' (n 4) 16.
[21] ibid, 27.
[22] Foucault (n 18) 138.

possibilities to acquire, use and contest individual rights—depends upon disciplinary power:

> Juridical systems, no matter whether they were theories or codes, allowed the democratization of sovereignty, and the establishment of public right articulated with collective sovereignty, at the very time when, to the extent that, and because the democratization of sovereignty was heavily ballasted by the mechanisms of disciplinary coercion.[23]

In other words, it is far too optimistic to assume that the contractual establishment of a democratic political community creates a form of peaceful co-existence wherein individuals can enjoy their individual freedoms. Since liberal social contract theory neglects disciplinary power relations, it blinds us to the fact that 'politics is the continuation of war by other means'.[24]

Second, Foucault's reconceptualisation of power disputes the liberal assumption of the pre-political individual. The juridical model conceives individuals as existing *prior to* power. It sees power as applied to individuals, such as when a sovereign threatens or kills an individual or where individuals contractually agree to accept legal coercion in order to safeguard their rights. Foucault, by contrast, considers the individual an *effect* of power: 'The individual, with his identity and characteristics, is the product of a relation of power exercised over bodies, multiplicities, movements, desires, forces'.[25] Foucault's account of subject formation includes a radical critique of mentalist understandings of subjectivity.[26] In his view, the interior mental aspects of self are not entities that can be separated from social-historical practices but are seen as effects of the submission to disciplinary power. The aspects of self that are often taken to be a 'non-corporeal' element, such as the soul, the psyche, personality, conscience or consciousness, actually emerge in virtue of the physical training, supervision, and correction of bodily forces:

> The soul is produced permanently around, on, within the body, by the functioning of a power that is exercised on those punished—and, in a more general way, on those who supervises, trains and corrects, over madmen, children at home and at school, the colonized, over those who are stuck at a machine and supervised for the rest of their lives. ... *this soul*, ... unlike the soul represented by Christian theology, is not born in sin and subject to punishment but *is born rather out of methods of punishment, supervision and constraint*.[27]

[23] ibid, 29.
[24] Foucault, '*Society*' (n 4) 15.
[25] M Foucault, 'Questions on Geography' in C Gordon (ed), *Power/Knowledge: Selected Interviews and other Writings 1972–1977* (London, The Harvester Press, 1980) 74.
[26] See ch 2, s IV.A.ii. for my discussion of Rawls' mentalist account of freedom.
[27] Foucault (n 18) 29 (emphasis added).

Importantly, the mind—or 'soul' as Foucault puts it—is not only an effect of power but is also crucially instrumental in sustaining and strengthening power relations. A central feature of Foucault's analysis of disciplinary power is that knowledge regimes target the consciousness of individuals to make them active participants in their submission to power. During this stage of subject formation—which Foucault calls 'subjectivation'—the subject consciously submits to disciplinary norms and thereby establishes herself as a subject of power.[28]

Foucault's analysis of the practice of confession offers a good illustration of this mechanism. In *History of Sexuality 1* Foucault shows how disciplinary knowledge regimes, such as psychiatry and psychological techniques like psychotherapy, tend to assume that subjects can be healed by sharing their inner secrets with a therapist. The therapist will ask the patient to confess her most private thoughts and desires and analyse these secrets in terms of a psychiatric standard: one is a neurotic, schizophrenic, and so on. These encounters teach the patient to recognise herself in terms of a particular criterion ('I am neurotic'; 'these thoughts and acts are irrational') and encourage her to submit her private thoughts and feelings to an ongoing analysis. Most likely the patient will continue to scrutinise her inner self and she might even develop a pleasure in categorising her private thoughts and feelings in terms of psychological norms. The effect of such practices is that they contribute to the depoliticisation of disciplinary power. By concentrating our critical attention on inner states of mind (feelings, desires, beliefs) they displace from view how these aspects of self—and their problematisations—are constituted by social-historical power relations. That is, the subject is mainly taught to see her problems as an individual mental problem rather than be stimulated to probe the power relations that constitute norms of subjectivity ('when and how did certain psychological standards become established as scientific norms?'). In other words, practices of confession strengthen the idea that the essence of self-hood resides in the inner self and thereby enact mentalist notions of self as an intricate part of our daily reality.

Finally, the last point of Foucault's critique of the social contract tradition that I need to address is his challenge to the self-understanding of the political philosopher as a neutral arbiter. The key problem for juridical liberal theory is to determine the legitimacy of power: it looks for criteria or principles that distinguish between exercises of sovereign power that are right or lawful and those that constitute an illegitimate breach of the contract.

[28] Foucault's account of subject formation distinguishes two interdependent processes. First, *subjection* refers to the subjugation of bodily forces to power, such as the aforementioned disciplinary techniques. Subjection designates the passive aspect of subject formation. Second, *subjectivation* denotes the more active side of subject formation or the sense in which the individual becomes an active participant in constituting his submission to power.

Foucault indicates that the philosophers who work in this tradition assume a position of a 'universal intellectual': they believe that their categories stand above competing forces and regard themselves as the 'bearer of values and significations in which all can recognise themselves'.[29] Put differently, the universal intellectual expects that by developing legitimate or just criteria, she will establish an order that achieves reconciliation between adversaries.[30] Foucault's understanding of the interdependence of power and knowledge challenges this view. Since he considers power a condition of possibility for knowledge production, and power relations are never morally or politically 'neutral', knowledge claims cannot transcend power struggles. That is to say, knowledge claims remain a temporary crystallisation of an endless power struggle, even though they may appear, or are presented, as conceptual tools that allow for neutral modes of conflict-resolution. The implication of Foucault's model for political philosophy is that the truth claims of political philosophy remain inherently partisan.[31] They remain indebted to historical power relations and participate in the production of new exclusionary power relations.

C. Confronting Foucault's Critique with Political Liberalism

Foucault presents a perturbing and suggestive critique of the juridical tradition in political thought. His analysis, however, is also quite generalist and mainly informed by seventeenth and eighteenth century political thought. For example, Foucault does not confront the fact that some contemporary social contract theories have become much more sensitive to the pitfalls of grand, universal theorising, and have revised their conceptions of reason accordingly. In this section I will examine the actuality of Foucault's critique by revisiting the work of John Rawls. Political liberalism—Rawls' recent reformulation of the social contract tradition—provides an excellent opportunity to analyse the strength of Foucault's critique. It is much less optimistic about the possibilities of developing universal values than earlier social contract theories from thinkers such as Kant. But it does make manifest the legitimist ambition of the social contract tradition: it uses reason to construct principles that claim to provide a justification for a just, stable society

[29] M Foucault, 'Truth and Power' in Faubion (ed) (n 3) 128.

[30] Foucault, *HS1* (n 4) 268.

[31] I should stress though that Foucault does not reduce knowledge to power. In his view, power and knowledge are two distinct, yet interdependent domains: power is a condition of possibility for the production and functioning of knowledge, and power relations cannot exist without knowledge relations, *cf* (M Foucault, 'The Concern for Truth' in L Kritzman (ed), *Politics, Philosophy, Culture: Interviews and other Writings 1977–1984* (London, Routledge, 1988) 264; Foucault, *HS1* (n 4) 94; Foucault (n 18) 43.

that is universally valid within the context of liberal-democratic societies. So how pertinent is Foucault's critique when we confront it with political liberalism?

It needs to be said that political liberalism does make conspicuous the fact that Foucault's criticism of the universal intellectual is somewhat overdrawn. As we saw in the previous chapter, Rawls does not assume that reason can transcend historical practices: he acknowledges that his theory of justice cannot completely rise above competing historical forces but remains indebted to a particular historical tradition ('the public culture of liberal-democratic societies'). For Rawls, the moral limits of a well-ordered society are the *contingent* outcome of a network of tentative theoretical texts and historical intuitions rather than a set of necessary limits. Moreover, Rawls agrees with Foucault that contingent moral knowledge claims must be submitted to a critique. To recap, his reflective equilibrium does not merely aim at a coherent defence of the status quo but is committed to bringing to light biases in hegemonic moral conceptions underlying liberal-democratic regimes. However, this commonality between Rawls and Foucault also allows us to see an important advantage of Foucault's perspective: Foucault's approach is much better suited to a critical revision of hegemonic moral notions than the methodology that Rawls designed and thereby does a better job in the democratic politicisation of political philosophy.

First of all, Foucault includes the ontological assumptions present in moral conceptions in his practice of critique. Unlike Rawls, Foucault does not *avoid* ontology as an object of critique but calls for a *politicisation of* these premises. In this way Foucault can improve upon a problematic consequence of Rawls' strategy of avoidance. We have seen in the previous chapter that Rawls' exclusion of ontology from his reflective equilibrium hampered the contestation of the mentalist, individualist biases in his theory of justice. In contrast, Foucault's critical scrutiny of ontology allows him to develop a critique of the mentalist-individualist paradigm and thereby to challenge the ontological assumption in political liberalism that identifies moral agency with mental capacities.

The second improvement offered by Foucault is an investigation of the historical genesis of moral theory. We have seen that this critical strategy enables Foucault to illuminate how the liberal social contract tradition remains indebted to a historically contingent juridical model of power that is insufficient for analysing modern types of oppression. Rawls, for that matter, acknowledges the historical contingency of moral conceptions such as social contract theory, but he does not analyse the historical context in which these notions emerge: the reflective equilibrium limits critique to a comparison of moral theories and intuitions. The consequence of this lack of historicisation, I want to suggest, is that Rawls' practice of critique is much less effective than Foucault's approach in scrutinising the historical biases of the social contract tradition. Consider, for instance, how Rawls uncritically imports the contentious juridical notion of power, central to the social contract tradition, into his conception of the political relationship:

> The political relationship we characterize as having at least two significant distinctive features. First, it is a relationship *of persons* within the basic structure of society. ... Second, political power is, of course always *coercive power backed by the state's machinery* for enforcing its laws. But in a constitutional regime political power is also the *power of equal citizens* as a collective body: it is regularly imposed on citizens *as individuals*, some of whom may not accept the reasons widely believed to justify the general structure of political authority (the constitution); or when they do not accept that structure, they may not regard as well grounded many of the laws enacted by the legislature to which they are subject.[32]

This definition of the political relationship replicates many of the flaws that Foucault identified in the juridical tradition of political thought. For Rawls, the political relationship consists of a relation of persons who appear to exist prior to power relations, excluding from his definition the disciplinary practices that constitute individuals. Power—be it the coercive power of the state or the power of the *demos*—'is imposed' upon individuals rather than being a condition of the possibility of individuality. And power is subjected to consent—citizens 'may not accept ... the general structure of political authority'—rather than being a political relation that produces the capacities of citizens to give consent. Foucault does not only indicate that this account is a contingent historical achievement (as Rawls does too) but his historical critique also alerts us to the occluding effects of the liberal understanding of the political relationship: by articulating this relation in terms of a cooperation between individuals, the juridical tradition blinds us to the disciplinary knowledge regimes that shape individuals and their 'just' system of social cooperation.

I explained that Foucault wants to remedy the blind spots of the social contract tradition with his alternative understanding of power. To illustrate the diagnostic potential of this account let me briefly return to the case of the handshake that I discussed in the previous chapter. One of the problems that we identified in a Rawlsian interpretation of this dispute was that political liberalism has no conceptual resources with which to analyse the role of cultural and bodily practices in realising or disabling mutual respect in the basic structure. Conversely, Foucault's notion of disciplinary power offers an analytical framework that does bring into view the cultural and bodily conditions of mutual respect and their exclusionary effects. For instance, one might think of the ritual of offering and accepting a hand as a form of bodily discipline. It has been transmitted historically through institutional sites

[32] J Rawls, *Justice as Fairness: A Restatement* (Cambridge, The Belknap Press of Harvard University Press, 2001) 182 (emphasis added).

such as families, schools and the workplace by inscribing itself on the bodies of the majority of Dutch citizens. Furthermore, the handshake has been supported by the circulation of various norms: for instance, many manuals on the usage of body language in social interactions, such as job interviews, specify how individuals should offer a handshake.[33] Due to the enactment of such power/knowledge relations the handshake has had the empowering effect typical of disciplinary power: the ritual has become an important part of the everyday practices that shape social interaction, convictions and feelings and thereby helps to produce democratic and social cooperation in The Netherlands. Seen in this light, it becomes understandable why many citizens resist giving up this practice: they experience the handshake as a natural and indispensable condition for maintaining mutual respect. Meanwhile, Foucault's notion of power also attends to the *exclusionary* effects of cultural customs of mutual respect. The ritual of the handshake realises its empowering effects through a hierarchical standard: accepting or offering a hand in a proper way is perceived as 'civil' while refusing to participate in this gesture is seen as 'disrespectful'. So religious customs that attempt to realise mutual respect by avoiding physical contact with relative strangers are considered abnormal in this view. In other words, the handshake illustrates how social-historical bodily practices both enable and hamper democratic agency: the gesture of the handshake helps to sustain the attitude of mutual respect for some while hampering the possibilities of mutual respect for others.[34]

In sum, the confrontation between Foucault's critique of the social contract tradition and political liberalism suggests that his analysis is still very much relevant to current political-philosophical debates. Although Foucault overstates his critique of the universal intellectual, he shows us that political liberalism is lacking important critical strategies to expose biases in universalistic moral claims. Furthermore, his analytic of power provides an important corrective to Rawls' reduction of a society's basic institutions to rights and economic opportunities. Unlike Rawls he shows us how liberal-democratic institutions are subjected to hierarchical practices that precede

[33] An effective handshake should be neither too soft (as this could convey a weak character) nor too firm (which could be perceived as intimidating). For an instructive video on the handshake from the United States, see: Expertvillage, *How to Prepare for a Job Interview: The Importance of the Handshake in a Job Interview*, available at http://www.youtube.com/watch?v=KwOskMOqGL4. The Dutch website *Groeten bij komen en gaan* includes a quiz that allows readers to test their own handshake abilities (F van Marwijk, *Groeten bij komen en gaan*, available at http://www.lichaamstaal.nl/groet.html.

[34] Foucault's emphasis on the exclusionary effects of cultural practices sets his account apart from Charles Taylor's plea for cultural recognition. While Taylor's proposal for cultural recognition underscores the empowering effects of cultural recognition, it does not discuss the fact that cultural recognition will also issue exclusionary effects.

the possibilities of becoming a liberal-democratic agent: free and equal citizens can take part in political relationships in virtue of cultural, bodily practices that empower some but exclude others.

But is this all that Foucault can do? Does his work only help us diagnose the exclusionary mechanisms inherent in liberal-democratic regimes? Or does it also offer normative orientation in the possibilities of how we might respond to such power relations in a democratic way? In the remainder of this chapter I will look more closely at the normative purpose and ontological background assumptions of Foucault's critique. What exactly is Foucault's alternative to the universal intellectual? Is his critique utterly lacking in criteria that can evaluate current democratic regimes? Or is he in agreement with Rawls that political thinkers have an educational role to play in the sense of teaching their fellow citizens 'ideals of personhood and political society' that can strengthen democratic practice?[35] Put differently, how and why is Foucault committed to democratic politics, including the democratic contestation of traditional power relations that have been transmitted by political philosophy?

IV. FOUCAULT'S ETHOS OF 'STIMULATING CONTEST'

Foucault's account paints a bleak picture of modern Western liberal democracies. He challenges any optimistic faith in freedom: we are constrained by historical power relations that do not only escape consciousness but constitute the very possibility of consciousness. Furthermore, the codification and expansion of legal freedoms has gone hand-in-hand with an increase in disciplinary control mechanisms, and the liberal juridical tradition lacks adequate conceptual resources to reveal this 'fact of domination in all its brutality and its secrecy'.[36]

In light of his sombre critique of the disciplinary coercion in modern Western societies one might think that Foucault would not wish to have anything to do with democratic practices. But even though he does not develop a substantive vision of democracy Foucault does not reject it entirely. During his life Foucault participated in democratic debates, providing various commentaries on the position of prisoners, psychiatric patients and stateless people, and he was engaged in numerous political actions to ameliorate their situation. Moreover, Foucault considers it to be an important civic responsibility for intellectuals to participate in democratic discussions. By disseminating through public debates a particular historical ontology,

[35] See ch 2, text to n 17.
[36] Foucault, *HS1* (n 4) 27.

the intellectual contributes to the democratic will-formation in a way that can contest the ruling truth regimes of society and could 'form a community of action' that will act differently to the established modes of conduct.[37]

How does Foucault distinguish his own political interventions from those of the universal intellectual? Foucault says that intellectuals need to practice their democratic duties as 'specific intellectuals' and sees his own participation in democratic debates as exemplary for this type of political engagement. The specific intellectual has a certain expertise on a particular truth regime, such as the institutionalisation of madness in hospitals, the enactment of educational discipline in schools or, for that matter, the intricacies of knowledge-production among academic political philosophers. Her familiarity with these truth regimes allows her to develop a well-informed contestation of these local knowledge domains but, in opposition to the universal intellectual in the juridical tradition, the specific intellectual does not assume to be a 'master of truth and justice' and does not try to legislate for the democratic public. Rather than attempting to transform the will of the citizenry, a specific intellectual limits herself to a local description of the intricate power-play in particular domains of modern societies:

> The work of an intellectual is not to *shape* others' political will; it is, through the analyses that he carries out *in his own field*, to question over and over again what is postulated as self-evident, to disturb people's mental habits, ... to dissipate what is familiar and accepted, to re-examine rules and institutions and on the basis of this reproblematization (in which he carries out his specific task as an intellectual) *to participate in the formation* of a political will (in which he has a role as citizen to play).[38]

Foucault's account of intellectual democratic activism, then, includes the possibility of what I have characterised as the democratic politicisation of political philosophy. When an intellectual has some expertise on an aspect of political philosophy, she should make an effort to question this tradition and circulate her critique within democratic debates. By showing other citizens that some aspects of political thinking should not be taken for granted, she can provide an impetus to the democratic will-formation about particular rules and institutions that have been shaped by these modes of thought. Foucault, however, also challenges an aspect that I treated as central to the democratic politicisation of political philosophy. In the introduction, I said that the democratic politicisation of political philosophy implies that political philosophers continue to develop normative and ontological premises of democratic politics but that they do so by submitting these accounts to

[37] M Foucault, 'Polemics, Politics, and Problematizations' in Rabinow (ed) (n 4) 115.
[38] Foucault (n 31) 265 (emphasis added).

democratic contestation. In contrast, Foucault's model of the specific intellectual suggests that political thinkers should develop critiques but make no attempt to give direction to democratic politics by developing an alternative normative and ontological framework. The normative and ontological task of the political thinker, then, is not displaced to the democratic arena, and political thinkers appear to be discharged of this task altogether.

How plausible is Foucault's account of the specific intellectual? Do political thinkers merely 'question', 'disturb', and 're-examine' thought and habits without anticipating an alternative framework of thought or calling for alternative habits? Do they merely '*participate* in the formation of a democratic will' and do they, unlike the universal intellectuals, make no attempt to '*shape* other's political will'? I want to suggest that, not unlike his account of the universal intellectual, Foucault has exaggerated the model of the specific intellectual in his attempt to rectify the biases of the juridical tradition in political philosophy. As we shall see, his local critiques are premised upon on a framework that offers both ontological and normative parameters for democratic will-formation and participation.

A. Foucault's Ontology of Power and Bodily Forces

One of the striking similarities between Rawls and Foucault is their refusal to elaborate on the ontological assumptions of their own political thought. Even though Foucault departs from Rawls in his attempt to criticise ontology, he, like Rawls, does not seek to develop a substantive, ontological position himself. Foucault's silence with regard to the ontological premises of his own critical project has been interpreted in various, conflicting ways. We shall see that some of his readers maintain that Foucault presents a political theory without an ontological foundation. Others defend an opposite stance which argues that Foucault foregrounds his political analysis with uncontestable, transcendental ontological claims. My own reading concurs with the latter view on the assumption that Foucault's political inquiries are premised upon implicit ontological claims, but suggests that he presents a historically contingent, rather than a transcendental, ontology. To explain this point, I will take a closer look at Foucault's notion of power and the body—the two characteristics of social life that, I contend, function as ontological conditions of subjectivity in Foucault's critique.

i. A Contestable Ontology of Power

We saw that Foucault's practice of critique is premised upon an innovative understanding of power: power relations are assumed to be a condition of possibility and an effect of knowledge production and social interaction.

Foucault has been notoriously reluctant in answering ontological questions with regard to his account of power:

> Nothing is fundamental. That is what is interesting in the analysis of society. That is why nothing irritates me as much as these inquiries—which are by definition metaphysical—on the foundations of power in a society or the self-institution of a society, etc. These are not fundamental phenomena. There are only reciprocal relations, and the perpetual gaps between intentions in relations to one another.[39]

Foucault wants to evade ontological inquiries into power in order to stimulate us to investigate power as specific intellectuals, that is, to look at how power is constituted in particular empirical contexts rather than to treat power as an abstract isolated phenomenon. He therefore finds it necessary to introduce the wager or 'suspicion' that 'power as such does not exist' and emphasises that this strategic denial of an ontology is 'not designed to introduce by stealth a metaphysics or an ontology of power'.[40] But this wager, I want to stress, is belied by many universalist claims that Foucault makes with regard to power. For instance, Foucault has explicitly argued that the ubiquity of power is not confined to the specific historical epochs that he has studied but is transhistorical. Though power relations obtain different shapes and techniques in various societies, the presence of power as such is constitutive of social relations in every society:

> What I mean is this: In a society such as ours—*or in any society*, come to that—multiple relations of power traverse, characterize, and constitute the social body … Power cannot be exercised unless a certain economy of discourses of truth functions in, on the basis of, and thanks to, that power. This is *true of all societies*, but I think that in our society, this relationship among power, right, and truth is organized in a very particular way.[41]

This claim suggests that Foucault's theory of power is not just a local account of the constitution of thought and action in the disciplinary regimes in modern Western societies. It seems rather that his conceptualisation of power is closer to an ontology: a set of presuppositions about the constitutive features of political life, such as human agency and interaction, that structure the empirical inquiries of intellectuals *prior to* their interpretation of particular truth regimes such as the prison, psychiatric discourse, and so on. But what is the epistemological status of this universal? Is the omnipresence of power a claim with never-ending, incontestable validity? Or is this foundation contingent and open to a critique?

Some of Foucault's readers have argued that Foucault's concept of power is transcendental. For instance, Jürgen Habermas accuses Foucault of

[39] M Foucault, 'Space, Knowledge, and Power' in Faubion (ed) (n 3) 356.
[40] Foucault, 'The Subject' (n 4) 337.
[41] Foucault, *HS1* (n 4) 24 (emphasis added).

raising power to a transcendental concept that has become incontestable and immune to revision in light of empirical facts:

> [D]iscourse formations ... maintain their transcendental power over whatever unfolds within the totalities shaped by them. This excludes a dialectical or circular feedback effect of either the ontic occurrence or the referents upon the history of the conditions of their possibility.[42]

Likewise, in her close reading of Foucault, Beatrice Han points at several passages where power-knowledge ceases to be a 'contingent and historically given configuration' but appears as a 'metaphysical entity'.[43]

The readings of Han and Habermas are not unwarranted. Foucault at times identifies the omnipresence of power as a necessary precondition of historical practice that is ill at ease with his insistence on the historical contingency of philosophical knowledge claims. For example, it is difficult to distinguish assertions such as 'it is pointless to dream of a day where knowledge would cease to depend on power' from a claim to a mastery of truth.[44] But it is important to note that while Foucault conceptualises power as an ontological condition of possibility of human practice he considers this universal to be contingent upon these very practices. As he puts it in *History of Sexuality 1*:

> Relations of power *are not in a position of exteriority with respect to other types of relationships* (economic processes, knowledge relationships, sexual relations) but are *immanent* in the latter; they are the immediate effects of the divisions, inequalities, and disequilibriums which occur in the latter, and conversely they are the *internal conditions of these differentiations*; relations of power are not in *superstructural* positions, with merely a role of prohibition or accompaniment; they have a directly productive role, wherever they come into play.[45]

In other words, Foucault's theory of power seems less a *transcendental* than an *immanent* condition of possibility of knowledge and interaction: it draws support from the phenomenal world and explicitly distances itself from any

[42] J Habermas, 'The Critique of Reason, Unmasking the Human Sciences: Michel Foucault' in M Kelly (ed), *Critique and Power: Recasting the Foucault/Habermas Debate* (Cambridge, The MIT Press, 1994) 62–63.

[43] B Han, *Foucault's Critical Project: Between the Transcendental and the Historical* (Stanford, Stanford University Press, 2002) 143. Han cites the following passage from *Discipline and Punish*: 'The subject that knows, the objects to be known and the modalities of knowledge must be regarded as so many effects of *these fundamental implications of power-knowledge and their historical transformations*. In short, it is not the activity of the subject that produces a corpus of knowledge, useful or resistant to power, but power-knowledge, the processes and struggles that traverse it and of which it is made up, that determines the forms and possible domains of knowledge' (Foucault (n 18) 27). According to Han, the idea that power '*determines* the forms and possible domains of knowledge' endowes power with a 'quasi-transcendental function'.

[44] M Foucault, 'Entretien sur la prison: le livre et sa méthode' in D Defert and F Ewald (eds), *Dits et Ecrits II* (Paris, Gallimard, 2001) 753. Cited in Han, ibid) 142–43.

[45] Foucault, *HS1* (n 4) 94 (emphasis added).

appeal to conditions of possibility that logically precede human practice.[46] This reading finds further support in a later text where Foucault explicitly affirms the contestability of his thesis on power. Here he acknowledges that the specific analysis of power relations presupposes an 'ongoing conceptualization' of power, and he underscores the need to submit this conceptual apparatus to a critique by confronting the thesis on power with the 'reality' that its attempts conceptualise.[47] This suggests that Foucault's ontology of power is not so much a transcendental, incontestable precondition of knowledge and interaction, but an immanent, contingent limit of subjectivity that is open to critical scrutiny by the concrete struggles within the empirical context that power tries to understand.

ii. The Body

Historically contingent power relations are not the only condition of subjectivity that Foucault identifies. As indicated in his critiques of modern Western societies, Foucault emphasises the crucial role of the body in subject-formation and he at times identifies the body as a force that exists prior to power. For instance, we saw that his account of subjection states that disciplinary power 'dissociates' the energies in the body and 'the power that might result from it', in other words, suggesting that the body is not only an *effect* of power (in terms of its capacities and aptitudes) but also a type of energy or force that *precedes* it. Another binary feature between bodily forces and historical power relations appears in his critique of the juridical concept of the individual, where the formation of individuality is conceptualised as the effect of 'power exercised *over* bodies, multiplicities, movements, desires, forces'.[48]

How should we interpret these allusions to pre-historical bodily forces in Foucault's analysis of Western modernity? Do they, like his theory of power, manifest yet another ontological claim? And, if so, how does Foucault negotiate the tension between, on the one hand, postulating a pre-historical force, and on the other hand, his insistent call to submit such pre-historical conditions to a critique?

To answer these questions it is instructive to take a look at Foucault's early essay 'Nietzsche, Genealogy, History'.[49] This text sketches the philosophical underpinnings of the historical critique that Foucault later applied

[46] I borrow the distinction between transcendental and immanent conditions of possibility from Christoph Menke. (C Menke, *Spiegelungen der Gleichheit: Politische Philosophie nach Adorno und Derrida* (Suhrkamp Verlag, Frankfurt am Main, 2004) 120).
[47] Foucault, 'The Subject' (n 4) 327.
[48] See ch 3 text to n 26.
[49] M Foucault, 'Nietzsche, Genealogy, History' in P Rabinow (ed), *The Foucault Reader* (New York, Pantheon Books, 1984).

to the social contract tradition, and that he developed further in the essay 'What is Enlightenment?' with which I opened this chapter.

In 'Nietzsche, Genealogy, History' Foucault challenges the idea that human history exemplifies a law, purpose or specific design by underlining the radical contingency of historical power relations. History consists of a dramatic quest for domination, 'the endless repeated play of dominations'; it is moved by a power struggle that exceeds the interpretations that impose order or a direction upon it: the 'forces operating in history are not controlled by destiny or regulative mechanisms, but respond to haphazard conflicts'.[50] Foucault's belief in radical historical contingency leads him to reject both traditional historical analysis and conventional ontological inquiries. Against the traditional historians who treat events as instances in a natural or teleological development, he holds that anyone who listens carefully to history will not find such a direction but confirm 'our existence among countless lost events, without a landmark or a point of reference'.[51] Against ontological inquiries that try to uncover a true identity or unity existing prior to or underneath such a historical chaos, he introduces 'discontinuity into our very being'.[52] For instance, in an oblique response to Kant, he challenges the separation between a noumenal and phenomenal world and the possibility of a noumenally free rational human being:

> [K]nowledge does not slowly detach itself from its empirical roots, the initial roots from which it arose, to become pure speculation subject only to the demands of the reason; its development is not tied to the constitution and affirmation of a free subject; rather it creates a progressive enslavement to its instinctive violence.[53]

In contrast to the search for foundations and, one might say, in line with the later essay on the Enlightenment, Foucault notes that the purpose of his own critique is the dismantling of foundations: historical critique 'disturbs what was previously thought unified'.[54] In fact, Foucault says that it is impossible to establish a firm ground for critique: '[n]othing in man—not even his body—is sufficiently stable to serve as the basis for self-recognition or for understanding other men'.[55]

Now, in light of this strong juxtaposition that Foucault constructs between foundational thought and his own critique, it is easy to assume that Foucault believes that his critique lacks any ontological ground whatsoever. For instance, the democratic theorist Wendy Brown contends that Foucault's

[50] ibid, 88.
[51] ibid, 155.
[52] I should note Foucault employs the term metaphysics rather than ontology in this essay.
[53] Foucault (n 49) 163.
[54] ibid, 82.
[55] ibid, 87.

historicisation of ontology makes way for a political theory that can avoid ontological claims. Reading 'Nietzsche, Genealogy, History' together with some of Foucault's later essays on the Enlightenment, she claims:

> [An] 'ontology of the present does not confuse itself with ontologically grounded politics. ... it doesn't tell us what is to be done, or even what is to be valued. It does not replace the truths and convictions it renders historically contingent and discursively containing; rather, it questions whether truths and convictions make up the right ethos for critical political consciousness.[56]

I agree with Brown that Foucault challenges traditional understandings of the relation between ontology and political reflection. But it seems to me that Brown misses the point that Foucault's problematisation of ontology is not so much leading towards a separation of political reflection from ontology, but rather presenting an alternative ontology. His critique on the faith in teleology and identity so typical for traditional ontology—such as the claim that the body does not offer a *stable* site of self-recognition—is not groundless but appears to be dependent upon an ontological belief in bodily contingency. Or, to put it in the terms of the later essay 'What is Enlightenment?', a critical ontology of ourselves is conditioned by an ontology of allegedly universal bodily forces.

The key to this reading comes in the early sections of 'Nietzsche, Genealogy, History' where Foucault plays with an underdeveloped distinction in Nietzsche's work between *Ursprung* (origin) and *Herkunft* (descent). On Foucault's reading, the quest for *Ursprung* signifies the search for certain foundations that he rejects. But he concedes that his own critique—which traces our historical descent (*Herkunft*)—resembles the traditional ontology of *Ursprung* in its attempt to conceptualise the roots of knowledge and morality. Yet, in opposition to the traditional ontologist, the theorist of *Herkunft* develops a hypothesis (*Herkunfthypothese*) that reveals the contingent quality of these sources and does not assume that these roots offer a stable ground.

Foucault's own *Herkunfthypothese* consistently centres on the body. He qualifies the body as 'the domain of *Herkunft*' and throughout the essay Foucault accounts for the contingency of morality and knowledge with reference to the body.[57] For instance, Foucault suggests that history can only

[56] W Brown, *Politics out of History* (New Jersey, Princeton University Press, 2001) 120. Brown does not cite 'What is Enlightenment?' but refers to another commentary of Foucault on Kant's essay (M Foucault, 'The Art of Telling the Truth' in L Kritzman (ed), *Politics, Philosophy, Culture: Interviews and other Writings 1977–1984* (London, Routledge, 1988). In this essay, Foucault employs the term 'ontology of the present' and 'ontology of ourselves' rather than a critical or historical ontology of ourselves.

[57] Foucault (n 49) 83.

produce the various cultural manifestations of the body in virtue of bodily forces that seem to precede power:

> The body is the inscribed surface of events ..., the locus of a dissociated self (adopting the illusion of a substantial unity), and a volume in perpetual disintegration. Genealogy ... is thus situated within the articulation of the body and history. Its task is to expose a body totally *imprinted by history* and the process of history's destruction *of the* body.[58]

Moreover, Foucault conceptualises this process of the cultural production of the body as a 'single drama'.[59] So even though Foucault claims to reject continuous historical narratives, he depicts the body as the universal scene upon which various struggles for power unfold.

These observations suggest that Foucault treats the body as an ontological condition that cannot be completely reduced to history and that he rather considers these bodily forces as primordial energies that social- historical power relations subject to disciplinary norms.[60] It is important to note however that, like his belief in the ubiquity of power, his faith in pre-historical bodily forces functions as a contestable wager that is itself open for contestation. He stresses that bodily forces can never be made fully intelligible within knowledge claims but give rise to 'desires, failings and errors'.[61] A thesis or *Herkunfthypothese* about the body will thus never secure a theorists' desire for certainty but remains a contingent, vulnerable knowledge claim: 'it is [not] an acquisition, a *possession* that grows and solidifies; rather, it is an *unstable* assemblage of faults, fissures and heterogenous layers that threaten the fragile inheritor from within or from underneath'.[62]

In sum, Foucault identifies two interdependent ontological conditions of subjectivity: the subject is constituted by historical power relations and bodily forces. Subjectivity and knowledge become possible in virtue of an ongoing taming process wherein historical power relations work upon and shape the body. This ontology renders him more universalist than Foucault

[58] ibid, 83 (emphasis added).

[59] ibid, 85.

[60] Foucault's references to the body seem to echo Nietzsche's belief in a naturalist 'will to power'. For instance, in 'Genealogy of Morality' Nietzsche explains that the moral subject is constructed by cultural practices that inhibit the release of animalist, expanding, bodily instincts. These bodily forces appear to exist prior to the socio-historical practices that constitute the subject, (F Nietzsche, 'Zur Genealogie der Moral' in G Colli and M Montinari (eds), *Kritischen Studienausgabe, Volume 5* (München, Deutscher Taschenbuch Verlag, 1999) 322). For the influences of Nietzsche on Foucault, see P Patton, 'Foucault's Subject of Power' in J Moss (ed), *The Later Foucault: Politics and Philosophy* (London, Sage Publications, 1998); J Butler, 'Foucault and the Paradox of Bodily Inscriptions'(1989) 86 *The Journal of Philosophy* 601; M Kelly, *The Political Philosophy of Michel Foucault* (New York, Routledge, 2009). For an account of Foucault's ontology of the body in light of Foucault's affinities to Deleuze, see R Coles, 'Foucault's Dialogical Artistic Ethos' (1991) 8 *Theory, Culture & Society* 99.

[61] Foucault (n 49) 148.

[62] ibid, 146 (emphasis added).

himself, and some of his readers, admit. In spite of Foucault's disavowal of a universal 'theory of the world', his undertakings as a specific intellectual—the analysis of local truth regimes—are structured by a belief in ontological historical power relations and primordial bodily forces. We have seen though that Foucault's ontology does not put a halt to critique. Both his account of power relations and bodily contingency are fragile, contestable interpretations of the conditions of subjectivity and open for critical revision. In this way, my reading of Foucault allows us to envision a relation between political thought and ontology that was lacking in Rawls' account. To recall, in Rawls' view the inclusion of ontology in political reflection would establish ontological notions as incontestable preconditions of politics and move us away from the democratic politicisation of political philosophy.[63] Foucault's perspective challenges Rawls' point. His ontology does not claim to possess the truth, but presents a tentative wager on ontological conditions that is, as Deleuze puts it, not 'apodictic but problematic'.[64] Moreover, his ontology of historical and bodily contingency accentuates the point that the knowledge claims that political philosophy draws upon—be it ontological and normative concepts or inherited historical identities—are inherently unstable due to numerous 'distinct and multiple elements' that resist these categories.[65] Foucault's ontology thereby provides a powerful impetus for the democratic politicisation of political thought. That is to say, when a political theorist tries to base an agreement on shared intuitions in a particular tradition—or, as Rawls would say, to look at settled convictions in 'public culture'—Foucault's ontology invites the democratic public to attend to the exclusions in these foundations. So taking to heart Foucault's commitment to critique the next section will address a problematic blind spot in Foucault's ontology.

B. 'The Great Carnival of Time': An Aesthetic Experiment with Plurality

Until now I have concentrated on the ontological parameters of Foucault's critique. In this section, I shift the focus to the normative assumptions of Foucault's project by looking at some of the writings from Foucault's middle period. Reconstructing the normative position that emerges during this phase serves two goals: it provides the first step in fleshing out Foucault's distinctive normative contribution to democratic thought, and contributes to the democratic politicisation of Foucault's ontology, that is, it helps to pin down a flaw in Foucault's ontology.

[63] See ch 2 s III.B.
[64] G Deleuze, 'Foldings, or the Inside of Thought (Subjectivation)' in Kelly (ed) (n 42) 332.
[65] Foucault (n 49) 94.

During his middle period Foucault presents himself mainly as a critic of morality and says very little about his own normative commitments. His refusal to explicate the normative horizon of his critique caused some alarm among his readers. In the words of Charles Taylor:

> He dashes the hope, if we had one, that there is some good we can affirm, as a result of the understanding these analyses give us. And by the same token, he seems to raise a question whether there is such a thing as a way out.[66]

In a certain sense, Taylor's analysis that Foucault's middle writings are lacking a collective good converges with Foucault's own suggestion that his critiques are not explicating a positive normative ideal.[67] In my view, however, even the middle stage of Foucault's argument sketches the normative contours of a way of living together that takes further shape in the later period. As we shall see, Foucault aspires to practices that, first of all, sustain a plurality of ontological, religious and historical identities and that, second, stimulate a contestation and experiment with these inherited categories. Still, I agree with Taylor that the middle writings of Foucault have difficulty explaining how human beings can revise dominating practices ('whether there is such a thing as a way out'). This problem emerges due to a deficit in Foucault's ontology: his early account of historical power relations and bodily contingency sees the subject merely as being instrumental in strengthening power relations and cannot account for the participation of subjects in the ongoing contestation of, and experiment with, identities that Foucault aspires to.

i. A Concerted Carnival

I already indicated that Foucault's critique provides a powerful impetus for the contestation of normative concepts. Foucault's critique is not, however, merely negating normative aspirations or depriving us of any normative guidelines for action whatsoever. To begin with, Foucault hopes that his critiques will assist people in particular struggles against the status quo. Even though critique cannot be a 'premise of deduction that concludes "this, then, is what needs to be done"', Foucault does envision it as 'an instrument for those who fight, those who resist and refuse what is'.[68] For instance, the analysis of disciplinary power might sensitise his public to forms of oppression in the prison that were previously not visible and initiate political initiatives to ameliorate the position of prisoners. Moreover, as we can see in

[66] C Taylor, *Philosophy and the Human Sciences: Philosophical Papers 2* (Cambridge, Cambridge University Press, 1985) 152.

[67] Wendy Brown's suggestion that Foucault's critique is not 'telling us what is to be valued' defends a similar stance, see ch 3 text to n 56.

[68] M Foucault, 'Questions of Method' in Faubion (ed) (n 3) 236.

'Nietzsche, Genealogy, History', Foucault is not just saying 'fight the status quo', he is also outlining a distinct ethos that provides some indication of the kind of practices, or alternatives to our current condition, that are worth embracing.

Foucault presents this evaluative horizon through an image rather than by means of a Rawlsian set of principles: he invokes the metaphor of 'a concerted carnival' which is a direct reference to 'the great carnival of time' that Nietzsche sets out in *Beyond Good and Evil.* Here Nietzsche observes that human beings cannot relinquish history. Even though man will remain deeply unsatisfied with his historical identities, they nevertheless remain indispensable for man, he 'absolutely requires a costume: he needs history as a storeroom of costumes. To be sure, he notices that none of the costumes fit him properly—he changes and changes'.[69] Foucault follows Nietzsche's insight on the indispensability of, and dissatisfaction with, historical identities. His critique does not attempt to deprive human beings of any markers of identification whatsoever, but aims for a *pluralisation* of the possibilities of identification. Rather than dissolving the category of identity, Foucault wants to replace the identification of our 'faint individuality with the *solid* identities of the past' with the '*excessive* choice of identities'.[70]

Foucault's acknowledgement of the need for historical identification bears some affinity with the communitarian insight on the constitutive role of historical practices in subject-formation. However, it is important to stress that Foucault does not so much aim, like Charles Taylor, for the strengthening of historical identities through recognition, but strives for a creative and experimental attitude towards history.[71] After the fashion of Nietzsche, he suggests that we need to develop a playful historical sensibility that parodies the 'morality, postulates of faith, aesthetic tastes and religion' in our historical heritage, rather than to recover or restore historical traditions.[72] The point of such an ongoing experiment with traditional metaphysical and historical identities is to provide a counterpoint to an uncritical glorification of history, and alter historical moods that are 'totally devoted to veneration'.[73]

Foucault's ethos finds methodological support in his attempt to give voice to ways of understanding that have hitherto been excluded. He calls such silenced discourses 'subjugated knowledges': 'naïve knowledges, hierarchically inferior knowledges ... the knowledge of the psychiatrized,

[69] Foucault (n 49) 94; F Nietzsche, *Beyond Good and Evil: Prelude to a Philosophy of the Future* (New York, Vintage Books, 1955) para 223.

[70] Foucault (n 49) 94 (emphasis added).

[71] See ch 2 s IV.A.i.

[72] Nietzsche (n 69) para 223.

[73] Foucault (n 49) 94

the patient, ... the knowledge of the delinquent'.[74] One might say that the excavation of marginalised discourses provides the positive or affirmative counterpoint to the negating aspect of Foucault's critique. It offers new modes of identification to the participants in a particular practice and thereby multiplies the possibilities for experimenting with hegemonic identities.

To make the normative impact of Foucault's ethos more tangible let me briefly recall the Dutch handshake debate. In the previous chapter, I mentioned that the Netherlands Institute for Human Rights and the mayor of Amsterdam at that time, Cohen, argued for a revision of Dutch customs of respect. They suggested that mutual respect could not only be enacted by a handshake but claimed that civility could also be demonstrated through a friendly nod (the Institute) or a respectful refusal of a handshake (Cohen). Foucault's plea for the pluralisation of, and experimentation with, historical identities offers important insights for construing a normative foundation of this position. For instance, the responses of the Institute and Cohen did not, as did Rawls and some Dutch commentators, overlook the importance of historical, bodily rituals in establishing mutual respect.[75] They took seriously the need of human beings for a particular mode of bodily, historical identification for sustaining respectful relations, but they also argued for an experimentation with established historical practices. By giving voice to excluded understandings of mutual respect, they tried to open up a space for people to resist hegemonic practices of civility and to pluralise customs of mutual respect.[76]

In short then, Foucault's middle period is committed to a distinct normative horizon: it aspires to the pluralisation of, and experimentation with, historical identities. And while this ethos does not offer clear prescriptions, it does offer some guidance in the evaluation of particular democratic disputes: it suggests that we take seriously the need for historical identification, but also strive to pluralise and experiment with historical identities.

There is, however, an unresolved ambiguity in this ethos: Foucault's overly submissive ontology of the subject seems at odds with his aspiration for an ongoing critical and concerted experiment with history. To begin with, while Foucault seems to assume and aspire to a subject that can critically distance herself from historical practices, his ontology of historical power relations and bodily contingency sees the subject primarily as the passive effect of such non-subjective forces. Consider, for instance, his account of

[74] Foucault *HS1* (n 4) 7.

[75] For the way in which some Dutch commentators neglected the importance of bodily rituals, see ch 1 text to n 5 and n 6. For Rawls' reduction of mutual respect to rights and political and economic opportunities, see ch 2 s IV.B.i.

[76] I should note, however, that Foucault had difficulty seeing the potential of state-sanctioned projects of pluralisation, such as carried out by law or policy-making. I criticise this aspect in Foucault's work in the next chapter.

resistance in *History of Sexuality 1*. Here Foucault explains that dominant discourses can be experimented with because power relations include a possibility of being reversed or altered:

> Where there is power, there is resistance, and yet, or rather consequently, this resistance is never in a position of exteriority to power ... Their existence [power relations] depends on a multiplicity of points of resistance: these play the role of adversary, target, support, or handle in power relations.[77]

For example, the discourse on homosexuality eventually gave rise to a counter-discourse in which gays started to criticise traditional homophobic norms: 'homosexuality began to speak on its own behalf, to demand that its legitimacy or "naturality" be acknowledged, often in the same vocabulary, using the same categories by which it was medically disqualified'.[78] On the one hand, Foucault implicitly assumes that such counter-discourses presuppose a capacity for critical agency. That is, he envisions an audience that is constituted by subjects that can question and deliberate over discourses: '[w]e must *question* them [discourses] on the two levels of their tactical productivity (what reciprocal effects of power and knowledge they ensure) and their strategical integration'.[79] Yet his conceptualisation of resistance makes no mention of an agent capable of a critical interrogation of discourse, and reduces the possibility of resistance to an amalgam of historical discourse and bodily pleasures. For example, it is the nineteenth century discourse on homosexuality that made possible the formation of a 'reverse' discourse' rather than agents who question and challenge discourse. And, to the extent that individuals do participate in resistance, they appear solely as bodily forces that are trained, operated upon and destroyed by forces beyond their control, as if they are merely passively subjected to bodily discipline: resistance is 'mobilizing ... individuals', 'inflaming certain points of the body', 'furrowing across individuals themselves', 'cutting them up and remolding them'.[80]

Furthermore, Foucault's ethos disregards the need for self-discipline in sustaining his evaluative horizon. In the last chapter of *The History of Sexuality 1*, Foucault imagines that nineteenth century political struggles arose from vital bodily instincts: 'what was demanded and what served as an objective was life, understood as the basic needs, man's concrete *essence*, the realisation of his *potential*, a plenitude of the possible'.[81] Here Foucault seems to endorse the predominance of bodily forces in politics, arguing that the counter-attack against disciplinary norms of sexual discourse ought to

[77] Foucault, *HS1* (n 4) 95–96.
[78] ibid, 101.
[79] ibid, 102 (emphasis added).
[80] ibid, 96.
[81] ibid, 145 (emphasis added).

depart from 'bodies and pleasures'.[82] But how do these 'bodies and pleasures' allow for Foucault's normative aspiration for a *concerted* carnival, that is, an ongoing experiment that is orchestrated to such an extent that it avoids the pitfalls of, on the one hand, a complete dissolution of historical practices and, on the other, an uncritical glorification of history? It seems that such an ethos is in need of bodies which are trained into particular kind of experimental dispositions and sensibilities.[83] Foucault's account of subject-formation, however, reduces disciplinary self-restraint to a practice that can only solidify oppression rather than of seeing it as a tool that can also support the aesthetic revision of historical power relations. These problems in Foucault's ethos are only solved at a later stage of his argument where the notion of agonic freedom and ethics play a central role.

V. THE STIMULATION OF *ENLIGHTENED* CONTEST

Foucault's later writings offer a much-needed second step in reconstructing his ontological and normative parameters for democratic politics. The ideal of freedom or autonomy that Foucault eventually came to affirm presents a significantly more agential notion of the subject than his initial focus on the passive docility constitutive of the self.[84] Foucault now explicates that power relations allow individuals an active role in questioning, evaluating, modifying, resisting and pluralising the strategic possibilities that power relations may open up. As he puts it in 'The Subject and Power':

> Power is exercised only over free subjects, and only insofar as they are 'free'. By this we mean individual or collective subjects who are faced with a field of possibilities in which several kinds of conduct, several ways of reacting and modes of behaviour are available.[85]

Foucault draws upon the aesthetic modernism of the French poet Baudelaire to exemplify his ethos of freedom. Baudelaire envisions the modern artist as someone who pays extreme attention to the current moment. He tries to intensify the present by looking for 'something eternal that is not beyond the present instant, nor behind it, but within it'.[86] The purpose of 'heroising' the present is not to freeze or to glorify reality but to transform current reality by imagining it differently than it is. Foucault transposes Baudelaire's ethos—that Baudelaire only intended for art—to the realm of ethics and politics. His notion of freedom aims for a creative, experimental attitude

[82] ibid, 157.

[83] After all, in light of Foucault's account of disciplinary power it would be difficult to argue that such an ethos would emerge naturally, that is, without constraining the body.

[84] See ch 3 s IV.B.i.

[85] Foucault, 'The Subject' (n 4) 342.

[86] Foucault, 'What is' (n 4) 310.

vis-a-vis oneself as well as for the worldly conditions that shape this self. Subjectivation—the process of self-discipline by which the individual consciously submits itself to disciplinary norms—is no longer reduced to the production of docile individuals but also opens up space for an ongoing process of reflective, experimental creation by which the self produces itself as 'a work of art' and reshapes given power relations.[87] By actively responding to current reality and by cultivating the capacity to re-imagine the present, the subject becomes attentive to possibilities 'of no longer being, doing, or thinking what we are, do, or think'. Rather than seeking to implement a blueprint of an ideal society, this ideal of freedom pursues possibilities for change by means of partial, experimental transformations of the status quo. How does Foucault conceptualise this notion of individual freedom or ongoing quest for 'transfiguration'?[88] And which conditions are necessary to sustain this ideal?

A. Foucault's Ontology of Agonic Freedom

Foucault's affirmation of autonomy situates him in closer proximity to Kant than do his earlier writings. Still, his understanding of freedom should not be mistaken for the Kantian idea of individual autonomy. The agency by which individuals self-consciously craft themselves and the world is not an interiorised mental capacity for self-determination but consists of a set of practical relations that Foucault designates with the term 'ethics'. Ethical activities provide individuals with a variety of ideals and techniques that are constituted by historically contingent power relations.[89] They structure the process of cultivation and

> permit individuals to effect by their own means, or with the help of others, a certain number of operations on their own bodies and souls, thoughts, conduct, and way of being, so as to transform themselves in order to attain a certain state of happiness, purity, wisdom, perfection, or immortality.[90]

The subject is not completely determined by his power-laden ethical context but can take an active role in questioning, problematising, resisting and modifying these norms and techniques. The later Foucault defines this

[87] M Foucault, 'On the Genealogy of Ethics: An Overview of Work in Progress' in Rabinow (ed) (n 4) 262.

[88] Importantly, Foucault's ideal of freedom aims for acts of 'transfiguration'—an imaginative transformation of the present—rather than a deed of 'transgression' that attempts to annul or destroy reality. P Rabinow, 'Introduction' in Rabinow (ed) (n 4) xxxii.

[89] See M Foucault, 'The Ethics of the Concern for Self as a Practice of Freedom' in Rabinow (ed) (n 4) 291. The later Foucault distinguishes ethics from power, defining the first as the relations that we participate in to govern ourselves and conceptualising power as the relations in which actions are effected upon the actions of others.

[90] M Foucault, 'Technologies of the Self' in P Rabinow (ed) (n 4) 225.

contestatory practice by the term 'thought': '*freedom* in relation to what one does, the motion by which one detaches oneself from it, establishes itself as an object, and reflects on it as a problem'.[91] But, importantly, these moments of detachment do not enable us to transcend power relations: the possibility to objectify or modify power remains dependent upon a complex web of knowledge, power and ethics.[92] I can, say, only criticise neo-Kantian conceptions of self by virtue of a competing framework—such as Foucault's theory of power—that renders the autonomous individual problematic. In other words, Foucault presents a heteronomous account of freedom that remains ontologically conditioned by power. The possibility for the individual to reflect, criticise, reinvent or decide upon rules cannot escape the predicament of being situated or thrown into a network of exclusionary aspirations and techniques.

Foucault also appears to maintain his ontological wager about the body. In addition to its dependence upon an intricate web of power, knowledge and ethics, the subject is constituted by wilful bodily forces. Drawing on the Greek term for combative game (*agon*), Foucault situates the subject in an 'agonic struggle' between historically contingent power relations, the quest for freedom, *and* a rebellious 'will':

> The power relationship and freedom's refusal to submit cannot therefore be separated. ... At the very heart of the power relationship, and constantly provoking it, are *the recalcitrance of the will* and *the intransigence of freedom*. Rather than speaking of an essential antagonism, it would be better to speak of an 'agonism'—of a relationship that is at the same time mutual incitement and struggle; less of a face-to-face confrontation that paralyzes both sides than a permanent provocation.[93]

So, to summarise, Foucault's notion of freedom of the subject consists of a heteronomous struggle that takes places at the crossing-points of competing history.

B. Agonic Freedom and the Enlightened Transfiguration of Ancient Ethics

In contradistinction to his earlier writings, the later Foucault develops a keen interest in the empowering possibilities of practices that intend to restrain and give form to the body. In *The Use of Pleasure* and *The Care of the Self,* he turns to Greek and Roman antiquity, a historical period,

[91] Foucault (n 37) 117 (emphasis added).

[92] Foucault uses the term 'practical system' for the forms of rationality that organise the freedom to react and modify existing rules. These practical systems 'stem' from the axis of knowledge, the axis of power and the axis of ethics (Foucault, 'What is' (n 4) 317–18).

[93] Foucault, 'The Subject' (n 4) 344 (emphasis added).

according to Foucault, where the ethical perfection of a beautiful individual existence was of great importance.[94] In these books, Foucault discusses various ethical techniques through which the Greeks and Romans tended to take care of the self, such as dietary regimes, memorisations of citations, keeping a diary, self-examination and collective games like sport. What is at stake in Foucault's interest in the Greek and Roman world? And what implications follow from his studies of ancient ethics for his understanding of agonic freedom?

It is important to emphasise that Foucault did not consider Greek and Roman ethics to be an alternative ethical ideal to modernity.[95] For the Greeks and Romans, agonic struggles aimed at maintaining and reproducing an ontological order that was set in a teleological worldview in which men, women and slaves had to accept and act according to hierarchical role models. This *telos* is diametrically opposed to Foucault's agonic ethos of Enlightenment which seeks to stimulate an agonic contestation and revision of ontological norms and role models. I want to suggest that Foucault rather treats ancient conceptions of morality as a subjugated knowledge regime that helps him to rethink problematic features of modernity which jeopardise the quest for agonic freedom.

For instance, one of the reasons why Foucault is drawn to antiquity is that this period helps to remedy some problems in contemporary ontologies of ethical subjectivity. The ancient 'arts of existence' focus our attention on the behavioural aspects of morality that have become neglected in the modern Kantian focus on principles, rules, law and doctrines. While ancient conceptions of morality gave prominence to the necessity of respecting laws, it stressed that a moral code is not sufficient to achieve moral action and needs to be supplemented with virtuous types of behaviour that support them: 'More important than the content of the law and its conditions of application was the attitude that caused one to respect them'.[96] Furthermore, Foucault turns to ancient ethics to unsettle the dichotomy prevalent in modern societies between, on the one hand, concern for the self and, on the other, an engagement with others. Central to Foucault's account of Greek and Roman ethics is the ontological insight that virtuous practices are in need of individuals who have learned how to take care of themselves. One could only establish ethical relations with others—as a citizen, as a

[94] M Foucault, *The Use of Pleasure: The History of Sexuality, Volume 2* (London, Penguin Books, 1992); M Foucault, *The Care of The Self: The History of Sexuality, Volume 3* (London, Penguin Books, 1988).

[95] Foucault (n 87) 256. This sets Foucault's project apart from the communitarian thinker Alisdair MacIntyre who, as we shall see in the next chapter, wants to replace neo- Kantian morality with an Aristotelian-Thomist ethics of virtue.

[96] Foucault, *History of Sexuality, Volume 2* (n 94) 31.

magistrate, as a spouse, as a friend—when one cultivated a proper relation with oneself and achieved self-mastery over one's desires and pleasures:

> To begin with, this exercise in domination implies an agonistic relation. The Athenian of the Laws reminds Cleinias of this: if it is true that the man who is blessed with courage will attain 'only half his potential' without 'experience and training' in actual combat, it stands to reason that he will not be able to become moderate ... 'if he has not fought triumphantly against the many pleasures and desires ... using the help of speech, deed, and art ... in games and in serious pursuits.'[97]

So, how did Foucault transfigure these ancient lessons on behalf of his ethos of Enlightenment?

First, Foucault emphasises the importance of restraining behaviour as a crucial condition for agonic freedom. Although agonic freedom is an ontological possibility of social life, Foucault does not envision it as the 'natural' outcome of human history. Human history has no teleological development and might just as easily culminate in a situation of 'domination' or 'antagonism'. 'Domination' refers to a situation where power has become consolidated to such an extent that the possibility to reverse power relations has been diminished, or has been reduced to a bare minimum. 'Antagonism' occurs when power relations lose their capacity to govern social interaction altogether. This state of affairs threatens human capacities to think and act, disables relationships, and 'paralyzes both sides'.[98] To encourage possibilities for agonic freedom, human beings need to be submitted to social forms wherein participants cultivate the possibilities and wilful energy to resist power relations and learn to transform them in an experimental spirit. These practices are committed to pluralisation: the proliferation of

[97] ibid, 66. Foucault's remarks upon Greek and Roman ethics at times allude to a rather self-indulgent ethical outlook that appears at odds with his commitment to the Stimulation of an Enlightened Contest. For instance, in his remarks upon the classic era Foucault emphasises that the care for the self had to precede 'care for the others' (Foucault (n 89) 287). This might give the impression that Foucault is after an ethics where individuals focus their attention and energy primarily on the self rather than to critically engage themselves with the power/knowledge relations that shape the world of themselves and others. However, when we treat Foucault's studies of Greek and Roman ethics as a subjugated knowledge regime we can see that Foucault's emphasis on the care for the self is not so much a plea to retreat into the self but rather part of his attempt to craft a more efficacious critical ethos for modernity. *cf* Foucault (n 89) 284: 'In the Greco-Roman world, the care of the self was the mode in which individual freedom—or civic liberty, up to a point—was reflected [se réfléchie] as an ethics. ... It is interesting to see that, in our societies on the other hand, at a time that is very difficult to pinpoint, the care of the self became somewhat suspect. Starting at a certain point, being concerned with oneself was readily denounced as a form of self-love, a form of selfishness or self-interest in contradiction with the interest to be shown to others or the self-sacrifice required.' Foucault suggests that the emphasis in Christian spirituality on renouncing the self contributed to the enactment of this dichotomy.

[98] Foucault, 'The Subject' (n 4) 342.

knowledge claims helps to challenge the self-evidence of existing knowledge regimes and thereby opens up a space in which to enact agonic struggles. But pluralisation is not identical to the abolishment of all disciplinary restraints: power relations remain crucial for giving the participants in a practice a sense of purpose, and allow for the development of particular skills.

Second, Foucault emphasises that the struggle for agonic freedom needs to be exercised and should not rely on the establishment and implementation of a moral code alone. He acknowledges the merit of collective political actions that concentrate on legal and institutional reform. Ending a state of domination often calls for practices of liberation: economic, military or political actions by which the participants break free from their oppressors. He also underlines the point that the codification of rights and institutional guarantees, such as the rule of law, are important practices for realising individual freedom. But when the quest for freedom is transplanted to the law, agonic freedom weakens like a muscle that is not in use. In Foucault's account, freedom can only be realised by the ongoing exercise of freedom:

> Liberty is a practice. ... The liberty of men is never assured by the institutions and laws intended to guarantee them. This is why almost all of these laws and institutions are quite capable of being turned around—not because they are ambiguous, but simply because 'liberty' is what must be exercised.[99]

A crucial exercise for realising agonic freedom is the regular exposure to critiques. The subjection to critiques nourishes a capacity to take notice when practices collapse into domination or antagonism, and helps todetermine where political interventions are most needed: 'the ethico-political choice we have to make each day is to determine which is the main danger'.[100] Such critiques are not limited to one specific domain or site in social life. The dangers of domination and antagonism can appear within representative institutions, such as parliament, but might just as well reside in topics that are (not) discussed between friends, the gossip of our boss, the sitcoms or talk-shows on TV, the gestures of a lover, and so on. For this reason, '[t]he analysis, elaboration, and bringing into question of power relations and the "agonism" between power relations and the intransivity of freedom is an increasingly political task—even, the political task that is inherent in all social existence.'[101] To stimulate the imagination critiques should not merely pass negative judgement on present circumstances but be accompanied by the circulation of subjugated knowledge regimes or alternative

[99] Foucault (n 39) 354. Foucault does not seem to distinguish between the terms 'liberty' and 'freedom'.

[100] Foucault (n 87) 256.

[101] Foucault, 'The Subject' (n 4) 343.

'signs of existence.' The exposure to new or relatively unfamiliar ways of life can stimulate our 'curiosity' to reinvent reality:

> Curiosity ... invokes 'care'; it evokes the care of what one takes of what exists and what might exist: a sharpened sense of reality, but one that is never immobilized before it; a readiness to find what surrounds us strange and odd; a certain determination to throw off familiar ways of thought and to look at the same things in a different way.[102]

For Foucault, then, the point of critical exercises is to attach us to the ongoing transfiguration of the world rather than to detach us from the world altogether. Furthermore, agonism needs to be sustained by the actual, regular subjection to agonic struggles with others, such as teachers, parents, friends, lovers and co-workers who challenge and provoke us. In this way, human beings could become accustomed to a certain degree of disharmony or 'mutual incitements' in social life and become more skilful in capitalising upon the possibilities for freedom that such disruptions entail. Put differently, agonic contests cultivate an eye for creative acts of transfiguration and foster a mood that conflict is perhaps not always pleasurable but liveable.[103]

To sum up, the ethos of the Stimulation of Enlightened Contest considers the exercise of agonic freedom its telos as well as its technique. The normative dimension of agonic freedom aims for individuals and practices that creatively, critically and experimentally contest and revise themselves and the world. This aspiration finds support in the ontology of agonic freedom: the agonic subject of freedom is constituted by an intricate web of plural social-historical power relations and bodily energies that, on the one hand, shape the individual and, on the other, can be resisted by that individual.

[102] M Foucault, 'The Masked Philosopher' in Rabinow (ed) (n 4) 325.

[103] One of the striking features in Foucault's writings on ancient ethics is his deep interest in Greek and Roman practices of consulting spiritual guides when one was going through a difficult time. The guide would challenge the person who sought direction to evaluate whether his public activities were in line with his values and recommended techniques that helped him to master desires that inhibited him from realising one's ethical aims. This focus on spiritual guidance indicates that Foucault's conception of freedom is very different from that of Kant. For Kant, the reliance on 'guardians' such as priests and doctors is tantamount to immaturity whereas Foucault suggests that guides might also give an impetus to individual freedom. However, it is important to read Foucault's interest in spiritual practices in light of his commitment to agonic freedom. One of the aspects that Foucault emphasises in the classic techniques of self-examination is that they had a very different aim than the Christian custom of confession. While the Christian examination of conscience intended to forge a relation of *dependence* between the priest and the believer, Greek and Roman practices of self-examination aimed to educate individuals into *independence*: they wanted to give individuals a sense of self-direction and make them more capable in deciding what to do with one's freedom. This might suggest that contemporary 'agonic' guides should take care not to diminish the wilfulness of the participants in a particular practice. In ch 5, I draw upon Foucault's interest in spiritual guidance to develop an account of the emotional dimension of democratic regimes.

To realise the possibility for freedom, it is crucial that individuals submit themselves to the discipline of various social forms that help them exercise the potential for freedom.

VI. AGONIC DEMOCRACY

Having fleshed out Foucault's normative-laden ontology of agonic freedom, we are now in a position to tie together some of Foucault's insights about freedom for an agonic account of democratic politics. This section discusses two features of such an agonic understanding of democracy by critically comparing it with political liberalism. I will show that the ontology of agonic freedom orients us in two normative aspirations for democracy that receive, unjustly, no attention whatever within political liberalism. First, it alerts us to the need of affirming agonic conflicts as a central aspiration for democratic regimes—a point that Rawls, given his commitment to the democratic contestation of justice, should not ignore. Second, agonism illuminates the point that democratic debates are in need of an agonic ethics of discussion that stimulates a critique of the 'settled' ontological and normative regimes in democratic regimes, and which thereby create better resources to stimulate the democratic politicisation of political philosophy than can Rawls' public reason.

A. Agonic Exercises and Political Liberalism

In the introduction, I tentatively defined democracy as a regime that aspires to give individuals a voice in the rules that govern them. Foucault's ideal of agonic freedom signals a distinct commitment to this aspiration: it suggests that individuals are capable of, and need to aim for, a critical and creative revision of the forms of authority that structure their lives, even though they can never entirely expel the effect of arbitrary power relations upon the establishment of such forms. Taking my cue from Foucault's perspective of agonism, I define democratic politics as the enactment of disciplinary provisions that encourage people to critique, creatively revise and pluralise power/knowledge relations. These provisions give form to the ontological possibility for agonic freedom and work to diminish the opportunities for domination and antagonism that are also inherent in social life.

Now, it is not difficult to see that the concept of freedom that supports my understanding of agonic democracy is poles apart from Rawls' understanding of freedom. We have seen in the previous chapter that the political liberalist view of freedom explicitly shies away from articulating a comprehensive way of life. Foucault's notion of freedom, in contrast, does amount to such a comprehensive view: it aims for a controversial view of human excellence in which social relations and types of character-formation stimulate people to engage in agonic struggles; importantly, furthermore, it treats this ideal of excellence to be just as crucial as the institutionalisation of rights. For this reason, Rawls would most likely consider the agonic ethos 'unreasonable': political liberalism claims that 'reasonable' political conceptions should consider rights as the most fundamental condition of human freedom, and would therefore reject the attempt to promote the realisation of human excellence to being on a par with the enactment of rights.[104] I contend, however, that political liberalism has good reasons not to dismiss these 'unreasonable' features of agonic democracy.

We have seen that Rawls and Foucault are both committed to a vital democratic debate on ruling notions of justice in a society. The Foucaultian ontology of freedom suggests that this democratic ideal is in need of citizens who regularly train their critical skills. That is, human beings can only become attached to an ideal of critique by means of an ongoing practice in critique: when citizens have 'come into collision with each other and with themselves, run into dead ends, problems, and impossibilities, been through conflicts and confrontations—when critique has played out in the real'.[105] To illustrate the orienting potential of this ontology, let me, for the last time, return to the handshake debate. In the previous chapter, we have seen that the Dutch Court which prescribed the handshake as a necessary greeting ritual in public schools justified this decision in respect of two aims: the necessity to prevent social conflicts in schools, and the need to familiarise the pupils with the dominant customs in Dutch society in order to prepare them for active citizenship and social integration. A striking aspect in this ruling is that the judge does not make any distinction between, on the one hand, social conflicts that ought to be prevented and, on the other hand, social conflicts that might stimulate the cultivation of important civic dispositions. The leadership of the school claimed that the practices of teaching and learning had become completely impracticable due to the consternation about the handshake. In Foucaultian terms: it highlighted the dangers of an antagonistic situation in which the practice at issue is put to a complete halt. The judge accepted the school's account without inquiring whether it was possible to revise antagonism into a situation of agonism; that is, to

[104] While political liberalism does not rule out that political regimes might appeal to ideas of human excellence in the implementation of rights and endorses the need for a 'freestanding' conception of political virtues, it argues that rights need to be realised first: 'An assignment of special priority to those rights, liberties, and opportunities, especially with respect to the claims that of the general good and perfectionist values' (J Rawls, 'The Idea of Public Reason Revisited' in *The Law of Peoples with 'The Idea of Public Reason Revisited'* (Cambridge, Harvard University Press, 1999) 141; *cf* Rawls (n 32) 152). Foucault's normative ontology challenges this priority by suggesting that the realisation of perfectionist values, such as the enactment of an agonic ethos, is just as fundamental as the institutionalisation of rights.

[105] Foucault (n 68) 236.

strive for the enactment of practices of teaching and learning that allow for some disharmony. In fact, it appears that the judge considered agonic conflicts undesirable. For instance, as noted in the previous chapter, refusing a handshake is 'experienced by the other person concerned as *confronting* and *unpleasant* and *puts pressure* upon cordial relations', and the judge advances this fact as an important reason to prohibit the refusal of a handshake.[106] This suggests that the Court has little patience with the presence of 'mutual incitements' in social life. The ontology of agonic freedom, in contrast, suggests that both the judge and the school lose sight of the fact that a certain degree of social disharmony in public schools could be of great importance for realising active citizenship. When pupils in schools become accustomed to the presence of agonic conflicts, they may learn that dissenting or unfamiliar acts need not necessarily put a complete halt to social relations, but that such disruptions could also provide a starting-point for experimenting with ruling ideas and customs within this practice. Such confrontations with agonic conflicts could eventually make the pupils more equipped and willing to participate in the conflicts that are inherent to democratic politics.

Now, in opposition to my Foucaultian understanding of agonic democracy, Rawls does not attend to the productive role of social conflicts in sustaining a contestatory democratic ethos. To be sure, Rawls acknowledges that the normative aspirations of a democratic regime need to be 'expressed in the character and attitudes of the members of society who realise its ideals'.[107] But in his discussions of virtues Rawls never explains how citizens cultivate dispositions that enable them to maintain a critical eye on the ruling principles of justice in the current regime. For instance, in the political liberalist account of education, the cultivation of political virtues concentrates only on the need to teach children to obey justice, to 'honor the fair terms of cooperation in their relations with the rest of society.'[108] Left out of this account is an understanding of the way in which children might acquire the skills to politicise particular principles of justice, such as by means of the regular participation in agonic struggles.

Rawls' theory of motivation suffers from a similar blind spot. Throughout *Political Liberalism* Rawls focuses solely on the way in which a liberal democratic regime can secure the *allegiance* to public principles of justice, that is, how citizens become willing to act on behalf of principles of justice. The political liberalist understanding of the motivational underpinnings of a democratic regime never explains how citizens might acquire the skills to resist or challenge ruling conceptions of justice. In light of its commitment

[106] See ch 2, n 78 (emphasis added).

[107] J Rawls, *Political Liberalism: With a New Introduction and the 'Reply to Habermas'* (New York, Columbia University Press, 1996) 12. *Political Liberalism* will hereafter be referred to as *PL*.

[108] Rawls, *PL*, ibid 199.

to the democratic politicisation of justice, it seems that political liberalism cannot remain satisfied with this lack of attention for the cultivation of contestatory dispositions and should give the enactment of such skills much more normative weight than it has done so far. The Foucaultian ontology of agonic freedom helps to flesh out this normative aspiration by emphasising that the regular exercise of agonic skills is a vital condition of possibility for realising democratic practices of critique.

B. Agonic Debates and Political Liberalism

Foucault's agonic freedom helps me to correct an important flaw in political liberalism: it suggests that a vibrant democratic debate on justice needs to be supported by ongoing exercises in contestation. But which kind of democratic debate does this perspective open up?

Before sketching my Foucaultian account of democratic discussion and confronting it with political liberalism, let me briefly recapitulate Rawls' notion of public reason and its underlying criterion of reciprocity. For Rawls, participants in democratic debates ought to propose fair terms of cooperation that they believe others will accept as reasonable. This exchange of reasons should not be manipulated by inequalities ('the pressure of an inferior political or social position')[109] and needs to draw on 'settled convictions' in public culture that Rawls represents as identical to distinct political liberalist values. I raised two objections to Rawls' conception of public reason: first, it treats the political-liberalist criterion of reasonableness as a criterion which precedes democratic contestation and, second, it disregards the critical function of ontological claims in the politicisation of dominant philosophical notions. In what way does Foucault's perspective help to remedy these flaws in the political liberalist model of democratic debate?

We have seen that Foucault affirms the importance of democratic debates: processes of collective critique are an important strategy for contributing to the democratic opinion and will-formation of a society's truth regimes. My reconstruction of Foucault's ethos of the Stimulation of Enlightened Contest gives us a better understanding of the purpose of such discussions. By problematising current forms of authority ('rules and institutions') and by introducing alternatives to these regimes (the subjugated knowledge regimes) democratic debates can nourish the quest for power relations that stimulate agonic freedom.

Note, however, how much Foucault's ontology of power is at odds with Rawls' notion of reciprocity. The ubiquity of hierarchical oppositions within social interaction suggests that no debate, including public reason,

[109] See ch 2, text to n 92.

can avoid situating some citizens in an inferior position. These exclusionary effects are issued, among others, by the various intuitions, norms, topics and styles of argument in public culture which put disciplinary pressure upon the democratic exchange of reasons. The effect of power upon democratic debates does not, however, imply that we should reject the aspiration for vibrant democratic discussions altogether. Foucault's ontology illuminates the potential and need to structure democratic debates in a more agonic fashion. This implies that we should try to cultivate habits of discussion that make room to challenge and experimentally readjust hierarchical oppositions.

The normative distinction that Foucault presents between 'discussion' and 'polemics' provides a helpful starting-point for such an agonic ethics of democratic debate. For Foucault, discussions ought to be construed as a game in which the participants contest each other's discourses by attempting to clarify the strengths and weaknesses of their accounts. He contrasts this model of 'reciprocal elucidation' with the practices of the polemicist who assumes that his truth regime is not in need of agonic contestation and, in fact, aspires towards domination, that is, the abolishment of opportunities of resistance:

> In the serious play of questions and answers, in the work of *reciprocal elucidation*, the rights of each person are in some sense immanent in the discussion. The person asking the questions is merely exercising the right that has been given him: to remain unconvinced, to perceive a contradiction, to require more information, *to emphasize different postulates*, to point out faulty reasoning, and so on. As for the person answering the question, he too exercises a right that does not go beyond the discussion itself; by the logic of his own discourse, he is tied to what he has said earlier, and by acceptance of dialogue he is tied to the questioning of the other. ... *The polemicist, on the other hand, proceeds encased in privileges that he possesses in advance and will never agree to question.* ... For him, then, the game consists not of recognizing this person as a subject having the right to speak but of abolishing him, as interlocutor, from any possible dialogue, and his final objective will be not to come as close as possible to a difficult truth but to bring about the triumph of the just cause he has been manifestly upholding from the beginning. The polemicist relies on a legitimacy that his adversary is by definition denied.[110]

As in Rawls' account of public reason, the participants commit themselves to the reciprocal exchange of reasons: our right to introduce a claim is tied to the duty to further elucidate our discourse when the other members of the democratic public confront us with a question, or an objection that our position is, say, inadequate or incorrect. However, this process of mutual contestation does not proceed under the assumption that some standards

[110] Foucault (n 37) 111 (emphasis added).

(such as political liberalism or the presumably 'settled convictions in public culture') precede democratic contestation.[111] The 'settled convictions in public culture' are not regarded as privileged norms that only need implementation, as in Rawls' conception of public reason, but are seen as needing to be unsettled so that the citizens can critically evaluate these leading intuitions. This implies that when someone presents his proposal as a reconstruction of the established ideas in public culture, the other participants treat such an articulation as a question or starting-point for further investigation rather than an answer. They look for the exclusionary effects in the representations of shared values and probe whether these exclusions are necessary or open for critical adjustments that increases agonic freedom.

With regard to the first point of critique that I raised (the failure to submit political liberalism to democratic contestation), a Foucaultian ethics of discussion proposes an important advantage over Rawls' conception of public reason. Unlike Rawls, a Foucaultian exchange of arguments does not exclude certain criteria, such as political liberalism, from critical contestation, but suggests that they ought to be submitted to an agonic learning process. In this way, the game of reciprocal elucidation places the participants in a better position to evaluate the strengths and weaknesses of the hegemonic standards within public culture than does political liberalism. But how does this game help to revise political liberalism with regard to the second critical point that I raised, that is, the restrictions on ontological claims in public reason?

We have seen that Foucault does not consider it fruitful for intellectuals to make their ontological claims explicit in democratic debate—a problematic aspect in his work that I have criticised throughout this chapter. With regard to citizens who do not lay a claim to intellectual expertise, however, Foucault does envision a need for ontologically-founded critiques. For instance, in a late interview Foucault suggests that marginalised political movements might strengthen the efficacy of their critical interventions by articulating a discourse of truth or, as I have put it, an ontology:

> It is within the field of the obligation to truth that it is possible to move about in one way or another, sometimes against effects of domination which may be linked to structures of truth or institutions entrusted to truth. [For example] there has been a whole so-called ecological movement … that was in opposition, as it were, to a science … But this same ecology *articulated its own discourse of truth*: … I believe the same holds true in the order of politics: here one can criticize … by playing a certain game of truth, by showing its consequences, by pointing out that there are *other reasonable options*, by teaching people what they don't know about their own situations.[112]

[111] As argued in ch 2, while Rawls' reflective equilibrium includes a critical learning-process of social–historical intuitions, his idea of public reason was lacking such a contestatory impulse.

[112] Foucault (n 89) 295 (emphasis added).

Foucault attributes ontological claims with having a similar function as marginalised discourses ('subjugated knowledge regimes'). Such discourses make the members of the public more sensitive to the exclusions in public culture, and introduce new conceptual tools into democratic debates that could stimulate a creative refashioning of power relations. For instance, by contrasting the dominant ontology in a public culture ('science') with a dissent or 'subjugated' ontology ('ecology'), citizens can make the democratic public mindful of the particularity of this dominant knowledge regime and open up reflexive space to experiment with other options.

The role that Foucault envisions for ontological claims in the politicisation of hegemonic truth regimes suggests that ontology could be given a much more critical function than that opened up by Rawls' notion of public reason: rather than introducing an ontological claim to strengthen the 'settled' discourses of public culture, such assumptions can be used to denaturalise these dominating regimes. Still, Rawls might object to this reading and note that citizens who use ontology critically cannot avoid appealing to these 'settled' discourses themselves. For instance, as we can see in the example of the ecology movement that I cited above, the citizens who introduce an ecological framework do not merely want to point out the existence of an alternative viewpoint, they also argue that other participants who do not share their outlook have good reasons to endorse this view ('there are other *reasonable* options'). So how should we envision this appeal to a shared notion of reasonableness? Does it not, say, imply that the members need to appeal to some set of 'settled' shared values in public culture?

It is true that an ontological claim can only be made effective as critique when the other members of the public can find points of affinity with this assumption: there is no point in circulating a critique within democratic debate without anticipating that some members might share some of our concerns. And, in their attempt to convince the others about the reasonableness of their position, the participants might adopt a strategy akin to Rawls' proviso, that is, the translation of ontological claims into 'settled' public values. In that case, we buttress our ontological assumptions with some notions or principles in our public culture that we do not wish to contest and that we assume to be persuasive enough for others. Then, we wait and see whether others agree with our appeal to reasonableness and, if necessary, elucidate or modify our interpretation of public culture. I should stress, however, that from the Foucaultian ontological perspective which I have construed so far, this articulation of reasonableness will remain exclusionary: at best, we persuade some participants in democratic debates into an unstable temporary coalition that could underpin further initiatives (a community of action).

Another strategy for forging such a coalition is to construe points of affinity between ontological traditions. When we believe that some themes of our ontological regime are analogous to certain aspects of other ontological traditions we can appeal to the possibility of what I call a 'cross-ontological analogy'. In this instance, we do not try to make our ontological claims more persuasive with a reference to publicly-shared values but invite our interlocutors to explore the connections between our ontological traditions. Such proposals are then submitted to a game of reciprocal elucidation: the other members of the democratic public can reject, modify or accept the suggestion for a 'cross-ontological analogy' and, in so doing, are committed to explain their refusal or counter-proposal. For example, let us imagine that a conservative communitarian tries to persuade an Islamic citizen that political liberalism is too individualist and fails to represent the concerns of citizens who aspire to increase mutual respect for cultural practices. He might do so by suggesting that both his ontology and certain Islamic notions of human dignity reject the liberal individualist conception of self and emphasise the need for cultural customs in living a good life. In turn, the Islamic citizen might accept the invitation to explore these differences and see opportunities to forge a coalition with communitarian citizens. But he may also resist a communitarian reading of his religion by highlighting how some themes in the Islamic tradition bear resemblance to liberal understandings of freedom or, for that matter, Foucaultian conceptions of self.[113]

The practice of bringing ontological regimes to democratic debates is risky. For example, it could stimulate the participants to focus too much on ontological disputes while disregarding other disagreements. For this reason, the appeal to ontological assumptions should be part of a cautious ongoing experiment: at times, we will consider it wisest to withdraw most aspects of ontology because we anticipate that ethical, social, historical or economic disputes are more in need of elucidation than ontological disagreements; at other times, we will introduce these contentious elements to clarify our position, criticise the discourse of others or, rather, to look for points of affinity with citizens who do not share our view. As William Connolly aptly notes:

> [T]o legitimate bringing fundamental orientations into the public realm does not mean it is either necessary or honorable to announce all the fundamentals you can marshal each time you address an issue. ... It means that when the issue is, say, the right to die, it is relevant to bring some dimensions of your theological or atheological perspective to the engagement, and when it is the just distributions of income another set may be pertinent.[114]

[113] For an argument about the compatibility between political liberalism and Islamic traditions, see A March, *Islam and Liberal Citizenship: the Search for an Overlapping Consensus* (Oxford, Oxford University Press, 2009). For Foucaultian readings of Islamic traditions that put more stress upon the differences between Islamic conceptions of self and liberalism, see T Asad, *Genealogies of Religion: Discipline and Reasons of Power in Christianity and Islam* (Baltimore, Johns Hopkins University Press, 1993); S Mahmood, *Politics of Piety: The Islamic Revival and the Feminist Subject* (New Jersey, Princeton University Press, 2004).

[114] W Connolly, *Why I am not a Secularist* (Minneapolis, University of Minnesota Press, 1999) 9.

The risks in experimentally including ontological regimes in democratic debates are worth undertaking, however, in view of the impetus that this practice might give to those debates. For a start, it does a much better job of stimulating democratic participation than the political liberalist strategy of avoidance. When a democratic regime allows citizens to introduce their contentious ontological premises into democratic debates, it will lessen the chance that some citizens will turn their back on the democratic process because of feeling forced to represent their claims in narrow political liberalist terms. Moreover, the reciprocal contestation of ontological regimes will mitigate the chance that one ontological regime will come to dominate democratic regimes, and encourages a learning process about the reflective underpinnings of these regimes, such as political philosophy. Provided that citizens are willing to bring to bear a critique of their own basic postulates, they can employ these claims for a critique of both the hegemonic ontological assumptions in a democratic regime, including those that are inherent to political liberalism, and the various dissenting views that challenge these norms. In this way, Foucault's ethics of discussion does a better job of stimulating the democratic politicisation of justice, including political philosophical accounts, than Rawls' conception of public reason.

i. Augmenting Foucault: A Plea for the Virtue of Listening

So far we have seen that my Foucaultian ethics of debate aims to orient citizens of a democratic regime in the various truth claims by means of agonic practices of contestation.[115] This process implies that citizens challenge each other's interpretations of the shared values in a public culture and opens up a space in which to introduce ontological claims that dissent from the hegemonic normative and ontological convictions in a public culture. I argued that this model has two advantages over Rawls' conception of public reason: it is more hospitable to citizens that want to use ontology

[115] As I do here, Moss argues that Foucault's focus on the effects of disciplinary power offers an important corrective to Rawls' public reason. Since disciplinary power can significantly hamper the exercise of freedom, Moss argues that the content of public reason needs to be revised by including economic issues and social marginalisation in the list of constitutional essentials (J Moss, 'Foucault, Rawls and Public Reason' in Moss (ed) (n 60). While I agree with Moss that these topics are central to democratic debates, I am not entirely convinced that his point is a persuasive critique of Rawls' conception of public reason. For Rawls, social and economic inequalities are issues of 'basic justice' and public reason applies just as much to these issues as to the constitutional essentials. So even though Rawls is blind to effects of disciplinary power, I don't think that Rawls would rule out that economic and social deprivation can be discussed in public reason. In contrast to Moss, I focus on Foucault's ontology of disciplinary power to dispute the ideal of reciprocity underlying Rawls' conception of public reason. And with regard to the content of public reason, I show that Foucault's critique of ontology helps us question Rawls' exclusion of critical ontological arguments. Perhaps because Moss is not critical of Rawls' separation between ontology and political thought, he does not discuss these issues.

in a critical vein, and encourages the democratic politicisation of justice. To end, I want to augment the game of reciprocal elucidation with the virtue of listening. In his studies on Greek and Roman ethics, Foucault repeatedly brings out the centrality of listening in ancient practices of education. In what follows I briefly note how practices of listening might nourish agonic discussions.[116]

Foucault narrates how Pythagorean sects and several Stoic and Epicurean treatises emphasised that pupils needed to refrain from speaking when learning a new truth. By not giving in to the temptation to intervene, to object or to give an opinion, the pupil could really appropriate and be affected by the discourse. Plutarch even recommended patient listening to adults. When forming a judgement about a particular discourse, the temporary suspension of speech was an important technique of getting a good grasp of the subject, and prevented a person from becoming a 'chatterbox':

> The ear of the chatterbox ... is not connected directly with his soul, but rather with his tongue. ... Everything the chatterbox receives through the ear immediately pours out, spills into what he says and, in spilling into what he says, what has been heard cannot have any effect on the soul itself.[117]

In his critiques of modern culture, Foucault suggests that the cultivation of silence offers a much-needed counterpoint to the centrality of speech in contemporary interactions.[118] His appreciation of silence does not address, however, in what way the suspension of speech might ameliorate public practices of critiques such as democratic debates. In fact, his remarks on democracy and ethics of debate appear to be very much speech-driven, emphasising the importance of *asserting* critiques and the questioning or answering of others, while paying no attention to the need for cultivating more *receptive* dispositions, such as the ability to listen patiently to others. This blind spot is troublesome for an agonic account of discussion. The reciprocal elucidation of truth regimes calls for citizens who do not merely assimilate questions and critique into their own categories but try to open these categories for contestation. To this extent it is important that they work against the temptation of immediately converting what one had heard into speech. For instance, when one is asked to give more information about one's postulates, it is important to get a good understanding of which ideas need further clarification. So instead of brushing off the questions of the interlocutor by a quick answer we need to listen patiently in order to get

[116] Rawls, I should say, mentions that democratic civility includes the willingness to listen but he does not develop this point (Rawls, *PL* (n 107) 217).

[117] M Foucault, in F Gros (ed), *The Hermeneutics of the Subject: Lectures at the Collège de France 1981–1982* (New York, Palgrave, 2005) 342.

[118] 'I think silence has been one of those things that has unfortunately been dropped from our culture. ... I am in favor of developing silence as a cultural ethos' (M Foucault, 'An Interview by Stephen Riggins' in Rabinow (ed) (n 4) 122).

a better sense of the perspective and particular concerns. Therefore, when someone judges our proposal to be insufficient, we can only respond to critique when we have *received* it, that is, when we do not immediately put it aside but take some time to absorb it and evaluate whether the contestation of our interlocutor calls for a revision, and a rather more persuasive defence, of our position.

Such practices of listening are dependent upon citizens who admit that their outlooks can be questioned. When we acknowledge that our discourses contain contestable aspects—some known to us; some not—we are more likely to listen carefully to others. This affirmation of contestability should not, however, be mistaken for a relativist stance in which we treat our truth regime as something that can be swapped for any other framework. The fact that someone doubts aspects of one's truth regime implies that one is convinced that one's perspective can be ameliorated and that democratic contests offer opportunities for such improvement. It does not mean that one is already convinced that other viewpoints have been more successful in construing answers. We allow ourselves to be persuaded by others but do not immediately surrender our truth.

VII. CONCLUSION

This chapter confronted political liberalism with Foucault's practice of critique, his ethos of agonic freedom and his ethics of discussion. This undertaking served a twofold aim. First, it presented an initial step in answering my question about the ontological conditions of democratic politics. I have shown that Foucault's ontology of freedom illuminates normative options for democracy that are missing in political liberalism. Second, it contributed to my investigation into the need for a democratic politicisation of ontology, by critically comparing the Foucaultian contributions to the democratic politicisation of ontology to Rawls' strategy of avoidance. Let me sum up how this chapter has accomplished these goals.

With regard to the latter goal (the need for a democratic politicisation of ontology) I first of all demonstrated the cogency of a critical attention to ontology by showing how Foucault's account of philosophical critique—the critical ontology of ourselves—corrects an important flaw in Rawls' reflective equilibrium. Foucault's historical critique of ontology helps to expose the mentalist bias in the social contract tradition. In this way, Foucault gives a more effective impetus to the democratic politicisation of political philosophy than Rawls' reflective equilibrium, which does not include a methodology of historicising the ontological notions in hegemonic moral traditions. This critique in turn paved the way for fleshing out a more orienting ontology that does address the relation between the body and democratic politics.

Second, I showed the merits of a democratic politicisation in my reconstruction of Foucault's own ontology. I emphasised that Foucault is not merely a critic of ontology but that he develops a competing contestable ontological perspective that foregrounds his critique of the social contract tradition. The strength of his ontology of power and bodily contingency is that it shows us, *pace* Rawls, that ontological inquiries need not preclude political contestation or reify dominant accounts of personhood. On the contrary, Foucault's ontology stimulates us to criticise hegemonic notions. But, obviously, Foucault's ontology is not free of contentious elements either. By confronting Foucault's initial ontology with his normative commitments to plurality and a concerted critical experiment with identities, I showed that this ontological regime presented an overly submissive account of subjectivity. This brought out the need to turn to Foucault's later ontology, which offers more orienting potential for democratic politics.

Third, I indicated how Foucault's ethics of democratic debate stimulates the politicisation of ontology. In opposition to Rawls' conception of public reason, Foucault's game of reciprocal elucidation makes room for a critical engagement with ontology, including the (implicit) ontological tenets of political liberalism. In this way, Foucault's agonic model of democratic discussion offers more opportunities for the democratic politicisation of political philosophy than does Rawls.

To highlight the illuminating potential of Foucault's alternative ontology for democratic politics, I showed that Foucault's later account of agonic freedom allows individuals to question and transform historical power relations, but that it remains embedded in power. This heteronomous practice of freedom cannot be taken for granted as if it were a 'natural' or teleological effect of social-historical practices, but can only be sustained when individuals regularly exercise their potential for freedom. A democratic regime seeks to give form to the ontological possibility of agonic freedom by enacting disciplinary practices that allow and stimulate people to pluralise, and experiment with, power/knowledge relations.

Furthermore, I showed that Foucault's normative-laden ontology of freedom makes visible two important normative aspirations for democratic regimes that are lacking in political liberalism. First, it helps to reveal the productive role of contests within social practices for sustaining that vibrant, democratic, critical ethos concerning justice that Foucault and Rawls are both committed to. Second, in contrast to Rawls' conception of public reason, Foucaultian agonism shows that the effect of disciplinary power upon democratic debates cannot and should not be avoided. Rather, disciplinary power needs to be productively employed to encourage an ongoing critical experiment with power relations, such as the 'settled' normative and ontological concepts inherent in public culture and political philosophy.

4

Agonic Democracy and the Exercise of Rights

I. INTRODUCTION

THE PREVIOUS CHAPTERS provided an important impetus towards answering the three central questions of this book. I investigated the first question about the plausibility of political liberalism via an analysis of Rawls' conception of justice. We have seen that Rawls' strategy of avoiding contentious ontological claims does not succeed and that Rawls appeals to a contestable ontology in his defence of freedom and mutual respect. The reconstruction of Foucault's ethos of agonic freedom contributed to answering the second question about the ontological conditions of democratic politics. I have shown that Foucault's normative-laden ontology of agonism helps us see that an ongoing democratic contest about justice is in need of some degree of social conflicts and an ethics of discussion that encourages the critical interrogation of hegemonic knowledge regimes. My third question evaluates the strength of the democratic politicisation of ontology in comparison to the political liberalist strategy of avoidance. I argued that the critical scrutiny of ontology is more helpful in stimulating orientation in, and the democratic politicisation of, normative ideals than the exclusion of ontology from democratic theory and practice.

In this chapter I revisit these questions by shifting the attention away from the ontological aspects of the normative foundations of liberal democracy (such as freedom), towards the ontological dimension of social theory, more precisely, towards a diagnosis of the social effects of individual rights. We have seen that much of what Foucault has to say about political thought and freedom is articulated in opposition to the centrality of individual rights in liberal thought. This displacement of juridical concerns in Foucault's work could convey the impression that his perspective has nothing to contribute to our thinking about individual rights and that democratic debates about rights fare better within political liberalist categories. I argue, however, that while Foucault's reflections about rights are underdeveloped, his ontology does offer important contributions for a theorisation of law and can, in fact, ameliorate some problems in political liberalist readings of rights.

The political liberalist theory of rights that this chapter investigates is taken from the work of the American political liberalist philosopher John Tomasi. Although Tomasi is not such an influential or well-known thinker as Rawls is, his contribution to the political liberalist paradigm is relevant for my discussion because he expresses worries about the marginalising effects of state action that are somewhat akin to the Foucaultian perspective on statehood that I develop here. In his critique of Rawls, Tomasi draws attention to the fact that the enactment of liberal state power can burden the ethical practices of citizens in ways that are not always aimed at by liberal ideals. For this reason, Tomasi claims that political liberalism should not only offer insights into the normative aims of rights but should also develop a social theory to diagnose the exclusionary implications of rights.

We shall see that Tomasi's proposal includes several innovative amendments that significantly enhance the orienting potential of political liberalism. I am troubled, however, by Tomasi's suggestion that his analytical framework can be constructed without appealing to contentious ontological claims. As Rawls does in the context of normative theory, Tomasi assumes that the ontological underpinnings of his social theory of rights are sufficiently impartial. The first aim of this chapter is to show that this assumption is implausible: I argue that Tomasi's social theory mobilises a contentious ontology that blinds us to the distinct concerns and struggles of agonic citizens. With this argument, I aim to further substantiate my answer to the first question of this book that scrutinises the plausibility of political liberalism. My second goal is to continue my investigation into the ontological conditions of democratic politics that is central to the second question of this book. I aim to bring out the strengths of my Foucaultian ontology of democratic politics by showing that it opens up fruitful possibilities for our thinking about the social effects of individual rights. My argument will draw upon some insights that Foucault presents in his later writings on 'governmentality'—a neologism of 'governmental' and 'rationality'.[1] In opposition to the political liberalist strategy of avoidance, this approach to statehood indicates that the conceptualisation of state action is structured by contentious ontological regimes. In addition, governmentality draws attention to the effect of state-sanctioned knowledge regimes upon the ethical and ontological self- understandings and practices of citizens. Throughout

[1] C Gordon, 'Governmental Rationality: An Introduction' in G Burchell, C Gordon and P Miller (eds), *The Foucault Effect: Studies in Governmentality with Two Lectures by and an Interview with Michel Foucault* (London, Harvester Wheatsheaf, 1991) 1. Thomas Lemke points out that the notion of governmentality was not invented by Foucault but already appeared in the work of the French literary theorist Roland Barthes in the 1950's (T Lemke, 'An Indigestible Meal? Foucault, Governmentality and State Theory' (2007) 8 *Distinktion: Scandinavian Journal of Social Theory* 43).

this chapter, I will extrapolate the frame of governmentality and apply this to individual rights by looking at the social consequences of legal knowledge regimes for the various understandings of religion in democratic culture.

Lastly, my aim is to pursue further my third question that aims to show the merits of a democratic politicisation of ontology in comparison to the political liberalist strategy of avoidance. Tomasi makes no attempt to submit his ontology to democratic contestation. That is to say, he neither investigates his approach in comparison to competing ontologies in democratic culture nor does he test his ontology in the light of actual struggles of democratic citizens. I will challenge his methodology by adopting two strategies of the democratic politicisation of ontology. First of all, I dispute the impartiality of Tomasi's ontological premises by confronting them with Foucault's ontology of power and agonic freedom. Second, I show the limitations of Tomasi's ontology by juxtaposing its descriptions with a case study drawn from the United States: the exclusionary effects of the American right to religious freedom. Taken together, these two strategies help us see the blind spots in Tomasi's ontology and thereby help to stimulate the democratic politicisation of political philosophy.

This chapter starts with a brief critical account of Foucault's position on modern statehood. I present his framework for analysing the exclusionary effects of modern welfare states and flesh out the normative purpose of such an analysis. The remaining part of this chapter applies this perspective in a comparison with political liberalism. I first introduce Tomasi's framework for analysing the exclusionary effects of individual rights. Next, I apply my methodology of the democratic politicisation of the ontology to his approach. I read Tomasi's work against the background of the ontological source that structures his analytical framework: the theory of tradition that has been developed by the communitarian thinker Alisdair MacIntyre. I first challenge MacIntyre's ontology of tradition by confronting it with some insights and concerns that are opened up by Foucault's ontology of power and freedom. I then show how Tomasi replicates some blind spots of MacIntyre's account in his theory of traditional life and in his concept of public culture. I conclude with a case study of the implementation of religious freedom in the United States. This case study will help to substantiate my claim that Tomasi's ontology of public culture opens up misleading interpretations about the exclusionary effects of individual rights.

II. THE GOVERNMENTALISED STATE

In the previous chapter, I explained that Foucault developed a distinct decentralised understanding of power in opposition to the more state-centred approaches of power in the juridical tradition of political thought.

His later writings maintain a certain reserve towards state theory but no longer shy away from conceptualising the state. In a series of lectures delivered at the Collège de France in 1978 and 1979, Foucault extends his research on power from an analysis of institutional discipline to an analysis of power at the level of state sovereignty.[2] These analyses are not carried out under the rubric of disciplinary power but undertaken through the lens of governmentality. This section looks at the implications of the governmentality perspective for understanding modern statehood and fleshes out the normative purpose of such an analysis.

A. Governmentality

The term governmentality has a wider scope than one which limits itself to meaning only government institutions, such as state policies and law. Basically, it connotes practices of power that, from the sixteenth century on, became operative in the context of modern European states in managing health, birth rates, race and religion, of populations. A governmentality analysis investigates these practices and looks at their techniques as well as at the political discourses that make these practices intelligible, or that provided them with a normative and ontological foundation.

One of the governmentality discourses that Foucault investigates is eighteenth century classical liberalism.[3] Central to this discourse is the idea that economic and social relations take place in an autonomous domain that is designated with the term 'society.' The processes of free exchange and voluntary association within 'society' are understood to organise themselves naturally, that is, they are depicted as if they can exist independently of power relations. Foucault observes how the idea that social and economic relations proceed naturally leads to a deep suspicion of state governance. For classical liberalism, the state should provide individuals with a set of rights and limit its interventions as much as possible.[4] In this way, it was believed that the state can contribute to the natural optimisation of free market exchange and voluntary association.

[2] M Foucault, in M Senellart (ed), *Security, Territory, Population: Lectures at the Collège de France 1977-1978* (New York, Picador, 2007); M Foucault, *Naissance de la Biopolitique: Cours au Collège de France, 1978-1979* (Paris, Seuil/Gallimard, 2004).

[3] Foucault develops his critique of classical liberalism in the first three lectures of M Foucault, *Naissance*, ibid. See also M Foucault, 'The Birth of Biopolitics' in P Rabinow (ed), *Ethics: Subjectivity and Truth* (New York, The New Press, 1997) 73–79. Foucault looks at thinkers such as Adam Smith, Condillac and Jeremy Bentham.

[4] This principle is neatly summed up by the formula 'one always governs too much' ('ne pas trop gouverner') that was invented by the French marquise d'Argenson who was the French secretary of state of Foreign Affairs from 1744 until 1747 and advocate of free trade.

Foucault challenges the classical liberal opposition between civil society and the state on two counts. First, he points out that this opposition is not a universal distinction but an effect of a social-historical power struggle: it was invented in the eighteenth century to delegitimise state interventions and to make way for free market exchange.[5] Second, he notes that this opposition leads to an idealisation of society while putting state action in a bad light.[6] In Foucault's view, this contrast is misleading: it blinds us to the fact that both sovereign power and society are constituted by complex power/knowledge relations which generate exclusionary effects. Like all power relations, both society and the state entail the risk of collapsing into domination.[7]

In contrast to the classical liberalist distinction between civil society and the state, Foucault proposes the notion of the 'governmentalised state'. In this view, the state is not seen as an abstract universal entity but understood as a changeable outcome of historically specific governmentality practices:

> [I] have tried to show you that the state, far from being a given natural-historical entity that develops according to its own dynamism—as if it is a 'cold monster' of which the germ has been thrown at a particular moment into history and which slowly expands itself—the state is the correlative of a certain manner of governing.[8]

More specifically, the way we define the state, how we come to recognise it as a separate sphere or entity, how we evaluate its competencies and how it is distinguished from other domains, such as 'society' or 'religion', are effects of a strategic network of power/knowledge relations.[9] In addition, states also help to consolidate governmental practice, that is, they produce and proliferate various knowledge regimes in order to arrive at a stable, safe and prosperous society. A central characteristic of these power/knowledge

[5] For instance, Foucault narrates how, in an anonymous article in 1751, d'Argenson recalls the invention of the famous classic liberalist principle of 'laissez-faire.' When the French minister of Finance Colbert met with the business man Legendre and asked him how the French state could help trade, Legendre responded 'Laissez-nous faire', Foucault, *Naissance* (n 2) 22.

[6] M Foucault, 'The Risks of Security' in J Faubion (ed), *Power* (New York, The New Press, 2000) 372.

[7] For the definition of domination, see ch 3 text to n 98.

[8] Translation by author. See, Foucault, *Naissance* (n 2) 7: '[J]'ai essayé de vous montrer que l'Etat, loin d'être une espèce de donnée historico-naturelle qui se développerait par son propre dynamisme comme un "monstre froid" dont la semence aurait été jetée à un moment donnée dans l'histoire et qui, petit à petit, la grignoterait, l'Etat c ene pas cela, l'Etat ce nest pas un monstre froid, c'est le corrélatif d'une certaine manière de gouverner.'

[9] Foucault stresses that the modern forms of governmentality, such as classical liberalism, emerged from spiritual forms of power. These so-called 'pastoral' power relations aimed to secure the salvation of a group in another world. For a discussion of Foucault's idea of pastoral power and its application to the contentious interaction between religion and politics in relation to Dutch conceptions of nationhood, see I Rosenthal, 'The Dutch Pastorate: Pluralism Without Pain?' in I ter Avest (ed), *Education in Conflict, Religious Diversity and Education in Europe, Volume 9* (Muster, Waxmann, 2010).

relations is that they manage the population through subjectifying effects. As in his theory of disciplinary power, Foucault's account of modern state power points out that knowledge regimes submit individuals to particular exclusionary identities or types of subjectivity. Modern state power is both 'totalizing and individualizing' ('Omnes et Singulatum').[10]

To explain the subjectifying effects of the governmentalised state, we might think of Dutch state law on religious freedom and its tendency to reinforce a distinct Protestant knowledge regime. In Protestantism, religion is typically defined in terms of beliefs. It treats inner convictions as the most important aspect of one's religious identity and does not, like Catholicism, Islam and Judaism, consider practices and rituals essential to religious experience. From its earliest codification in 1579, the Dutch right to religious freedom has progressively included religious worldviews that dissent from Protestantism, and nowadays protects many publicly visible religious practices.[11] However, the Protestant emphasis on beliefs is still present in Dutch laws on religious freedom. Citizens who claim protection in virtue of the right to religious freedom are required to show that their custom is supported by a coherent belief-system. This implies that practices which can be defended as expressions of a belief are much more eligible for protection through appealing to religious freedom than citizens who cannot frame their custom in terms of a coherent doctrine. For instance, in 2005 the Netherlands Institute for Human Rights identified dreadlocks as a religious custom because this hairstyle found support in the rastafari belief-system. Nine years earlier, however, a citizen with a Mohawk haircut was denied important exemptions in virtue of religious freedom because his hairdo did not find support in a worldview.[12] So, in other words, Dutch citizens who go to court to claim protection or aspire to certain legal privileges are subjected to exclusionary identities that the state has authorised.

B. The State and Plurality

In analytical respects the differences between Foucault's perspective and the classical liberalist view of the state are not very difficult to discern. Instead

[10] M Foucault, 'Omnes et Singulatim': Toward a Critique of Political Reason' in Faubion (ed) (n 6).

[11] The so-called Union of Utrecht of 1579—a founding document for the Republic—rejected the Spanish Inquisition and recognised the religious freedom in the private sphere (that is, freedom of conscience and the right to have private ceremonies) for Jews, Lutherans and Catholics.

[12] Both citizens were fired because of their hairstyle and argued that this constituted a violation of their religious freedom. I discuss these two cases and some more exclusionary effects of the Dutch right to religious freedom in I Rosenthal, 'Dreadlocks, hanenkammen en de juridische constructie van een godsdienstig domein' in O Tans, W Veraart, B Wolthuis and J Zwart (eds), *De grenzen van het goede leven: rechtsgeleerde opstellen aangeboden aan Prof mr A Soeteman* (Nijmegen, Ars Aequi Libri, 2009).

of envisioning the state in mere juridical terms, Foucault confronts us with the network of power/knowledge relations that structure state action. And, whereas classical liberalism depicts the state law as a form of regulation that *facilitates* individual freedom and 'natural' processes of social interaction, Foucault confronts us with the *subjugating* effects of modern state power. In the words of Nikolas Rose, a governmentality perspective reveals how the state becomes intertwined with 'projects, plans and practices of those authorities—economic, legal, spiritual, medical, technical—who endeavour to administer the lives of others in the light of conceptions of what is good, healthy, normal, virtuous, efficient or profitable.'[13] However, when we consider Foucault's stance on the state *normatively*, that is, by looking for the ethical aim or *telos* of an analysis of governmentality, it is not so easy to grasp how to distinguish his perspective from classical liberalism. In fact, Foucault's normative reflections on state action sometimes collapse into the very derogatory terms that he sees as symptomatic of classical liberalism.

For instance, in his article on agonic freedom, Foucault depicts the state as the primary locus of critique and resistance:

> The conclusion would be that the political, ethical, social, philosophical problem of our days is not to try to liberate the individual from the state, and from the state's institutions, but *to liberate us both from the state and from the type of individualization linked to the state*. We have to promote new forms of subjectivity through the refusal of this kind of individuality that has been imposed on us for several centuries.[14]

Foucault's claim here—the idea that citizens should liberate themselves from state practices of identity-formation—gives the impression that state interventions are prima facie bad. He disregards the fact that the production of homogeneous or constraining identities in other institutions than the state—such as the labour market—might be in need of a much more urgent critique than state power. And he does not discuss the possibility that state interventions could also offer some support in the struggle for agonic freedom and pluralism. Take, for instance, Dutch law on religious freedom. I already mentioned that Dutch law is somewhat biased in favour of a Protestant notion of subjectivity. However, Dutch jurisprudence on religious freedom shows that the law can also be mobilised on behalf of *decreasing* the authority of such understandings. For example, we have seen in chapter two that the Netherlands Institute for Human Rights constructed an exemption for citizens who do not want to shake hands with members of the other sex by authorising dissenting greeting rituals. In this way the Institute contributed

[13] N Rose and P Miller, 'Political Power beyond the State: Problematics of Government' (1992) 43 *The British Journal of Sociology* 175.

[14] M Foucault, 'The Subject and Power' in Faubion (ed) (n 6) 336 (emphasis added).

to the pluralisation of permitted religious identities in the labour market and opened up a space for citizens to critically experiment with the prejudices against certain religious rituals. This suggests that state power, not unlike disciplinary power, contains possibilities of resistance, or 'strategic reversal', that may support a pluralisation and experimentation with identities.

Furthermore, state practices can actively try to make their knowledge regimes more responsive to pluralism. For instance, it is now to some extent customary in Dutch law to give claimants a voice in the legal definition of religion. When citizens appear before a judge to claim a particular exemption or good from the state in virtue of their religious freedom, the judge should take into account how these claimants themselves define their religion. In this way, the chances that the judge will only recognise predominant or elitist religious practices decrease and allows the possibility of making the law more hospitable to various new and marginal religions.[15] So, in light of the support that state practices can give to a pluralisation of identities, Foucault's categorical rejection of modern state power seems much too overdrawn. Rather than a rejection of state practices *tout court*, I want to suggest that it makes more sense to adopt his normative ethos of agonic pluralism as an evaluative standard that can help us distinguish between better and worse state practices. In this approach, one gives prima facie support to a state that supports pluralism and investigates how state practices could contribute to agonic experiments with plurality.[16]

In his reflections on gay rights, Foucault seems to move toward this position. He indicates that institutions, such as the state, create problematic burdens for the plurality of ethical practices that constitute agonic freedom: 'We live in a relational world that institutions have greatly impoverished. Society and the institutions which frame it have limited the possibility of relationships because a rich relational world would be very complex to manage'.[17] But he also envisions a possibility for challenging state-sanctioned exclusions by means of the enactment of rights. That is to say, in addition to affirming the importance of institutionalising human rights to protect dissenting sexual practices, Foucault suggests the possibility of inventing a radically new right: 'We should try to imagine and create a new relational right that permits all possible types of relations to exist

[15] This practice is to some extent customary in both US and Dutch jurisprudence of religious freedom but remains contested. For the American context, see E Penalver, 'Note: The Concept of Religion' (1997) 107 *The Yale Law Journal* 791; for the Dutch context, see A Soeteman, 'De religieuze dwergwerper. Over de consequenties van een beroep op de grondrechten' (1992) 21 *Rechtsfilosofie & Rechtstheorie* 100; Rosenthal (n 12).

[16] For Foucault's ethos of pluralism, see ch 3 s IV.B.i.

[17] M Foucault, 'The Social Triumph of the Sexual Will' in P Rabinow (ed), *Ethics: Subjectivity and Truth* (New York, The New Press, 1997) 158.

and not be prevented, blocked, or annulled by impoverished relational institutions'.[18]

This relational right seems to endorse legalist practices that actively try to pluralise their knowledge regimes, such as the aforementioned examples from Dutch jurisprudence. I am troubled, however, by Foucault's expectation that this new right 'permits all possible types of relations to exist'. This anticipation of such a complete inclusion is belied by his own crucial insights into the inevitable subjectifying effects of governing populations. Even though the enactment of a right can decrease marginalisation by pluralising the relations it authorises, it will remain dependent upon exclusionary power/knowledge regimes to realise such effects. So, in contrast to Foucault's somewhat naïve musings about an all-inclusive right, I argue that the pluralisation of legally sanctioned identities may diminish exclusion but that it can never completely surmount marginalisation. And this is exactly why a critique of specific practices of state governmentality, such as the institutionalisation of rights, will remain a permanent task.

III. A POLITICAL LIBERALIST APPROACH TO STATE-SANCTIONED EXCLUSIONS

Let us sum up the discussion so far. We have seen that Foucault's account of the governmentalised state attends to the way in which views of the state are influenced by distinct power/knowledge claims, and how state practices, in turn, help to strengthen particular identities. Making apparent these relations, I suggested, serves the purpose of criticising overly homogenous state practices of identity-formation and helps to open up a space for pluralising the identities that are authorised by state interventions. Nonetheless, I argued, against Foucault, that it is not possible to overcome the problem that legal state interventions aiming to decrease marginalisation will also produce exclusionary effects for some citizens.

The remaining part of this chapter examines this governmentality perspective by confronting it with political liberalism. I will look at the work of John Tomasi, a political liberal who, like Rawls, tries to develop a 'freestanding' conception of justice that can accommodate a plurality of ways of life. Tomasi, however, is much more sensitive than is Rawls about the exclusionary effects of liberal state interventions in modern welfare states. To bring these exclusions into view, Tomasi suggests that political liberalism needs to supplement its normative framework with a social theory that addresses the consequences of implementing individual rights. Such an

[18] ibid.

account helps political liberals to diagnose the disadvantageous effects of legal institutions and also offers orientation in normative proposals that can mitigate these exclusionary effects.[19] In this way, Tomasi hopes that political liberalism becomes more hospitable for the various citizens that inhabit political liberalist regimes who experience a tension between individual rights and other commitments, such as religious customs. I will first give an overview of Tomasi's position and then politicise his proposal with the help of Foucault's governmentality perspective.

A. Political Liberalism and Unintended Effects

In *Liberalism beyond Justice: Citizens, Society, and the Boundaries of Political Theory* John Tomasi develops an elegant criticism of the political liberalist conception of political philosophy.[20] He agrees with Rawls that political liberalism should accommodate citizens that adopt a critical stance towards traditional customs ('comprehensive liberals') as well as those who attempt to conform to such practices. But Tomasi says that political liberalism does not succeed in realising this aim. In his view, political liberalism creates disproportionate burdens for communal ways of life, thereby violating its commitment to the equal treatment of comprehensive liberals as well as to those citizens who are less prone to critically detach themselves from traditions.

To understand Tomasi's critique, I need to say a little about the distinction between so-called 'intended' and 'unintended' effects of moral principles. Political liberals qualify the practical consequences that are aimed for by its regime as 'intended' effects. For instance, political liberalism considers it crucial that citizens are able to make use of their rights.[21] This implies that while schools do not have to actively encourage pupils to leave their

[19] With this plea for a diagnosis of the social effects of individual rights, Tomasi envisions a very different task for social theory than Rawls does. For Rawls, the purpose of a social theory is restricted to showing that his moral ideal is feasible, or at least not unrealistic (J Rawls, *Political Liberalism: With a New Introduction and the 'Reply to Habermas'* (New York, Columbia University Press, 1996) 88). *Political Liberalism* will hereafter be referred to as *PL*. For instance, when Rawls appeals to social theory, he aims to show that most citizens are capable of fulfilling the requirements of political autonomy, such as the mutual recognition of rights. Tomasi, in contrast, holds that a social theory must also provide insight into the social consequences of implementing these requirements. So instead of arguing only that citizens ought to recognise each other's rights and can be taught to do so, Tomasi says that political liberalism needs also to pay attention to the negative side-effects of political liberalist identity formation.

[20] J Tomasi, *Liberalism beyond Justice: Citizens, Society, and the Boundaries of Political Theory* (New Jersey, Princeton University Press, 2001).

[21] '[C]itizens have a normally effective sense of justice, that is, one that enables them to understand and apply the publicly recognized principles of justice' (J Rawls, *Justice as Fairness: A Restatement* (Cambridge, The Belknap Press of Harvard University Press, 2001) 9).

traditional backgrounds, they must teach them how they can exercise a right to exit. Political liberals acknowledge that this demand may jeopardise the communal ways of life of people who reject the political liberalist tenet that citizens are entitled to leave their traditional backgrounds. Such practices will, after all, fare much better in a society where citizens need not obtain any understanding about a right to leave. Political liberalism, however, does not regret the harm done to these practices: since it aspires to a society where everyone appreciates its principles of justice and its underlying 'political ideals of person and society', the marginalisation of norms and customs that challenge political liberalism's basic principles (such as the right to leave), is an intended effect.[22]

More problematic for political liberalism are its 'unintended' effects: the practical implications of principles that are not formally required by political liberalism and that might, in fact, be at odds with basic political liberalist norms. For instance, communitarians and feminists have often argued that individual rights do not only provide citizens with an option to assert individual claims vis-a-vis communal practices, but actually encourage people to detach themselves from communities and other sorts of relations. By teaching citizens to review the practices in which they participate from a detached, individualist point of view, legal regimes cultivate individualist modes of conflict-solving and interest-identification that unintentionally undermine the affective ties constitutive of communities, families and friendships.[23] Political liberals typically do not deny that rights may have such effects. Rawls, for instance, admits that political liberalist education could in effect collapse into a comprehensive liberal education: teaching pupils how to make use of rights could indeed stimulate them to pursue individualist ways of life and may thereby structurally disadvantage admirably communal ways of life.[24] Rawls does not, however, consider it the task of democratic theory to engage with these structural exclusions. For him, unintended effects are a sad but inevitable fact of social life that need to be acknowledged, but that does not prompt him to any theoretical or practical adjustments in the political liberalist framework:

> We must accept the facts of commonsense political sociology ... Neutrality of effects or influence political liberalism abandons as impracticable ... There is no social world without loss; that is, no social world that does not exclude some ways of life that realize in special ways certain fundamental values.[25]

[22] Rawls, *PL* (n 19) 200.

[23] See eg, M Sandel, *Liberalism and the Limits of Justice* (Cambridge, Cambridge University Press, 1982); M Glendon, *Rights Talk: the Impoverishment of Political Discourse* (New York, Free Press, 1991).

[24] Rawls, *PL* (n 19) 199.

[25] Rawls, *PL* (n 19) 193–200.

John Tomasi challenges the Rawlsian way of treating unintended effects. He suggests that by paying so little attention to the unintended effects of political liberalist principles, political liberalism provides an inadequate justification of its conception of justice. Many citizens—whose comprehensive doctrines support political liberalism's public norms—may not give their consent unless they have been shown how public norms affect the viability of their comprehensive doctrines. These citizens are interested in the kind of culture or way of life that political liberalism implicates, and ask political liberals to explain the social implications of liberalism rather than to be 'mere technicians of justified coercion'.[26] Furthermore, Tomasi thinks that the neglect of unintended effects hampers the realisation of stability. He believes that the eroding effects of liberal democratic justice are an important reason why many societies are still confronted with citizens who reject political liberalism. And even though political liberalist theorists cannot soothe all the worries citizens may have in this regard, they can offer a diagnosis of these effects and think of ways of mitigating them. In doing so, political liberalist theorists can reduce the unwillingness of citizens to consent to political liberalism and deepen the allegiance of those who are already convinced by it.

In sum, political liberalists must expand the boundaries of political theory with a social theory that provides insight into the unintended effects of political liberalist principles.

B. Tomasi's Proposal

To provide insight into the unintended effects of political liberalist regimes, Tomasi conceptualises rights as a social practice rather than a as set of formal requirements necessary to achieve justice. Put somewhat differently, he suggests that we look at what rights actually do instead of what rights ought to do.

His theory of the social effects of rights distinguishes between a 'public' domain and a 'non-public' sphere. The 'public' point of view ('the personal uses of public reason'), is shared by all citizens and consists of an awareness of the rights that each citizen has in order to exercise one's political autonomy. Like communitarians, such as Sandel, Tomasi points out that rights structure the personal lives of citizens in an individualist fashion: 'Rights mark lines between people. But by that very fact they set out social

[26] Tomasi, *Liberalism* (n 20) 34. For Rawls, as we explained in ch 2, a conception of justice needs to be supported by the various comprehensive doctrines. Tomasi notes, however, that by framing justification as a 'fit' between principles and the core tenets of comprehensive doctrines, political liberalism makes the test for justification appear much too easy.

markers by which people can recognize when *individualistic* lines have been benevolently crossed'.[27] Yet, he also notes that rights can contribute to the *strengthening* of traditional ties. If citizens refrain from exercising their right to exit but continue to participate in a community, they send out a message to the other participants that this particular communal practice is worth maintaining, and in doing so affirm the value of traditional practice.

The main part of Tomasi's analysis of unintended effects concentrates on the way that the 'non-public' commitments of citizens ('the machinery of non-public virtue'), affect the exercise of rights. To deepen the understanding of the identities and basic understandings that constitute this 'non-public' sphere, Tomasi borrows an idea from the communitarian thinker Alisdair MacIntyre, who famously conceptualises human life as an enacted narrative. For MacIntyre, individuals are part of ongoing stories that offer various role models, such as the parent, the academic or the citizen. These role models, or social identities, are historical: they are taught and sustained through 'traditions' that MacIntyre defines as 'a mode of understanding … which has been transmitted often through many generations.'[28] Building upon MacIntyre's idea of a narrative tradition Tomasi develops an account of society in terms of 'comprehensive groupings'. With this notion—a reconceptualisation of Rawls' notion of 'comprehensive doctrines'—Tomasi wants to convey the point that citizens do not only identify with various doctrines but are also shaped by customs and tacit knowledge claims that cannot always be rationalised in a set of beliefs. In fact, one of the profound disagreements between narrative traditions is exactly how they evaluate doctrinal thought: most citizens, says Tomasi, do not wish to understand their commitments in terms of a doctrine. Another disagreement between comprehensive groupings is their usage and their evaluation of rights. While some have no objections to individual claim-making in more intimate relationships, others find legal reasoning deeply at odds with their ideal of community, friendship, family or love.

To clarify the various differences between comprehensive groupings, Tomasi conceptualises society in terms of four ideal types. The first type (the 'A-people') is made up of citizens who strive for a relentless critical reflection on traditional customs and who are comfortable with legal reasoning, such as comprehensive liberals and others who aspire to 'experimental, fallibilist, reflective, and self-aware' lives.[29] The second type ('B-people') pursues traditional habits without rejecting critical detachment completely.

[27] ibid, 43.

[28] A Macintyre, *After Virtue: a Study in Moral Theory*, Second (corrected) edition (London, Duckworth, 1985) 221.

[29] Tomasi (n 20) 17.

These citizens experience their 'non-public' lives as a 'complex and unsettled mixture ... of commitment and of detachment, of reflection and of acquiescence, of certainty and of doubt'.[30] While they affirm the value of rights in public life, they do not want to structure their entire personal life around this mode of conflict-solving. Instead, they aspire to 'forms of personal life based on spontaneity and non-reflective expressions of trust'.[31] To illustrate the values of the B-people Tomasi recalls the custom of stewardship and solidarity among some American farmer families. The bond that these families experience with inherited land prevents them from selling their land even if the exercise of property rights would be economically beneficent. Tomasi also points out the tradition of elderly care among African-Americans and the Jewish custom of charity (*tzedakah*): these customs can give participants in these traditions a strong incentive to provide other citizens with welfare even if such actions are not required by any legal obligations. Finally, the third and fourth types ('C-people' and 'D-people') are made up of citizens who are committed to traditional practices that are at odds with liberal norms. These citizens might, for instance, be attached to religious practices that pursue hierarchical gendered role patterns or dogmatic identities that leave little space for individual dissent. Even more than in the case of 'B-people', these citizens do not wish to critically reflect on traditional practices. But whereas 'C-people' subscribe to political liberalism as a public morality, the 'D-people' reject political liberalism entirely and strive for another type of regime.

Tomasi highlights the fact that 'B' and 'C-people' are confronted with deep difficulties when trying to reconcile political liberalist norms with their relational fabric.[32] Although political liberalism allows citizens to use rights in regard of traditional practices or even refrain from exercising them, the very requirement of knowing how to make use of individual rights is much more attuned to the legalistic ways of life of liberal 'A-people' than the habitual or faith-based practices of 'B' and 'C-people'. For instance, political liberalism allows marital partners to pursue deeply gendered role patterns, but also demands that they are able to see their spouses as equal citizens that can file for divorce and challenge gendered norms. While this requirement may not demand that citizens consciously reflect on their right to divorce, it does ask for a set of skills, 'a settled disposition', that allows them to affirm each other's rights.

[30] ibid, 19.
[31] ibid, 51.
[32] Since the D-people are 'unreasonable' from the political liberalist perspective, Tomasi does not elaborate upon the concerns within this group.

Tomasi agrees with Rawls that political liberalism cannot completely assuage the worries of 'B' and 'C-people': there remains a tension between the demands of political liberalist justice and the social fabric of traditional ways of life that cannot be relieved. However, political liberalist regimes can decrease the structural disadvantages for these citizens who affirm political liberalism by limiting those state interventions that burden traditionalist practices. For instance, Tomasi supports the so-called 'Religious Freedom Restoration Act' (RFRA), a 1993 American law prohibiting the state from substantially burdening the practice of religion, and giving citizens much more leeway to claim exemptions from laws on the grounds of religious exercise.[33]

IV. THE ONTOLOGICAL REMNANTS IN TOMASI'S SOCIAL THEORY

Tomasi's theory of unintended effects offers an innovative adjustment to political liberalism. To begin with, his notion of 'comprehensive groupings' offers a much more satisfactory account of pluralism than Rawls' idea of comprehensive doctrines: unlike Rawls, Tomasi takes seriously the centrality of habits in the lives of many citizens. And, by showing the social-cultural effects of individual rights Tomasi provides an insight into the functioning of political liberalist regimes that is removed from view when the analysis of political liberalism is limited to the intended or formal requirements of principles of justice.

To some extent, Tomasi's argument to deepen the understanding of liberalism bears resemblance to the perspective that have I developed so far. Tomasi and I both agree that a political philosophy which is committed to pluralism should not limit itself to an explication of the normative basis of liberal democratic states but needs to analyse the exclusionary or subjectifying effects of state action. Therefore, it is crucial that normative views on the state are supplemented by a social-diagnostic account of state action.[34] There are also important differences though. First, I emphasise the need for a critical analysis of the ontologies that influence the normative and analytical conceptualisation of the state. Tomasi, in contrast, sees no need to subject to critical scrutiny the ontological premises of political reflection

[33] This law is no longer in force on the federal level, but many states have implemented their own versions of the RFRA. My case-study will look at some problems in the implementation of this law in the state of Florida. See below s V.B.i.

[34] Or, to put it in more political liberalist terms: political theorists need to become more responsive to justificatory questions of ordinary citizens that arise in the second and third stages by expanding the justificatory argument in the reflective equilibrium in the first, *pro tanto* stage, with a social theory. For the various stages in the reflective equilibrium, see ch 2.

on state action. He believes that his analysis of the interaction between state and society is 'free-standing' and will give way to an

> ideal of society that [is] *genuinely* and not merely formally inclusive. It is the ideal of a society that, beyond being just, is as much as possible *a home* to people affirming diverse but politically reasonable views of value and spirituality.[35]

My perspective disputes Tomasi's anticipation of a just and fully inclusive society: by my account, no normative or social theory of the interaction between state and society will eradicate marginalisation.

The second difference between Tomasi and my perspective is methodological. The Foucaultian governmentality critique that I draw upon here underlines the need for an empirical investigation of state power. Tomasi, in contrast, attempts to provide insight into the exclusionary effects of political liberalism by abstracting from the empirical reality of liberal democratic regimes. That is to say, Tomasi looks for exclusionary effects that are unavoidable for political liberalist regimes and sees no need to investigate how individual rights are applied in variable empirical circumstances. Even though he acknowledges that rights are applied in 'various branches of law', he claims it is sufficient to model the legal background culture in terms of a very general notion of rights: '*Of course*, our main concern is with this process as it applies to rights in the broadest political sense'.[36] I question the self-evidence of Tomasi's approach to rights. First, his abstract approach makes it difficult for him to analyse the exclusionary effects of the concrete proposals that he recommends, such as the RFRA. While Tomasi endorses this law as a means to mitigate marginalisation, he does not reveal how the implementation of this law has issued various new exclusionary effects. And, second, Tomasi is blind to the fact that empirical investigations into the exercise of rights can be of help in putting into question the ontological tenets of his social theory. One of the attractive features of Tomasi's work is that he illustrates his social diagnosis of rights with various lively examples taken from American culture. The empirical practices of the United States are, however, not only an archive for illustrating theoretically established ideas but can also serve a more critical function, that is, they can alert us to the limitations of theoretical frameworks, such as the ontologies that we bring to bear in our diagnosis of rights.

The first step in my evaluation of Tomasi's framework is to bring out the exclusionary effects of Tomasi's ontology of 'non-public culture' via a critical confrontation between MacIntyre's view of tradition and Foucaultian ontology of power and agonic freedom. I will then address some conceptual problems in Tomasi's ontology of 'public culture' and, finally, introduce an

[35] Tomasi (n 20) 125 (emphasis added).
[36] ibid, 43 (emphasis added).

example of an actual struggle taken from American culture to expose the blind spots in Tomasi's interpretation of rights.

A. 'Life as a Narrative': A Precondition or Site of Contest of Democratic Politics?

As noted earlier, Tomasi regards it essential to political liberalism that it includes a theory of the constituent features of 'non-public' attachments. Tomasi implicitly concedes that such a theory could implicate the theorist in an ontological dispute: a conflict regarding the conditions of possibility of political life. He writes:

> Any description of the sources of those very basic forms of self-perception and of non-public value pluralism can at best be rough, especially in conditions of reasonable value pluralism. We are speaking, after all, about how humans pursue value over the course of a life. But there is one very general way of describing the sources of compass concepts that may be useful here, in part because of a feature for which it is often criticized: its extreme flexibility. This is the idea of life as a kind of narrative.[37]

Although Tomasi does not use the term metaphysics or ontology, his attempt to provide understanding in 'non-public' life is similar to what I have identified as an ontological investigation: illuminating the 'sources of those very basic forms of self-perception and of non-public value pluralism' invokes a set of presuppositions about the fundamental conditions of political existence, in this case, our status as moral or political agents.[38] And we can see that Tomasi senses that the inclusion of such a thesis in his reflective equilibrium could jeopardise his attempt to offer a 'freestanding' justification of his social theory. On the one hand, an account of 'non-public' life needs to be rich enough to deepen the understanding of political liberalist principles, and to diagnose a tension between those principles and the attachments of citizens. But, on the other hand, this theory should remain so general or 'rough' that it will be acceptable for the plurality of self-understandings that constitute the citizenry.

Tomasi negotiates this dilemma by introducing the notion of 'life as a narrative': the assumption that most citizens in his public will understand themselves as enacting traditional narratives. Tomasi does not, however, treat this idea as a site of contest of pluralistic democratic cultures. On the contrary, his celebration of the 'extreme flexibility' and generality of this notion suggests that he considers it to be a rather uncontroversial precondition of political life. But is the ease with which Tomasi assumes his notion

[37] ibid, 46.

[38] His description is also similar to what Rawls takes to be a metaphysical claim: see ch 2 s III.A.

of traditional narrativity to be uncontentious not somewhat surprising? Take, for instance, the fact that Tomasi adopts his ontology from Alisdair MacIntyre, a distinctly anti-liberal, communitarian thinker. He makes no effort whatsoever to defend this account for citizens who do not identify with communitarianism, such as comprehensive liberals or, for that matter, citizens with a more agonic sensibility who struggle with traditional narratives without believing that they can completely transcend traditions.[39] These citizens will deservedly ask whether Tomasi's ontology of society is adequate enough to account for their self-understandings and struggles. To see whether the idea of traditional narrativity is indeed not contentious let me briefly turn to the theorist who developed this notion: Alisdair MacIntyre.

B. MacIntyre's Ontology of Tradition

MacIntyre develops his notion on traditional narrativity in *After Virtue*—a book that challenges post-Enlightenment moral philosophy and wants to restore an Aristotelian tradition-based ethics of virtue.[40] Central to MacIntyre's argument is his criticism of individualist notions of self that emphasise our capacity to exercise independent choice. Like Foucault and the communitarian thinker Charles Taylor, whose conceptions of self we discussed in the previous chapters, MacIntyre rejects the Kantian premise of autonomous reason and argues that 'all reasoning takes place within the context of some traditional mode of thought'.[41] Human identity is not the result of a set of independent decisions but is produced through a narrative 'quest': a practice in which we connect our current actions and self-understanding with our individual past and a wider traditional framework.

MacIntyre stresses that human beings are dependent upon others to achieve narrative unity. But he also points out that our sociability puts the achievement of narrative identities at risk: the stories that give our actions a sense of purpose challenge the self-understandings of others. For MacIntyre, enacting a narrative is not a peaceful undertaking but implicates us in a dramatic struggle:

> We enter upon a stage which we did not design and we find ourselves part of an action that was not of our making. Each of us being a main character in his own

[39] The idea of agonic freedom is perhaps closest to Tomasi's depiction of the 'B-people'. Like the 'B-people', citizens who aspire to agonic freedom do not attempt to relinquish all traditional ties but try to open a space in which to question and experiment with these practices. Also, like 'B-people', their way of life includes various ethical practices and does not only center on systemic thought (as the 'A-people'). The centrality of critical reflection and experiment in agonic freedom, however, are typical 'A-people' sensibilities.

[40] Since Tomasi draws upon MacIntyre's seminal work *After Virtue*, I limit my discussion of MacIntyre's theory of tradition to this work. See Macintyre (n 28).

[41] MacIntyre, ibid 222.

> drama plays subordinate parts in the dramas of others, and each drama constrains the others. In my drama, perhaps, I am Hamlet or Iago or at least the swineherd who may yet become a prince, but to you I am only A Gentleman or at best Second Murderer, while you are my Polonius or my Gravedigger, but your own hero. Each of our dramas exerts constraints on each other's making the whole different from the parts, but still dramatic.[42]

Traditions provide human beings direction in such struggles. They situate social conflicts in a historical framework that pursues a particular good, and teach the necessary virtues to choose between conflicting goods. But MacIntyre does not suggest that participants in traditional practice can transcend disagreements. In his view, vital traditional practices are constituted by an ongoing disagreement with regard to the criteria that constitute a good, such as, say, parental care, academic excellence, or religious piety. A living tradition embodies 'continuities of conflict', more specifically, 'an historically extended, socially embodied argument, and an argument precisely in part about the goods which constitute that tradition'.[43]

One reason why MacIntyre considers traditional practices to be so important is that they provide an indispensable safeguard against the degenerate effects of institutions such as the market and the state. To be sure, he acknowledges that such institutions provide essential background conditions for perpetuating traditional life: 'no practices can survive for any length of time unsustained by institutions'.[44] But he also underlines the point that institutions are a great threat for traditions: by dividing participants in a competition for resources and institutional privileges, institutions always threaten to undermine the integrity of a practice. To counter the corruption inherent in institutional life, MacIntyre suggests that institutions must actively support traditional self-understandings. Traditional practices can only flourish if virtues 'can be and are exercised in sustaining the institutional forms which are the social bearers of a practice'.[45]

MacIntyre's defence of traditional virtues bears some resemblance to Foucault's plea for ethics.[46] Both argue that the quality of institutions depends upon ideals and skills that are taught and exercised in socio-historical practices. And the two theorists agree that traditional practices implicate the participants in continuous conflicts. However, in opposition to Foucault, MacIntyre neglects to analyse power relations within traditions.

[42] ibid, 213.

[43] MacIntyre explicitly distances his understanding of tradition from the conservative position defended by the thinker Edmund Burke, in which 'the stability of tradition can be contrasted with reason and conflict' (ibid, 222).

[44] ibid, 194.

[45] ibid, 195.

[46] For an account of Foucault's understanding of ethics, see ch, 3 ss V.A and V.B.

As we can see in his differentiation between institutions and practices, MacIntyre regards power as a force that is *external* to traditional practices:

> Practices must not be confused with institutions. Chess, physics and medicine are practices; chess clubs, laboratories, universities and hospitals are institutions. Institutions are characteristically and necessarily concerned with what I have called external goods. They are involved in acquiring money and other material goods; *they are structured in terms of power* and status, and they distribute money, power and status as rewards.[47]

Since MacIntyre does not investigate power in traditional practices, he does not confront how hierarchical exclusions within traditions affect the livelihood of traditional narratives. For instance, he says that the most important condition for the success of a traditional practice is the virtuous performances of the participants who affirm this notion of excellence: the 'key answer' to the strength and decay of traditional practices resides in 'the exercise or the lack of exercise of the relevant virtues'.[48] So when we want to understand why a particular standard of excellence with regard to, say, parenthood, is more successful than other standards, MacIntyre suggests that we look at the qualities of character of the fathers and mothers who affirm this notion of excellence. Surely, however, the achievements of successful practitioners cannot only be accounted for by the fact that these participants are more skilled in performing their duties than fathers and mothers who have tried to establish different arrangements. Successful role models are *also* sustained by power relations within traditions, such as the fact that dominant conceptions of the good often take a derogatory view of relatively less established competing standards of excellence.

MacIntyre's inattentiveness to power relations within traditions brings us to another problem in his account. Unlike Foucault's analytics of governmentality, MacIntyre does not look at the way in which traditional power relations shape institutions and how institutional support, in turn, affects power relations within traditions. When an institution, such as state law, sets out to stimulate the exercise of virtues, it needs to decide which interpretation of a traditional practice it takes as authoritative in the distribution of institutional privileges. And in the case that institutions draw upon the most powerful traditional narratives, institutional support could reinforce existing power relations and thereby pressurise more marginal role models. For example, a powerful traditional practice such as the classic gendered nuclear family has profited from the fact that laws and markets have replicated its role models. Practitioners of less established ideals of care and nurture, however, have been further marginalised by the fact that they were denied access to legal and economic privileges.

[47] MacIntyre (n 28) 195 (emphasis added).
[48] ibid, 223.

In sum, MacIntyre's theory of traditional narrativity shows that traditional role models are a continuing source of conflict and argumentative disagreements—an insight that many agonic citizens and comprehensive liberals will agree with. However, he does not acknowledge that the possibilities of strengthening conflicting traditional narratives are structured by power relations in institutions and in the traditional practices themselves. In light of these problems it becomes difficult to sustain the assertion, as Tomasi does, that MacIntyre's theory of traditional narrativity offers a relatively uncontroversial understanding of 'non-public' life. For citizens who struggle with traditional role models it is crucial that an account of public life includes a diagnosis of the interaction between power relations within institutions, on the one hand, and within traditions on the other. For them the question is bound to arise as to why it is sometimes so hard to challenge traditional norms, and why some traditional role models are more successful in establishing themselves than others. Put differently, it is not just the relation between history and identity, but rather the relation between history, identity and power that is of special interest.

C. A Political Liberalist Appropriation of MacIntyre's Ontology

In light of Tomasi's commitment to plurality one might expect that his own account of tradition would be more acceptable to comprehensive liberals and agonic citizens than would MacIntyre's view. But, strangely enough, Tomasi's reworking of MacIntyre's account of tradition has even less to say to citizens who challenge traditional role models than MacIntyre's. Unlike MacIntyre, Tomasi treats narrative traditions as relatively secure background conditions and does not discuss the point that traditional role models are also subjected to ongoing disputes. That is to say, he addresses neither the diversity nor the tensions in traditions and instead gives the impression that traditions are static and organic wholes. Consider, for instance, Tomasi's account of citizens who strive for more dogmatic traditional identities (the 'C-people'). Tomasi rightly points out that some of these citizens affirm and try to enact traditional role models without actively questioning them. His claim that public liberal culture may infuse these traditional practices with more detached dispositions than these citizens would see fit is also plausible. But the stark opposition that Tomasi sets up between the centrality of 'conscious reflection' in the practices of 'A-people' and the 'spontaneity and non-reflective expressions of trust' in practices of 'C-people' occludes the fact that self-awareness and the questioning of traditional backgrounds are *also* cultivated by practices which do not treat critical detachment and individual experimentation as central to the good life.[49] In fact, the idea that

[49] ibid, 51.

traditions open up moments of self-awareness and conscious choice-making is not just pointed out by MacIntyre but accepted by most twentieth century philosophers. Even philosophers who consider our pre-reflective habitual practices as much more fundamental than conscious reflection, such as Heidegger and Foucault, acknowledge that these ontological background conditions do not preclude possibilities for conscious reflection.[50]

Tomasi's blindness to the reflective dimension of traditional practice can be illustrated with his narration of Hasidic Judaism in The United States. Tomasi points out that the gendered role patterns among Hasidic Jews leave women very little room to exercise their rights: they are, for instance, not allowed to pursue careers other than caretakers. Further, he notes even if Hasidic men and women appreciate each other's status as political equals, the pressures within such a group render meaningless this admission, because it remains highly questionable whether these citizens can actually make use of their rights. While I agree with this part of Tomasi's analysis, it seems that his ontology of tradition makes it difficult for him to see that critical reflection is not completely foreign to orthodox religious practices. Even members of tightly integrated communities, such as American Hasidim, often reflect and disagree on the question of how they ought to perform a religious duty of custom. Certainly, they deliberate on such matters in order to obey tradition rather than to distance themselves from traditional authority, but this does not mean that critical reflection is completely alien to orthodox religious ways of life and, as Tomasi suggests, is imposed upon them by the public culture of liberal legalism.[51]

Furthermore, like MacIntyre, Tomasi completely omits the presence of power in his diagnosis of traditional life. Take, for instance, Tomasi's representation of citizens who aspire to traditional ways of life but who try to enact traditional narratives in a somewhat unorthodox way (the 'B-people'). Tomasi interprets the concerns of this group primarily in terms of the attempt to safeguard traditional practices against liberal modes of perception and ways of reasoning. He does not mention, however, that people in this group might also have to engage in struggles with power relations *within* traditions, such as contests between traditional practices that allow for flexible modes of reasoning vis-a-vis more orthodox ones.

In other words, Tomasi's account of 'non-public' life is not as neutral as he makes it appear to be, and merits much more democratic contestation than he suggests. Tomasi addresses neither the presence of conflicts nor the role of power relations within traditions, and therefore cannot explain

[50] For Heidegger, see ch 1 s II. For Foucault's idea of agonic freedom, see ch 3 s V.A.

[51] For an overview of some conflicts and debates in an Hasidic community in the state of New York, see W Sullivan, 'Competing Theories of Religion and Law in the Supreme Court of the United States: an Hasidic Case' in special volume entitled 'Religion, Law and the Construction of Identities' (1996) 43 *Numen* 184.

many of the struggles that confront citizens who struggle with traditional role models. The next section will reveal some blind spots in Tomasi's ontology of public culture and explain how they represent a flawed interpretation of the exclusionary effects of state action.

V. POLITICISING TOMASI'S CONCEPT OF LEGAL CULTURE

So far we have seen that Tomasi's ontology of 'non-public culture' imports a problematic flaw of MacIntyre's understanding of tradition into his social theory: a neglect of the existence of power relations within traditions. In this section, I turn to Tomasi's theory of public culture and show how this account, like MacIntyre's, displaces the agonic concerns of citizens who struggle against the effects on law of traditional power relations. I will further illuminate the blind spots of Tomasi's diagnosis of individual rights with a case study drawn from American jurisprudence of religious freedom. Whereas Tomasi suggests that the usage of an individual right excludes citizens who tend to conform to traditions, we will see that the American implementation of the right to religious freedom reveals how an individual right tends to exclude citizens who challenge established traditional practices. While political liberalism can mitigate some of these current disadvantages, its public legal culture will remain biased against citizens who tend to dissent from hegemonic, traditional, interpretations.

A. The Displacement of Agonic Concerns

Liberal legalism, including political liberalism, is committed to the rule of law, a principle that serves to provide citizens with some reliability when exercising their rights. An important implication of the rule of the law—'justice as regularity' as Rawls calls it—is that judges and citizens must frame their practices within legal definitions that are clear enough to ensure some predictability.[52] These definitions are tied to important privileges that affect the viability of traditional practices. To begin with, they determine which citizens can make use of material benefits, such as subsidies and tax deduction: citizens are only eligible for the privileges associated with particular rights, such as marital rights, if the practice they engage in is legally recognised as such. Moreover, legal definitions have a symbolic effect. When the state recognises a particular traditional custom in law, it provides these

[52] J Rawls, *A Theory of Justice: Revised Edition* (Cambridge, The Belknap Press of Harvard University Press, 1999) 207. Hereafter, *A Theory of Justice* will be referred to as *TOJ*.

practices with a sense of approval and prestige that is not conferred upon unrecognised customs.[53]

Legal theorists have often pointed out that the definitions determining the usage of rights bear the imprint of historical power relations in a democratic community. That is to say, the definitions that designate the scope of a particular right, such as 'marriage' or 'religion', typically reflect the values and self-understandings of hegemonic traditions and tend to exclude the identities of citizens who dissent from predominant traditional knowledge claims.[54] Due to the impact of these legal definitions upon the viability of ethical practices, many current liberal democratic regimes engage in long and tiresome democratic struggles against the traditionalist prejudices that shape the production of public meaning.

The first problem in Tomasi's ontology of public culture is that he, like MacIntyre, blinds us to the effect of powerful traditions on the production of meaning in legal institutions, including the disputes that these power/knowledge relations open up. Tomasi mentions in passing that the scope of the law will remain a source of ineradicable disagreement, even in the ideal political liberalist societies that are the object of his social theory: 'the exact reach of those branchings [that is: all the branches of public law] can be expected to be a matter of ongoing dispute and discovery *even within a society that is more or less well ordered*'.[55] But while conflicts about the scope of rights are apparently an intrinsic part of political liberalism, Tomasi's ontology of public culture structurally ignores the ongoing presence of such disputes. In Tomasi's accounts of legalistic practices, participants never seem to dispute the public significatory regimes that condition the exercise of rights and the enjoyment of legally-sanctioned privileges.[56] In fact, Tomasi suggests that citizens are free to advance legal claims in regard of their

[53] For instance, one of the reasons why some gay activists object to same sex-marriage campaigns is that the legal recognition of marriage renders unmarried citizens less respectable than married ones. By setting up a distinction between legally recognised and unrecognised sexual relations the state contributes to the century-long stigmatisation of sexual relations that do not conform to the traditional institution of marriage. As Michael Warner puts it, the legalisation of the institution of marriage 'sanctifies some couples at the expense of others' (M Warner, *The Trouble with Normal: Sex, Politics, and the Ethics of Queer Life* (Cambridge, Harvard University Press, 1999) 82).

[54] For instance, in most Western constitutional law regimes marital law is still indebted to Christian self-understandings of the majority. Even though some regimes now also support monogamous partnerships along with monogamous marriages, polygamous partnerships have not obtained equal juridical standing in most Western legal codes. For a criticism of the prohibition of polygamy in the American context, see M Nussbaum, *Liberty of Conscience: In Defense of America's Tradition of Religious Equality* (New York, Basic Books, 2008) 179–98.

[55] Tomasi (n 20) 43 (emphasis added).

[56] Bert van den Brink's raises a similar concern in his review of Tomasi's book (B van den Brink, 'Liberalism beyond Justice: Citizens, Society, and the Boundaries of Political Theory' (2002) 112 *Ethics* 872).

own traditional self-understandings (the '*non-public* compass concepts'). This sketch of legal claim-making is far too voluntarist: it hides from view the fact that citizens cannot appeal to their own traditions at will, but that they must always take into account whether their legal claims conform to the contentious *public* definitions that determine the scope of a right. As the legal theorist Carol Smart so aptly puts it, law functions by 'narrowing down the possible interpretations of behaviour'.[57] The fact that Tomasi provides no orientation in the relation between public significatory regimes and the usage of individual rights is especially troublesome for citizens who are engaged in agonic struggles against hegemonic traditional interpretations in law. They will look for a diagnosis of legal public cultures that offers insight into their disputes and, for instance, addresses which possibilities exist to challenge established interpretations.[58]

This brings me to the second problem in Tomasi's account: his ontology of legal public culture fails to address the point that citizens who try to experiment with established traditions face a structural disadvantage in challenging hegemonic interpretations of rights. Earlier in this chapter, I suggested that the exclusionary effects of individual rights for citizens who do not conform to authoritative traditions cannot be extinguished entirely, but remain an essential part of liberal legal regimes. Political liberalism cannot escape this predicament. For sure, political liberalism, like other liberal legal cultures, may adopt flexible definitions and thereby grant citizens the opportunity to introduce and clarify their unfamiliar ethical practices to the judge. But the rule of law demands that citizens will account for their practice with reference to legally authorised criteria. Without such standards, judges and other citizens would no longer be able to verify or predict in which cases a right can be claimed. Such acts of translations are especially burdensome for citizens who try to dissent from, or experiment with, well-established traditions. Consider, for instance, a citizen with an idiosyncratic, unorthodox understanding of religion who claims a particular benefit in regard of the right to religious freedom. Like everyone else, this citizen will need to depart from a purely subjectivist interpretation of what he considers to be a 'religious' custom and appeal to a legal criterion. There might be various ways which the law prescribes for this citizen to account for his practice: he may refer to well-known texts, established customs,

[57] C Smart, *Feminism and The Power of Law* (New York, Routledge, 1989) 34.

[58] Such as the possibility for flexible definitions which I discussed in ch 4 text to n 15. There I noted that liberal democracies can actively try to make individual rights more responsive to plurality by giving citizens a voice in the definitions that determine the applicability of a right. These flexible definitions can open up some space for agonic citizens to challenge the exclusionary implications of ruling interpretations of individual rights. For instance, a flexible definition calls upon the judge to listen to the account that citizens give of their own ethical practices rather than to treat legal definitions as settled in advance.

organisations, authoritative legal precedents, or scientific expertise. But all these attempts fit uncomfortably with the self-understandings and experiences of citizens with an agonic religious sensibility, that is, with a self-identity that dissents from dominant traditional practices and struggles against established authority. In comparison to orthodox citizens, these citizens are less likely to have such authoritative resources available to them and may even reject appealing to authority as such.[59] Tomasi does not mention that the rule of law limits the possibilities of questioning the scope of individual rights in political liberalist regimes. Nor does he show that the mode of representation demanded by the rule of law includes a structural bias against citizens whose practices resist clear categorisation, or who reject the establishment of univocal standards. His account thereby fails to illuminate an exclusionary effect of individual rights that is particularly troublesome for citizens who struggle with established traditions. That is, the ongoing dispute concerning the public interpretations of rights structurally disadvantages agonic citizens in comparison to those citizens who acquiesce in established traditions.[60]

The consequence of Tomasi's neglect of the intimate link between traditional power relations and the determination of legal meanings is that he presents an overly individualist diagnosis of the social construction initiated by political liberalist regimes. To be sure, I do not wish to dispute that individual rights have some individualising effect. In fact, I agree with Tomasi that rights contribute to individualist patterns of perception: the fact that participants in traditional practices are always entitled to leave this practice implies that they will not only perceive each other as sharing a similar collective commitment but also view one another as, to some extent, separate individuals. This assumption alone, however, does not warrant the conclusion that rights structurally disadvantage citizens who try to conform to traditions. We need also to attend to the fact that liberal acts of legal claim-making, including those sanctioned by political liberalism, are dependent

[59] A lack of institutional support was one of the main reasons for denying a prisoner an exemption on the grounds of religious freedom in *Africa v Commonwealth of Pennsylvania*, 662 F.2d 1025 (3rd Circuit 1981). In this case a prisoner required a diet of raw vegetables in light of his status as a minister of 'Move', an organisation 'absolutely opposed to all that is wrong.' The plaintiff explained his request for raw food in light of the commitment of Move to purity and harmony with the natural world. His claim was not granted however, for the reason, among others, that the judge held that Move was lacking the structural characteristics of religion such as formal services, ceremonies and a clergy. For a criticism on some Western biases in this case, see Penalver (n 15).

[60] Tomasi's silence about the rule of law is especially surprising since one of the reasons why political liberalism insists on the rule of law is to protect the equal treatment of citizens. The usage of clear standards aims to decrease the chances that the application of law becomes infused with the personal or historical prejudices of public officials that are discriminatory of some groups (J Rawls, *TOJ* (n 52) 207). But, while this requirement of the rule of law *intends* to diminish discrimination, I show here that it *unintentionally* yields new forms of exclusions.

upon modes of representation which are structurally more beneficial for citizens who conform to established hegemonic traditions than for those that challenge them.

B. A Case Study: The Exclusionary Effects of Religious Freedom in the United States

We have seen that Tomasi's account of public culture is ontologically contentious because it ignores the impact of well-established traditional power/knowledge regimes on the usage of individual rights. Indeed, his diagnosis of the unintended effects of individual rights completely overlooks how political liberalism—due to the principle of the rule of law—enacts a structural bias against citizens who contest and struggle with hegemonic traditions. For this reason, Tomasi's voluntarist ontology of public culture offers little orientation for agonic citizens.

In this section I will further unsettle Tomasi's social theory by juxtaposing his interpretation of unintended effects with a case study about the exclusionary effects within US jurisprudence on religious freedom. As suggested by Foucault's governmentality approach, I will study the effects of individual rights in regard of the contingent social-historical web of power/knowledge relations that condition their usage rather than, as Tomasi does, abstract and detach rights from such contexts. This approach has two advantages. First, it allows me to bring to light how a legal culture that is governed by the principle of the rule of law enacts exclusions for citizens who do not conform to dominant traditions, and to further substantiate my argument that the focus in Tomasi's ontology on the individualist effects of rights is one-sided. Second, analysing the way in which rights are used contextually can help to diagnose some of the exclusionary effects of the legal proposals that Tomasi endorses. I mentioned that Tomasi presents the American RFRA as an exemplary proposal to ameliorate the position of citizens who adhere to traditional practices. But, in opposition to the governmentality approach, his perspective has no tools with which to diagnose how this law works in practice. For instance, Tomasi's abstract analytics offer no insight into the new exclusions that the enactment of this law might bring about.

i. US Jurisprudence

As we have seen, Tomasi claims that the legal background culture places citizens who affirm a type of religious traditional authority ('C-people') in a structurally disadvantaged position in comparison to secular citizens whose lives centre around values such as individuality, experimentation and critical reflection ('A-people'). From the perspective of Tomasi's ontology of the legal public culture, this diagnosis seems plausible. Tomasi clarifies the role of legal claim-making in such rationalist terms that legal practices appear to be much more welcoming to citizens who are accustomed to detaching themselves from customs and beliefs ('A-people'), than to the dispositions of those citizens who are not so habituated to questioning their social roles (the 'C-people'). For instance, he says that participants in legalistic practices make '*decisions* to withhold right-claims' that 'may gain positive appraisals from third-party community members who may *observe* the benefits of rewarding human encounters'.[61] Such a practice—the critical reflection of one's attachments—seems to be much more comfortable for a rationalist 'A-person' than 'C-people' whose interactions are prompted by 'spontaneity and non-reflective forms of trust'.[62] But if you depart from an ontology of legal public culture that emphasises that rights are always subjected to exclusionary public significatory regimes, the interpretation of the social effects of individual rights undergoes several important shifts. Consider, for instance, how the right to religious freedom is signified, or—as Foucault would say, 'governmentalised'—in the United States. Analysing the American interpretative regime of religious freedom reveals that legalistic practices do not so much burden citizens who identify with traditionalist narratives, but rather, create disadvantages for citizens who struggle *against* powerful traditional practices, such as dissenters, non- conformists and new minorities.

The United States is well known for its strict separation of church and state: the first amendment of the United States Constitution explicitly prohibits the legal establishment of religion. From the time of its founding in the eighteenth century, however, American law has granted religious citizens important privileges. Religious institutions are eligible for tax benefits and religious citizens can claim exemptions from drug laws, mandatory military service and unemployment laws.[63] Tomasi, as noted earlier, considers such policies an essential feature of the state's obligation to minimise its unintended effects. Since religious customs are eligible for important privileges, many American citizens have gone to court to have their actions and beliefs designated as 'religious', including some secularists (a group that

[61] Tomasi (n 20) 44 (emphasis added).

[62] ibid, 51.

[63] The First Amendment of the American Constitution states that 'Congress shall make no law respecting an establishment of religion, or prohibiting the free exercise thereof; or abridging the freedom of speech, or of the press; or the right of the people peaceably to assemble, and to petition the Government for a redress of grievances.' The meaning of this Amendment is much debated in American legal theory: even though the American state accommodates religious institutions, commentators disagree if and to what extent the Constitution allows for state support for religion. See K Greenawalt, *Religion and the Constitution, Volume 1: Free Exercise and Fairness* (New Jersey, Princeton University Press, 2006) 11–34; Nussbaum (n 54)) 115–74; W Sullivan, *Paying the Words Extra: Religious Discourse in the Supreme Court of the United States* (Cambridge, Harvard University Center for the Study of World Religions, 1994) 59–68.

Tomasi qualifies as 'A-people'). This has involved the American courts in the difficult task of deciding which actions merit the qualification 'religious'. Initially, the Supreme Court identified religion with a belief in a 'Supreme Being', and required that the teaching of the claimants conformed with the mainstream morality of 'all civilized Christian countries'.[64] This theistic definition excluded secularists and citizens from minority religions that do not worship a deity or whose customs challenge prevalent Christian norms, such as the Mormons, who regard polygamy a central practice of their religion. During the twentieth century this legal definition of religion has been increasingly challenged, partly due to immigration that multiplied the number of non-Christians and religious sects in the United States. The Court progressively moved to a more flexible definition to include this increasing plurality of religious identities. For instance, in 1961 the Supreme Court finally dropped the majoritarian bias in its concept of religious freedom and granted protection to non-theistic belief-systems.[65] And, four years later, in a 1965 conscientious objector case, the Court included in its understanding of religion a 'sincere and meaningful belief which occupies in the life of its possessor a place parallel to that filled by the God of those admittedly qualifying for the exemption'.[66] In this way, religious freedom could now also accommodate non-theistic minority religions such as Buddhism as well as secular worldviews such as humanism. In 1972, however, the Court introduced a more narrow definition and excluded secular citizens from the jurisdiction of religious freedom. The Court now said that a way of life based upon purely 'secular considerations'—such as the non-conformist belief-system elaborated by the philosopher Thoreau—could not make use of the benefits secured by religious freedom.[67] This brief survey of US jurisprudence on religious freedom suggests that it is a sweeping generalisation to claim, as Tomasi does, that religious citizens are structurally disadvantaged by the exercise of individual rights. A non-religious citizen who constructs his entire life around a secular philosophy and finds this commitment as meaningful and profound as a faith in god might be for a religious person, is not as eligible for tax benefits or exemptions on drug laws as his fellow citizen who aspires to a religious way of life.[68] In other words, religious citizens can often claim important privileges that are denied to secular citizens that form part of Tomasi's 'A-people'.

[64] *Davis v Beacon*, 133 US 333 (1890).
[65] *Torasco v Watkins*, 367 US 488 (1961).
[66] *United States v Seeger*, 380 US 163 (1965).
[67] *Wisconsin v Yoder*, 406 US 205 (1972).
[68] Aesthetic convictions and practices are subjected to similar exclusions. Nussbaum gives the example of a fan of Mahler who would want to use drugs. While exemptions on drug laws have been granted to Native Americans on the grounds of religious freedom, an aesthetic commitment is not sufficient to claim such an exemption in American law (M Nussbaum, *Women and Human Development: The Capabilities Approach* (Cambridge, Cambridge University Press, 2000) 206–10).

Citizens who affirm a conception of religious authority with a somewhat agonic sensibility ('B-people') are also confronted with exclusionary effects when they appeal to the American right to religious freedom. For instance, religious citizens that do not identify with, or even resist, doctrinal belief-systems or institutionalised religions are confronted with substantial difficulties in obtaining privileges granted to religiosity. The benefits of this right are the easiest to obtain for members of relatively well-established religious groups. The legal and religion scholar Winnifred Sullivan has traced such an exclusionary dynamic in her analysis of the case *Warren v Boca Raton*.[69] This trial was the first in the state of Florida where the judge was asked to interpret the (Florida) RFRA, the law which Tomasi endorses to mitigate the unintended effects for religious citizens. Sullivan's detailed analysis of the way in which this law was put to use reveals that the RFRA yields new exclusions for citizens who dissent from hegemonic religious traditions.

At issue in this trial was the struggle of a group of American citizens who had decorated graves of relatives on a non-denominational cemetery with big, vertically placed handmade objects (varying from Jesus figures and stars of David to flowery crosses etc.) These decorations were too large according to the burial regulations issued by the city: though religious symbols were allowed, they were subjected to restrictions in size. The group claimed that the city placed a substantial burden on their exercising of religious rights and had thus to demonstrate that their practices could be designated as 'religious'. Sullivan's focus of the different concepts of religion that were employed in this trial shows the extent to which the legal determination of religion remains embedded in traditional power relations. Even though the act at issue employed a flexible definition of religion, the judge used his discretionary power to advance a narrow, distinctly Protestant criterion to establish the religiosity of the practices of the plaintiffs. In his opinion, customs had to reflect 'some tenet, practice or custom of a larger system of religious beliefs'.[70] A practice that did not meet this test was qualified as a 'purely personal preference' and could not claim exemption on the grounds of religious exercise. Rights were thus, in Sullivan's words, attached to 'views, not to the actions that one takes'. The judge's definition of religion also revealed a distinctly elitist understanding of religion. The plaintiffs explained the significance of their practices by reference to very local, cultural and familial circumstances: they referred mostly to the authority of family members and the specific characteristics of the deceased rather than religious leaders or textual obligations. The judge, however, qualified the grave markers as a purely personal preference: in his view, 'nowhere in the

[69] W Sullivan, *The Impossibility of Religious Freedom* (New Jersey, Princeton University Press, 2005); *Warren v Boca Raton* United States District Court for the Southern District of Florida. West Palm Beach Division. Case No 98-8054-CIV-/CIV-KLR.

[70] ibid, 97.

sacred texts, doctrines or customs of either the Jewish or Christian faith can the *principle* be found that grave markers or religious symbols should be displayed vertically rather than horizontally'.[71] Sullivan notes that by reducing the practices of the plaintiffs to one principle rather than seeing them as a complex cultural practice the judge's decision displayed a bias towards more informal or 'embodied religion, one less intellectual and doctrinal than that often expressed by religious elites'.[72]

ii. Back to Political Liberalism

My discussion of the American right to religious freedom applied some insights of Foucault's governmentality perspective: it attended to the way in which the usage of a right is embedded in a web of publicly-sanctioned significatory exclusionary regimes. This case study showed that citizens who conform to established traditions have benefitted much more from the exercise of an individual right than citizens who practice their traditions in a more agonic way. It indicates a problematic limitation of Tomasi's voluntarist ontology of public culture: his diagnoses of the usage of rights blind us to the problems that agonic citizens may encounter in the exercise of them. For example, we have seen that liberal legal regimes which enact Tomasi's suggestion for mitigating exclusionary effects, such as the RFRA, could yield new exclusions by discouraging experimentalist types of character-formation. Citizens who practice their religion with an experimental and anti-authoritarian sensibility—'B-people' that practice virtues typical for 'A-people'—are confronted with many more difficulties in exercising their religious freedom than religious citizens who tend to conform to traditional religious authorities ('C-people').[73] But, in opposition to my governmentality perspective, Tomasi's ontology of public culture has no conceptual resources with which to analyse the anti-agonic effects of this law.

Now, I want to emphasise that many aspects of this case study are not fixed or necessary attributes of liberal democracies but are open for contestation. For example, the way in which the judge uses his discretionary power, or the quality of the defence, are dependent upon contingent circumstances that can be revised and ameliorated. It is not unlikely that, say, the cultivation of a more sympathetical disposition towards listening within the judiciary might make judges more responsive to unfamiliar religious practices. Furthermore, the proliferation of critiques of current jurisprudence

[71] ibid, 98 (emphasis added).

[72] ibid, 140.

[73] Note, however, that Sullivan's analysis confirms Tomasi's point that legal regimes are biased against citizens who cannot, or do not, aspire to rationalise their customs in terms of a set of principles or a doctrine: the informal religious experiences of the plaintiffs in Sullivan's trial resemble the 'less unreflective anchors' of Tomasi's 'B-people'.

might increase the sensitivity to legal exclusions and mobilise citizens to organise against marginalisation. And, surely, such strategies can also be adopted by political liberalism: by making visible, and encouraging disputes about, the interpretations of rights, a political liberalist society could diminish the exclusion of religious citizens with a more experimental sensibility. Still, it is important that we do not overestimate the possibilities for both responsiveness, and for pluralising religious freedom, in legal cultures, including political liberalism. Due to principle of the rule of law, not even a well-ordered political liberalist regime such as that defended by Tomasi, will completely extinguish the biases against informal or experimental practices in religious freedom. As the rule of law requires citizens to support their practices with a recognised standard, this principle simply works against citizens that participate in religious practices which depart from established traditions. Seen in this light, the exercise of individual rights, such as religious freedom, will more likely stimulate citizens to consolidate traditions than to dissent from, or experiment with, them. So, *pace* Tomasi, the public legal culture of political liberalism includes an inherent bias against citizens who strive for an agonic relation with traditions.

VI. CONCLUSION

This chapter investigated whether political liberalism can plausibly arrive at an ontologically impartial social theory of rights. I focused on the social theory of Tomasi, who seeks to increase the orienting potential of political liberalism by illuminating two, presumably uncontroversial, ontological conditions of democratic politics: an ontology of tradition and an ontology of the legal dimension of political liberalist public culture. I have argued that Tomasi's attempt to avoid ontological controversies in his social theory fails. Tomasi's ontology of tradition conceptualises traditional life in terms of the enactment of narratives. I showed that this ontology was much more contentious than he suggested: it ignores the existence of conflicts and power-relations within traditions and cannot account for the struggles of agonic citizens. Tomasi's ontology of the legal political liberalist public culture treats legalistic practices as an exchange of legal claims that obtains meaning in light of political liberalist norms as well as in the various traditional self-understandings that inhabit liberal democratic regimes. I emphasised that this ontological account suffered from two blind spots. First, it does not address the effect of traditional power relations on the production of meaning in legal institutions, including the disputes that these power/knowledge relations open up. In addition, it does not confront the structural bias that effects agonic citizens in this contest with legal knowledge regimes. These ontological flaws have two problematic consequences. First, Tomasi's account of public culture does not respond to the needs for orientation of citizens who contest or struggle with traditional practices. Second, Tomasi all-too-easily assumes that political liberalist legal cultures contain an inherent bias against citizens who do not aspire to challenge traditions. A diagnosis of the social implications of rights should also take into account the fact that political liberalist legal regimes enact structural biases against agonic citizens.

I also showed how my Foucaultian ontology helps to ameliorate the blind spots in Tomas's ontology. Unlike Tomasi, Foucault's governmentality approach highlights the presence of conflict and power in traditional practices and state institutions. Further, this approach offers tools to help interpret in what way the usage of rights structurally disadvantages citizens who participate in agonic struggles. A social theory that aims to illuminate the exclusionary effects of rights in democratic regimes needs to address these effects.

Finally, I made clear that the democratic politicisation of ontology offered critical assistance in fleshing out the contentious aspects of Tomasi's ontology. I employed two strategies of the democratic politicisation of ontology: I staged a confrontation between Tomasi's ontology and Foucault's ontology of power, and challenged Tomasi's view of public culture with an American case study. These two strategies allowed me to make visible the point that Tomasi's ontology is contentious and results in a flawed interpretation of the struggles of citizens who are burdened by the effects of individual rights.

5

Transit: Renegotiating Political Liberalism and Agonic Democracy

THE PRECEDING CHAPTERS were spent on a critical comparison between political liberalism and Foucaultian insights. This undertaking demonstrated that contentious ontological ideas affect our understanding of democratic politics and, how, in turn, democratic regimes might benefit from the democratic politicisation of ontological claims. I also developed an ontology of agonic freedom and sketched some of its implications for democratic politics. We have seen that political liberalism and my account of agonic democracy concur with the view that political philosophy, public debates and individual rights can contribute to democratic life, but that we offer very dissimilar readings of these practices. Not only have I underlined the need to illuminate ontology within democratic theory and practice, I also drew attention to the role of exclusionary arbitrary power relations and the body in shaping democratic politics—two ontological constituents of political life that are missing in political liberalist readings of politics. My findings might leave one wondering whether the differences between political liberalism and the perspective developed here are insurmountable or open to negotiation. This transit reflects upon the consequences arising from the disagreements between political liberalism and my account by revisiting some of the insights of the previous chapters. With this short exposé, I end my critical comparison between political liberalism and my Foucaultian account of agonic democracy and set the stage for the last chapter in which I turn to psychoanalysis to address and amend an important drawback of the perspective of agonic democracy that I have developed so far.

We have seen that from the perspective of agonism, democratic politics denotes the enactment of disciplinary provisions that encourage people to contest, influence and pluralise power/knowledge relations on the level of local institutions and at the level of the population at large. Political philosophers can contribute to agonic democratic politics by critically investigating how hegemonic power/knowledge regimes that shape democratic politics support or hamper agonic struggles. In opposition to the political liberalist attempt to ground democracy on the 'settled' intuitions in public culture, my democratic perspective seeks to disturb these convictions by highlighting their exclusionary effects. In this way, the political philosopher tries to loosen the hold of hegemonic power/knowledge relations and aims to open up space for resistance to, and/or transfiguration of, the disciplinary effects that they effectuate in democratic cultures. Obviously, such critical interventions of political philosophers are not immune from disciplinary effects either. When challenging a particular democratic ideal, the political philosopher remains part of a controversial ontological and normative regime that both enables and constrains possibilities for thought and action. My agonic perspective does not only acknowledge its dependence upon such disciplinary regimes, but actively seeks to explicate contentious ontological and normative premises in order to enhance agonic struggles. For example, by presenting the ontological and normative contours of agonic freedom, I have tried to mobilise the democratic public on behalf of important aspects of democratic politics that political liberalism does not sufficiently attend to, such as the role of body rituals in constituting freedom, the relevance of experimenting with bodily customs and other historically transmitted forms of identification, and the need for sustaining some degree of social conflicts in democratic regimes.

My critical readings of political liberalism do not imply that I reject more typical political liberalist forms of democratic politics. For instance, we have seen that my understanding of democracy endorses individual rights—a practice which forms the heart of political liberalist democracy. I should stress, though, that political liberalism and my agonic perspective have not reached an overlapping consensus about individual rights. From my perspective, rights are important because they can open up possibilities for agonic struggles, but I consider the actual participation in such practices of contestation and experimentation just as essential to democratic regimes as the enactment of rights. This view is incompatible with the political liberalist understanding of democracy that neglects the realisation of agonic practices, or, to the extent that it would make room for such practices, will not allow them as much normative weight as it gives to rights. Furthermore, political liberalism and my account of agonic democracy disagree about the ontology of the social consequences of individual rights. I conceptualised rights as power-laden, exclusionary constructions that contain possibilities for agonic freedom but that also enact a structural disadvantage for agonic citizens. The political liberalist ontology, in contrast, focuses one-sidedly on the exclusionary implications of rights for conservative citizens while neglecting the marginalising effects of rights for citizens with more agonic concerns.

Are these disagreements so profound that political liberalism and my account of agonic democracy can never work together in democratic politics? Perhaps not. There might be possibilities for social cooperation between these two perspectives that will not be as stable as the political liberalist ideal of an overlapping consensus but that can nonetheless be made productive for democracy by means of an unstable coalition. For example, when public support for religious pluralism decreases significantly in a particular democratic regime, it is not unlikely that political liberals and agonic democrats might try to initiate an alliance to challenge laws and policies that enact a too homogeneous account of public culture.

One of the problems, however, that such a coalition would have to confront, is that political liberalism and agonic democracy have conflicting views about the kind of virtues that the participants in this coalition need in order to sort out mutual disagreements. The political liberalist conception of public reason asks citizens to exclude from the discussion ontologies that are critical of political liberalism when they reflect upon constitutional legislation, such as religious freedom. In other words, when agonic citizens deliberate with their fellow political liberalist citizens over institutional proposals for mitigating the exclusionary effects of individual rights, they cannot challenge the ontological vision that structures the political liberalist account of law. In contrast, the disciplinary virtues that I have proposed—the game of reciprocal elucidation—encourages the critical contestation of ontology, including ontological regimes that challenge political liberalism or, for that matter, agonic democracy.

Even though these conflicting accounts of democratic virtues are an obstacle for forging a coalition between political liberalism and agonic democrats, they need not necessarily undermine it. If agonic democrats and political liberals are capable of renegotiating their mutually incompatible set of political virtues, they may construe possibilities for concerted action. Agonic democrats would have to take some ontological disagreements off the table—a concession they might be prepared to make for the sake of the greater good—in order to enact important agonic struggles (such as the contestation of homogenising effects of law). Political liberals would need to open up space to experiment a little with the democratic politicisation of ontology; they might be willing to engage in such an experiment because they are mindful of the fact that 'all theories are presumably mistaken in places' and are always trying to reach a wide reflective equilibrium about competing democratic ideals.[1]

It is not unlikely that such a careful, limited exploration of ontological regimes would focus on the ontological underpinnings of a social theory of rights. Political liberals and my agonic perspective acknowledge that rights can undermine plurality; there is some agreement about the need to analyse these effects with the help of ontological premises but we are in disagreement about the ontological regime that needs to inform such an analysis. By my account, it would be deeply worrisome when the democratic public and,

[1] See ch 2 text to n 25.

for that matter, the legislator and judiciary, would adopt the communitarian ontology about the exclusionary effects of individual rights that Tomasi seems to endorse. It would blind these participants in democratic politics to agonic concerns and decrease the chances that these concerns are taken into account in the enactment of individual rights, such as religious freedom. By introducing a Foucaultian ontology into discussions about rights and by showing concrete examples of agonic conflicts within legal culture, agonic democrats would try to persuade political liberals that political liberalism is not attentive enough to the presence of power and conflicts within traditions, and the way in which legal public culture tends to disadvantage new or marginalised knowledge regimes.

Perhaps such a reciprocal elucidation of ontological regimes transfigures the ontological frame through which political liberals both see traditions and tend to interrogate individual rights. The exposure to an unfamiliar ontological regime may capture the curiosity of political liberals, evoke a sense of care for agonic experiences, and make them 'throw off familiar ways of thought and to look at the same things in a different way.'[2] But, surely, the democratic politicisation of ontology might also encourage political liberals to formulate strong objections to agonic ontology—critiques that the game of reciprocal elucidation commits us to listen to.

For example, a communitarian-inclined political liberal, such as one of Tomasi's 'C-people', could ask whether the centrality of contest within the agonic ontology of social-historical practices is not too neglectful of the need for comfort and ease that so many people seek in traditional groups. In my critique of Tomasi's appeal to communitarian ontology, I pointed out that traditions do not only open up agreeable experiences for citizens, such as the comfort of relating with others on the basis of familiarity and spontaneity, but are also constituted by ongoing power struggles. But in this challenge to the communitarian ontology of tradition, I have said nothing about the way in which my own ontology accounts for the longing of people to retreat into the comfort of familiar surroundings. In fact, it is not difficult to see that agonic democracy works against the yearning for a relatively safe environment. To begin with, agonic contests challenge the commitments that people tend to take for granted and thereby confront the participants with numerous and painful experiences of rejection, loss and failure that upset the longing for a sense of ease and comfort. Moreover, since my understanding of democracy treats all social practices as potential *loci* of agonic contests, there are no sites in a democratic regime that are completely safeguarded from critical contestation and the distressing emotional experiences that they potentially animate.

[2] For Foucault's ethical disposition of curiosity, see ch 3 text to n 102.

The tension between the longing for safety and the challenges that agonic democracy poses to this desire indicates a problematic drawback of my perspective. Even if citizens have cultivated the skills to enact agonic struggles and have obtained sufficient critical insight to determine where critiques are most needed, it will also be the case that they will come to resent agonist democratic politics because it is often such a painful and tiresome quest. And, if the emotional burdens of agonism are left unanswered, this blind spot could seriously undermine the willingness to engage in agonic politics and eventually jeopardise the viability of an agonic democratic regime. So what resources does agonic democracy have to account for and mitigate the emotional burdens of its politics? The next chapter addresses this question by turning to an ontological regime that Foucault was perhaps even more critical of than liberal social contract theory: the tradition of psychoanalysis.

6

Drained by a Democratic 'Burn-out': The Emotional Burdens of Agonic Democracy

I. INTRODUCTION

THE VISION OF democracy that I have developed so far is emotionally demanding. Agonic struggles open up possibilities for more freedom but also produce painful experiences of loss for citizens who have to accept defeat in a particular contest. The centrality of civic failure in agonic democratic regimes suggests that citizens need to be able to face the disappointments that democratic participation confronts them with. Without the capacity to endure civic defeat, citizens might lose their motivation to initiate another democratic contest, acquiesce in existing exclusions or, for that matter, lose the desire to reconnect themselves to the democratic process altogether. But how do citizens deal with civic loss on an emotional level? Which capacities help to realign citizens to democratic struggles after a defeat?

This chapter seeks to answer these questions by focusing on citizens who are most vulnerable to the experience of democratic loss: individuals who are committed to a dissenting view or practice that they try to realise in opposition to dominant truth regimes. I offer a diagnosis of the affective dynamics of civic loss and consider a possible political response that might strengthen the democratic resilience of disempowered citizens. With this account, I first of all provide the final step of my ontological account of democratic politics. In light of my commitment to the pluralisation and democratic politicisation of power relations, I need to pay attention to the emotional burdens of challenging power in my ontology. An ontological account of these burdens can help us diagnose the emotional obstacles for agonic democracy, and also stimulate reflection about the disciplinary provisions that might increase democratic resilience.

Unfortunately, the two thinkers that have played the most prominent role in this thesis—Foucault and Rawls—do not offer much assistance in developing such an account. While both thinkers are—to a greater or lesser extent—committed to a vibrant democratic regime that includes a variety of dissenting views and practices, neither of the two offers an account of the emotional conditions of democratic resilience of disempowered citizens, or even ponders the emotional burdens involved in defending or practising a dissenting standpoint.[1] It is my wager that the psychoanalytic tradition offers important resources to repair that lacuna. Not unlike Foucault, psychoanalytic thought takes notice of the fact that individuals tend to participate in their own submission.[2] Psychoanalysts, however, do not explain this point so much by focusing on social-historical power relations, but by bringing into view the workings of the unconscious: sexual instincts and infantile wishes that remain largely hidden from awareness but which, at times, enter our consciousness in the shape of dreams, fantasies and emotions.[3] This affective dimension of subjectivity, I want to suggest, is worthy of exploration when considering how individuals cope with civic disappointments: as we shall see, it may offer insight into the mechanisms that prompt individuals to acquiesce in, creatively appropriate or resist dominant truth regimes.[4]

The second aim of this chapter is to highlight, for the last time, the merits of a democratic politicisation of ontology. The articulation of psychoanalytic ontologies of subjectivity will be central to fleshing out affective aspects of subjectivity that are underexposed in the ontology that I have developed so far. However, I need also to address some of the depoliticising tendencies in the psychoanalytic tradition. To begin with, this mode of thought

[1] We have seen in ch 2 that Rawls tries to address the psychic conditions of democratic agency in terms of mutual respect. However, Rawls does not reflect on the specific emotional challenges of the democratic participation for disempowered citizens, let alone ponders the question of how to ease such burdens. Foucault mentions the empowering possibilities of insular disempowered groups who share a particular pleasure but his account does not address how such groups empower citizens emotionally to maintain or cultivate their pleasure in the face of hostile rejections. I briefly discuss Foucault's remarks below.

[2] In a very general sense, one might say that the psychoanalytic thinkers and Foucault have both made important contributions to the twentieth century displacement of the Kantian subject: like Foucault, psychoanalysts do not consider reason to be an autonomous faculty but assume that thought and moral agency are constituted by intersubjective practices that the individual cannot transcend.

[3] The term unconscious was coined by the eighteenth century German Romantic philosopher Riegel but has become practically synonymous with Freud. Freud introduced his thesis on the unconscious in 'The Interpretation of Dreams' where he analysed dreams as attempts to fulfill unconscious desires (S Freud, 'The Interpretation of Dreams' in J Strachey (ed), *The Standard Edition of the Complete Psychological Works of Sigmund Freud* Volume 5 (London, Hogarth Press and the Institute of Psycho-Analysis, 1953). In his work Freud uses the term unconscious both as an adjective—denoting all mental states that are not present in consciousness—as well as a psychic mechanism that consists of instinctually-driven fantasies, emotions, and wishes that are repressed and that can only become conscious in a distorted form. For a succinct account of Freud's usage of the phrase unconscious and other psychoanalytic terms, see, J Laplanche, JB Pontalis, *The Language of Psycho-Analysis* (New York, WW Norton & Company, Inc, 1973).

[4] *cf* J Butler, *The Psychic Life of Power: Theories in Subjection* (Stanford, Stanford University Press, 1997) 102. See also, W Brown, *Regulating Aversion: Tolerance in the Age of Identity and Empire* (New Jersey, Princeton University Press, 2006) 225.

has often and deservedly been accused of depicting psychological processes as autonomous forces that structure human subjectivity independently of social-historical practices.[5] Moreover, the emphasis in psychoanalytic theory on inner states of mind and childhood experiences may discourage one to look at other influences on our affective life, such as social movements that develop collective strategies for political resistance. This analytical focus appears to be at odds with a key feature of my agonic ethos: the assumption that the analysis of power cannot be confined to just one setting (the family), but remains a task in all domains of life. I contend that while these flaws and dangers in psychoanalytic theory warrant vigilance when using psychoanalytic concepts, they need not prompt us to reject this mode of inquiry altogether. In fact, I hope to show in this chapter that by remaining mindful of the democratic politicisation of ontology, it becomes possible to reappropriate some of the more fruitful psychoanalytic insights on behalf of the quest for agonic freedom. I will submit psychoanalytic ontologies to a democratic politicisation by means of the normative commitment to agonic freedom, Foucault's historical critique of the psychoanalytic ontology, and by recalling the ubiquity of power relations.

I start by explaining the salience of addressing the emotional burdens of democratic contest by elucidating Seneca's treatise *De tranquillitate animi* ('On the Tranquility of Mind'), an example of ancient ethical practices that Foucault concentrates on. I then turn to the psychoanalysts Sigmund Freud and Donald Winnicott to explore the emotional dynamics of civic loss and the conditions of democratic resilience. Winnicott's work, in particular, is helpful for the perspective that I am developing, because his notion of subjectivity has an agonic structure that demonstrates a strong ontological analogy to that of Foucault.[6] Like the Foucaultian account of agonic freedom that I developed in chapter three, Winnicott's theory of subjectivity suggests that the individual is structured by, yet also resistant to, social-historical discipline. Winnicott, however, is much more attentive to the affective aspects of agonic subjectivity than Foucault and thereby offers a crucial amendment to the agonic democratic ontology that I presented so far. I will arrive at Winnicott's distinct contribution to democratic agonism via a critical reading of Freud's influential theory of mourning. My critical discussion of Freud will, first of all, serve as an introduction to some of the general tenets of the psychoanalytic framework that Winnicott appropriates and, second, help us to appreciate the distinct agonic potential of Winnicott's work. The Winnicottian account of democratic resilience that I develop next focuses on three capacities: a capacity to mourn, a capacity for

[5] See, for instance, N Fraser, 'The Uses and Abuses of French Discourse Theories for Feminist Politics' (1990) 17 (2) *Boundary* 82.

[6] For the notion of ontological analogy, see ch 3, text to n 113.

dissent and a capacity to invent new techniques for interaction. After presenting these capacities, I politicise some limitations in Winnicott's ontology with the critical assistance of the work of Arlie Hochschild. Finally, I introduce the practice of emotional boundary-marking as a possibility to renew strategies for democratic resilience.

II. A DEMOCRATIC 'BURN-OUT'

In one of his lectures on Greek and Roman ethics, Foucault offers an extensive treatment of Seneca's treatise *De tranquillitate animi* ('On the Tranquility of Mind').[7] This treatise consists of an exchange between the Stoic philosopher Seneca and Serenus, a commander of Rome's police and fire brigades. Serenus is suffering from great psychic unrest. He is deeply committed to leading a life according to Stoic principles, like frugality and public activity, but at times finds himself drawn to illicit pleasures such as a luxurious residence and silent retreats into introspection. These desires upset him: even though he is still capable of controlling himself most of the time, he dislikes the fact that his daily thoughts, feelings and actions are not in line with his principles.

To ameliorate his condition, Serenus turns to his friend Seneca for advice. In his response, Seneca suggests a number of techniques that may help him achieve a more tranquil mind. For instance, Seneca recommends Serenus to increase his self-knowledge, that is, to critically examine himself so as to evaluate whether his plans and activities suit his particular character. He also praises an ascetic lifestyle and argues for the need to alternate public participation with solitude ('solitude will heal our hatred of the crowd, and the crowd will heal our hatred of solitude'). Moreover, it is important to seek out friends who calm our anxieties rather than to suffer from pain in isolation. And, not unlike contemporary stress management manuals, Seneca underlines the need to relax the mind with sufficient sleep and leisure.[8]

One might, as Foucault does, read Seneca's text as a powerful illustration of the significance of techniques for realising freedom. As argued in chapter three, Foucault turned to Greek and Roman antiquity to correct the emphasis on principles in modern day conceptions of morality. The case of Serenus

[7] M Foucault, in J Pearson (ed), *Fearless Speech* (Los Angeles, Semiotext(e), 2001). Foucault refers to L Seneca, 'On Tranquility of Mind' in *Moral Essays* Volume 2 (Cambridge, Harvard & Heineman, 1928).

[8] In his latest version of justice Rawls includes leisure-time in the list of primary goods (see J Rawls, *Justice as Fairness: A Restatement* (Cambridge, The Belknap Press of Harvard University Press, 2001) 179).

indeed suggests that rules are not adequate for living a good life: although Serenus has sufficient knowledge about the basic tenets and practical rules of his Stoic doctrine, he is still unable to align his behaviour, thoughts and feelings with these principles. This supports Foucault's point that individual autonomy is in need of specific techniques or spiritual exercises that help one to put ideals into practice, 'making them as permanent and effective as possible in our life.'[9]

There is, however, another suggestive lead in Seneca's text that is just as relevant for our modern ethical-political condition, but which Foucault's discussion of Seneca's text does not address. One of the striking features in this treatise is the relation that Seneca brings to light between civility and the affective condition of the individual or, more specifically, the dependence of the exercise of civic virtues upon the resilience of the individual citizen in the face of civic disappointment. In his letter, Serenus explains how the disappointments and frustrations of public life tempt him to turn his back on the political arena:

> I resolve to obey the commands of my teachers and plunge into the midst of public life; I resolve to try to gain office and the consulship, ... by the desire to be more serviceable and useful to my friends and relatives and all my countrymen and then to all mankind. ... And then, whenever something upsets my mind, which is unused to meeting shocks, whenever something happens that is either unworthy of me, and many such occur in the lives of all human beings, or that does not proceed very easily, or when things that are not to be accounted of great value demand much of my time, I turn back to my leisure, and just as wearied flocks too do, I quicken my pace toward home. I resolve to confine my life within its own walls: ... let my mind be fixed upon itself; let it cultivate itself, let it busy itself with nothing outside, nothing that looks towards an umpire; let it love the tranquillity that is remote from public and private concern.[10]

Seneca empathically situates the inner turmoil of his friend in an analysis of the emotional perils of civic participation. He notes that fear is a powerful obstacle to the exercise of civic duties. Citizens might easily be put off by anxiety when considering the dangers involved in confronting popular opinion in the public arena. And those that do muster enough courage to fulfil their public tasks have to reckon with the inability of realising a particular public aim, and cope with the frustration and resentment that civic disappointment may entail. Typically, citizens who suffer from civic loss tend to fall prey to two distinct, equally problematic attitudes. Some citizens become so depressed that they tend to retreat into the self when the current state of affairs in public life affords few possibilities to realise their ambition. Though Seneca acknowledges that such a turning away from public

[9] Foucault (n 7) 166.
[10] ibid, 155–56.

tasks is an understandable and even necessary reaction in order to recover from civic disappointment, often enough citizens become so entangled in a depressive web that they do not succeed in surmounting their loss, but rather, become fixated on their pain:

> From this aversion to the progress of others and despair of one's own their mind becomes incensed against Fortune, and complains of times, and retreats into corners and broods over its trouble until it becomes weary and sick of itself.[11]

Other citizens, in contrast, never seem to be depressed by painful losses and appear imperturbable in their exercise of public tasks. On closer inspection, Seneca suggests that these hyperactive citizens participate in the democratic arena without a sense of purpose, wandering around aimlessly while being at the complete disposal of external stimuli. Being distracted by every event, responding to all requests, they are so reactive that public participation will eventually exhaust them:

> They have been rushing to pay a call to someone who will not return it ... having attached themselves to some litter, have in some places even carried it. Afterwards, when they are returning home wearied to no purpose, they swear that they themselves do not know why they left home.[12]

Seneca suggests that the cultivation of a tranquil mind helps citizens to ward off both depression and exhausting hyperactivity when suffering from civic loss. In the context of civic action, such a disposition steers a middle ground between an uncompromising fixation on one's ideal and the immediate surrender of one's goal to the demands of others. Put somewhat differently, it underlines the importance of participating in civic life with a sense of purpose but also emphasises the need for flexibility in adjusting our plans if current circumstances do not allow for the realisation of our ideal.[13]

Seneca's discussion of the emotional burdens of civic participation has not lost its relevance to this very day. In fact, our large-scale, fragmented, modern pluralist democracies seem to confront citizens with even greater pressures than the small, relatively cohesive Roman city state in Seneca's time. While Serenus had to reckon with the difficult challenge of shaping his political aims in changing circumstances, he could rely on a relatively stable ontological and normative horizon in public life. The modern day citizen, however, is faced with an ongoing questioning of this horizon in the democratic arena due to the plurality of worldviews. This increases the possibility of resentment against public participation and the chances of a democratic

[11] Seneca (n 7) 219.

[12] ibid, 264–65.

[13] ibid, 229. For example, if we are disappointed because we have not been elected for a particular position, we should not obsess over our loss or completely retreat from public life, but rather look for alternative possibilities to fulfil civic tasks.

'burn-out': today, citizens need not only cope with the disappointment of being unable to realize a political goal but they must also endure the fact that many citizens do not even take for granted the shared background of their particular contributions. Moreover, in opposition to the classic era, civic participation is no longer assumed to be the quintessence of the good life. In this age, most citizens consider it just as important, or even more worthwhile, to devote their lives to family, work and leisure. So those citizens who do make an effort to exercise their democratic freedoms are no longer supported by a widespread belief that they are pursuing the ultimate human good, but will often experience doubt as to whether their energy and time are not better spent otherwise.

The emotional stress of democratic participation is especially burdensome for citizens who question the dominant truth regime in a democratic culture. We have seen that my agonic perspective attempts to make room for democratic struggles by aiming, among others, for legal responsiveness to plurality, by opening up space in democratic debates for dissenting knowledge regimes, and by cultivating the virtue of listening. These characteristics of agonic democracy do not, however, guarantee the success of citizens who struggle to enact dissenting views or practices. As we saw in chapter four, legal institutions contain a structural bias against alternative ways of life. And even if majorities make an active attempt to listen to disempowered citizens, there is obviously a likely chance that a dominant truth regime will resist all attempts of democratic politicisation; for that matter, it could rather strengthen its hegemonic position in the face of critique. In such cases, disempowered citizens are faced with the difficult challenge of maintaining their resolve in enacting agonic struggles and are, as Bert van den Brink and David Owen put it, in need of a disposition for 'civic endurance'.[14]

But how do disempowered citizens cultivate civic endurance or, as I put it, democratic resilience? What if Serenus were a woman in a patriarchal society, an immigrant in a xenophobic nation-state, a pacifist in a democracy that glorifies violence, or a practitioner of a minority religion in a secularist society? How do such citizens keep up their emotional spirits to persist in their democratic struggles rather than, say, acquiescing in majority exclusions, or turning their backs on democratic politics? Put differently, what are the conditions of possibility for developing democratic resilience?

In his reflections on gay politics, Foucault muses about the agonic potential of insular groups that are brought together by shared experiences of

[14] B van den Brink, 'Liberalism without Agreement: Political Autonomy and Agonistic Citizenship' in J Christman and J Anderson (eds), *Autonomy and the Challenges to Liberalism* (Cambridge, Cambridge University Press, 2005); R Bentley, D Owen, 'Ethical Loyalties, Civic Virtue and the Circumstances of Politics' (2001) 4 *Philosophical Explorations: An International Journal for the Philosophy of Mind and Action: Special Issue Civic Virtue and Pluralism* 223.

pleasure. Such groups could give the participants a strong impetus to enact alternative ways of life that are difficult to realise in established institutions and dominant knowledge regimes:

> A culture that invents ways of relating, types of existence, types of values, types of exchanges between individuals that are really new and are neither the same as, nor superimposed on, existing cultural forms. ... Rather than saying what we said at one time, 'Let's try to re-introduce homosexuality into the general norm of social relations,' let's say the reverse—'No! Let's escape as much as possible from the type of relations that society proposes for us and try to create in the empty space where we are new relational possibilities'.[15]

Foucault wagers that these new habits could eventually trickle down into other practices: 'gay culture will be not only a choice of homosexuals for homosexuals—it would create relations that are, at certain points, transferable to heterosexuals.'[16]

Foucault's reflections about gay politics offer a refreshing alternative to the strategies of democratic politics that I have pursued so far. It suggests that when the possibilities of articulating a critique in mainstream democratic arenas are barred, or confront disempowered citizens with too many emotional burdens, these citizens might take their refuge in the pleasures of relatively secluded groups which offer alternative opportunities to persist in agonic struggles. The pleasures of enacting new cultural forms, one might say, could contribute to the pluralisation of power relations by experimenting with, and habituating people into, new, alternative ways of life, rather than by circulating a critique of mainstream culture or a subjugated knowledge regime in democratic fora.[17] Still, I am not confident that the affirmation of pleasure suffices for enhancing democratic resilience. Citizens who adopt insular strategies can never completely isolate themselves from mainstream culture: even if one does not seek recognition in legal institutions, nor aims to participate in forums of democratic opinion-formation, various other domains in social life, such as the workplace, the media and public spaces, could give rise to various conformist demands and, indeed, pressure one into giving up one's pleasure. In fact, an alternative politics of pleasure might even become a central target of majoritarian rejections and obdurate already existing exclusions.[18] This suggests that democratic resilience is not just in need of alternative forms of pleasure but also calls

[15] M Foucault, 'The Social Triumph of the Sexual Will' in P Rabinow (ed), *Ethics: Subjectivity and Truth* (New York, The New Press, 1997) 160.

[16] ibid, 160.

[17] In ch 6 s III.F. I discuss a Catholic welfare movement that enacts a dissenting ideal by practising an alternative way of life rather than by actively interrogating institutions.

[18] *cf* Connolly's concise account of the tendency of majorities to resist alternative forms of sexual pleasure (W Connolly, *Pluralism* (Durham, Duke University Press, 2005) 127).

for empowering strategies that enable citizens to resist surrendering their pleasure when they are faced with a hostile environment. Unfortunately, Foucault's scarce intimations about insular groups do not confront the fragility of pleasure.

III. A PSYCHOANALYTIC READING OF CIVIC LOSS

I contend that the psychoanalytic tradition offers a more fruitful starting-point than Foucault's project from where to diagnose and alleviate the emotional burdens of democratic agonism. Like Foucault, the British psychoanalyst and pediatrician Winnicott emphasises the empowering potential of pleasurable forms of creative resistance when individuals are faced with demands to comply with current reality. Winnicott, however, is much more attentive than Foucault to the inherent vulnerability of pleasure. For instance, Winnicott shows how the pleasure of creative agency can become thwarted when individuals have not been taught how to endure their aggressive impulses. Before elaborating upon Winnicott's account, however, I will first address Freud's theory of mourning. Freud's account of mourning forms the basis of many post-World War II psychoanalytic reflections on coping with loss, including that of Winnicott, and is therefore a good introduction to the psychoanalytic model of development. However, we shall see that Freud's theory of mourning is deeply troublesome in light of my ideal of democratic agonism: it rests on a punitive model of authority that leaves little room for creative resistance. Winnicott redresses this problematic aspect in Freud's work and paves the way for a much more agonic account of coping with civic loss. Yet, I need to say from the outset, however, that while my reading of civic loss is mostly indebted to Winnicott, I part ways with Winnicott's claim that the family is the most important site for enacting democratic resilience. *Pace* Winnicott, I bring into view the influential effects of emotional forms of authority that are transmitted by social movements. The sociologist Arlie Hochschild will serve as my accomplice in this move in the next section.

A. Freud on Mourning and Omnipotence

Seneca's reflections on the tendency of disappointed citizens to fall prey to depression or hyper-activity bear some resemblance to 'melancholia' and 'mania'—the two affective states that Freud discusses in his early essay on mourning, 'Mourning and Melancholia'. In this essay, Freud offers a somewhat broader definition of mourning than its everyday meaning of responding to the loss of a loved person (bereavement). Mourning does not only occur when one loses a person but also denotes our reaction to the loss of any object that we have loved, including an abstraction, such as a political ideal.[19] In a general sense, a normal mourning process is characterised by a painful, depressive mood in which the mourner loses his interest in the world except for activities that are associated with the lost object. Some people, however, do not only react to loss with a disinterest in the world but seem to extend their dismissive attitude towards themselves. Freud characterises this state as 'melancholia', a mood in which the individual suffers from profound feelings of inferiority, believes himself unworthy of love, anticipates punishment, and expects to be excluded by others: 'In mourning it is the world which has become poor and empty; in melancholia it is the ego itself.'[20] This lack of self-esteem is accompanied by a rigid and fixated attachment to the lost object; in opposition to the regular mourner, the melancholic seems to be incapable of redirecting his energies to another, more realistic, attachment. The lost object lives on as an intrinsic part of his identity, the melancholic has 'incorporated this object into himself'.[21]

In some cases, melancholia manifests itself in terms of 'mania', a response which appears in many ways to be the opposite of melancholia. Instead of drowning in a loss, the manic does not seem to be affected by his loss at all, suffers neither from a sense of inferiority nor a lack of interest in the world, but idealises himself or others and appears to be deeply engaged in the world. For example, when a manic citizen is disappointed by the lack of transparency in representative democratic institutions, he will frantically commit himself to any new political movement that promises to heal the faults of the system. The melancholic, in contrast, will much rather turn away from these institutions under the conviction that his vote will not make any difference in this 'corrupted' system whatsoever.[22] From a psychoanalytic point of view, however, the manic response is simply a mirror of, and defence mechanism against, melancholia: the incapability of processing a loss leads to the denial of loss and when the manic can no longer repress the experience of loss and realises the inherent imperfections of democratic institutions, he will suffer from the same painful sense of inferiority and paralytic fixation typical of the melancholic.

Freud initially thought that melancholia was deeply pathological and not necessarily the destiny of every mourner. In his definitive account of

[19] S Freud, 'Mourning and Melancholia' in J Strachey (ed), *The Standard Edition of the Complete Psychological Works of Sigmund Freud* Volume 14 (London, The Hogarth Press and the Institute of Psycho-Analysis, 1961) 243.

[20] ibid, 246.

[21] ibid, 249.

[22] This example is mine, but it seems to be in line with Freud's suggestion that the loss of political ideals (such as, in this example, the aspiration for transparent democratic institutions) may lead to melancholia or mania.

mourning, though, he argued that the melancholic incorporation of lost objects—and its accompanying self-loathing—was a normal and essential feature of the mourning process.[23] To account for the punitive fear associated with mourning Freud developed the idea of the so-called Oedipal conflict: an inter-generational struggle during which young children (between three and five years old) are faced with the inevitable loss of omnipotent fantasies.

In the psychoanalytic development model, the infant initially relates to the world in a narcissistic manner. This entails that he does not experience boundaries between himself and others, but believes that the outside world—such as his caretaker—is an extension of his own wishes and can be subjected to his control. Most psychoanalysts believe that narcissism is an essentially normal feature of human beings.[24] Up to a degree, we are attracted to another person or ideal because we see a part of ourselves, or an idealised version of ourselves, in the other.[25] But, while narcissism is crucial in forming attachments, it is just as crucial that individuals learn to cope with the frustration of omnipotent desires. Someone who cannot differentiate between himself and the external world will lash out towards anyone who defies his own wishes and has not developed the basic ethical capacity to take into account the interests of others.

Freud treated the Oedipal stage as the key experience in mourning the loss of omnipotence. During this phase the child has to come to terms with the fact that he cannot forge an exclusive attachment to his mother and accept that there is a third person, his father, who is his mother's primary love object. The realisation that he has to give up the desire to be at the centre of his mother's universe confronts the child with a difficult conflict. On the

[23] The experiences of World War I and the death of his daughter had made him realise that his initial distinction between regular mourning and melancholia did not sufficiently capture the ongoing pain and self-loathing that loss could invoke (T Clewell, 'Mourning beyond Melancholia: Freud's Psychoanalysis of Loss' (2004) 52 *Journal of the American Psychoanalytic Association* 43). Freud presents his definite account of mourning and subjectivity in general in 'Ego and Id'. Here Freud assumes that the psychic structure is constituted by three agencies: 'Id', the 'ego' and the 'super-ego'. Basically, the 'Id' denotes the sexual instincts, the 'super-ego' refers to our conscience or censor and the 'ego' serves as the mediator between the Id and the super-ego. While the contents of the Id are unconscious, the ego and the super-ego can also work unconsciously (S Freud, 'The Ego and the Id' in J Strachey (ed), *The Standard Edition of the Complete Psychological Works of Sigmund Freud* Volume 19 (London, The Hogarth Press and the Institute of Psycho-Analysis, 1974).

[24] S Freud, 'Narcissism: An Introduction' in Strachey (ed) (n 19) 74. For Winnicott's affirmation of narcissism, see ch 6 s II.D.

[25] For example, Freud says that it is our tendency to 'narcissistic self-complacency' that explains why groups often select a leader who seems to magnify the characteristics that the members admire or wish to realise in themselves (S Freud, 'Group Psychology and the Analysis of the Ego' in J Strachey (ed), *The Standard Edition of the Complete Psychological Works of Sigmund Freud* (paperback) (New York, WW Norton & Company, 1959) 79).

one hand, he experiences profound aggressive feelings towards his father: 'a wish to get rid of the father in order to take his place with his mother.'[26] But, on the other hand, he fears that the father will punish him for this desire, and this feeling is so frightening for the child that he refrains from actually attempting to carry out his wish. The Oedipus complex is solved when the child replaces the desire for the mother by an identification with the powerful father. From this point on, the child tries to live according to his father's prohibition rather than to pursue his omnipotent desire for the mother. A crucial step in giving up this fantasy is the establishment of the 'super-ego' or conscience. This censuring part of the psyche induces feelings of guilt whenever the child is tempted to transgress paternal norms.

B. Freud's Oedipus Complex and Agonic Democracy

Freud regards the introjection of patriarchal authority during the Oedipal stage to be the 'most important' method that human civilisation can rely on to pacify aggression.[27] It is not difficult to see why. A successful resolution of the Oedipal complex allows the child to face reality without being devastated by the loss of an omnipotent fantasy. Though he has to accept that he cannot control the world, the child does not become completely helpless but is ethically empowered: he becomes capable of controlling himself and learns to adjust his own wishes by taking into account the interests of others. In this way, one might say that the Oedipal resolution provides the psychic condition of possibility for individual autonomy and responsibility.[28] It enables the individual to experience a norm or ideal as an intrinsic part of himself (as a so-called 'ego-ideal'), and makes it possible to hold oneself accountable whenever one fails to realise these ethical standards. But how fruitful is the Oedipal resolution in light of our ideal of agonic democracy? Or, to be more precise, to what extent does it benefit disempowered citizens who are confronted with civic loss to persist in questioning authority or to look for creative solutions that may help them to perpetuate their struggles?

[26] Freud, 'The Ego' 32.

[27] S Freud, 'Civilization and Its Discontents' in J Strachey (ed), *The Standard Edition of the Complete Psychological Works of Sigmund Freud* (paperback) (New York, WW Norton & Company, 1961) 37.

[28] Freud's autonomy should not be mistaken for the Kantian notion but remains intersubjective: its condition of possibility is identification with the paternal other, not a purely autonomous reason.

Freud makes clear that the Oedipal stage structures our relation to external authorities in later life:

> As the child grows up, the role of the father is carried on by teachers and others in authority; their injunctions and prohibitions remain powerful in the ego ideal and continue, in the form of conscience, to exercise the moral censorship.[29]

This suggests that whenever a citizen senses a conflict between his own wishes and hegemonic norms within a democratic regime, he will to some extent replicate the pattern that helped the child to overcome his murderous hostility towards the father. He will be tempted to transform the aggression towards, and fear of, authority into an incorporation and idealisation of authority, and develop a desire to acquiesce in current power relations. Seen in this light, the establishment of the super-ego appears to militate against opening up space for the ongoing critique of, and creative experiments with, power that we considered crucial to democratic politics.

The cost of the Oedipal structure for democratic agency also becomes apparent when we take into account that the super-ego announces itself in the psychic life of the individual by aggressive and unconditional commands. In each instance that the individual obeys current power relations, the super-ego will intensify his aggressive hold on the subject: 'The effect of instinctual renunciation on the conscience then is that every piece of aggression whose satisfaction the subject gives up is taken over by the super-ego and increases the latter's aggressiveness (against the ego).'[30]

Furthermore, Freud emphasises that the super-ego governs the individual through an unconditional voice: the super-ego expresses itself in absolute terms, 'in the form of a categorical imperative.'[31] This suggests that the individual will most likely experience the power relations that he identifies with as harsh and non-negotiable standards. Even if a hegemonic norm or practice in democratic regimes opens up agonic possibilities for critique or compromise, the individual in the Oedipal stage will prima facie envision these power relations in terms of domination, that is, as standards that do not allow for creative adjustments or compromise.[32]

[29] Freud (n 23) 37. *cf* 'the differentiation of the super-ego from the ego is no matter of chance; ... indeed, by giving permanent expression to the influence of the parents it perpetuates the existence of factors to which it owes its origin.' (ibid, 35); 'Although it is accessible to later influences, it nevertheless preserves throughout life the character given to it by its derivation from the father-complex—namely, the capacity to stand apart from the ego and master it' (ibid, 48).

[30] ibid.

[31] ibid, 35. This is a direct reference to Kant, for as Freud explains elsewhere 'Kant's Categorical Imperative is thus the direct heir of the Oedipus complex' (S Freud, 'Economic Problem in Masochism' in Strachey (ed) (n 23) 167).

[32] For the distinction between agonism and domination, see ch 3 text to n 98.

Finally, the anti-agonic effects of the Oedipal stage emerge from the longing for suffering that the Oedipal stage may bring about. Most individuals do not completely succeed in overcoming the Oedipus complex and experience profound guilt feelings when their prohibited desires announce themselves. In many cases, however, the repression of these desires does not so much manifest itself in terms of guilt or fear of transgressing norms, but lives on as a need for punishment. Freud qualified this affective condition as 'moral masochism' or the attachment to suffering itself.[33] He wagered that by seeking out pain and humiliation, the individual unconsciously tries to satisfy his interdicted love.

Freud mainly discussed moral masochism in the context of his psychoanalytic practice: it helped him to understand the puzzling experience that some patients seem to be so attached to a condition of illness that they can only be cured of their particular disease when they encounter another unfortunate circumstance, such as an unhappy marriage or economic hardship.[34] The thesis of moral masochism might, however, also help us understand a difficult obstacle that disempowered citizens may encounter when they are confronted with civic loss. In her suggestive reading of Freud, Wendy Brown mobilises Freud's insights on the desire for punishment to account for the peculiar longing for domination in democratic practice.[35] Brown observes that many citizens tend to fall prey to the condition of 'victimization': they either insist on claiming a status as victim or appear unable to give up an excluded position.[36] In the case of disempowered citizens, this attachment to victimhood can manifest itself by an active searching for narratives, gestures, statements or acts that confirm their status as underdogs. As Brown notes, the eagerness with which incidents of sexual harassment or racial violence are sometimes embraced and reported brings to mind the hyperconscious focus on potential insults from authority figures that Freud considered typical for moral masochism:

> People who harbour fantasies of this kind develop a special sensitiveness and irritability towards anyone whom they can put among the class of fathers. They allow themselves to be easily offended by a person of this kind … I should not be

[33] Freud (n 31) 165. Freud already discerned this tendency in his early essay on mourning when he observed that melancholics often take a particular enjoyment in communicating their pain: '[T]he melancholic does not behave in quite the same way as a person who is crushed by remorse and self-reproach in a normal fashion. … One might emphasize the presence in him of an almost opposite trait of insistent communicativeness which finds satisfaction in self-exposure' (Freud (n 19) 247).

[34] Typically, these patients also tend to reject any suggestion on the part of the therapist that their condition is improving.

[35] W Brown, *Politics out of History* (New Jersey, Princeton University Press, 2001).

[36] ibid, 54.

> surprised if it were one day possible to prove that the same fantasy is the basis of the delusional litigiousness of paranoia.[37]

Now, at first one might say that moral masochism harbours a certain readiness for critique and action that is productive for democratic agonism. For instance, a heightened awareness of dominating effects could be made useful as a kind of necessary distrust that is needed when we check upon, or participate in, powerful institutions.[38] The problem, however, is that the moral masochist is deeply incapable of relinquishing his lamentable, excluded position and will, in fact, do whatever he can to perpetuate his exclusion. As Freud puts it:

> In order to provoke punishment from this later representative of the parents, the masochist must do what is inexpedient, must act against his own interests, must ruin the prospects which open out to him in the real world and must, perhaps, destroy his own real existence.[39]

In the context of democratic politics, I want to suggest that such an 'acting against one's own interests' can manifest itself by a deep awareness of the political avenues that are closed to someone, but that produce a blindness for possibilities that do occur. For instance, a citizen might utter a much-needed critique of sexist practices but fail to see opportunities for dissenting acts or alternative cultural forms that do exist and that may help to mitigate, or even displace, persistent exclusions. Or, more abstractly, a moral masochist will insist on looking at the faults and exclusions of prestigious democratic modes of conflict-regulation, such as law and democratic debate, while resisting any attempt to think of ways to ameliorate these defective institutions or, for that matter, to think of better alternatives. Put somewhat differently, the critical watchfulness, or readiness for action, of the moral masochist is *static* rather than *creative*: it looks for a confirmation of the status quo, is committed to a perpetual re-injury and is incapable of using the capacity for critique in the service of a cautious transformation of power relations.[40]

[37] S Freud, 'A Child is Being Beaten': A Contribution to the Study of the Origin of Sexual Perversions' in P Rieff (ed), *Sexuality and the Psychology of Love* (New York, Collier Books, 1963). *cf* Brown (n 35) 58.

[38] For the fear of authority as an important attitude in democratic regimes, see B Honig, *Democracy and the Foreigner* (New Jersey, Princeton University Press, 2003) 120.

[39] Freud (n 31) 169–70.

[40] The academic version of moral masochism might be a strong resistance towards reappropriating, or even reading, thinkers who are associated with faulty regimes, such as Carl Schmitt. Or, the tendency to construct a straw man of thinkers representative of defective regimes such as liberalism, as is often done with Rawls.

C. A Historical Ontology of the Oedipus Complex

Freud's mourning theory makes us mindful of the fact that the implementation and contestation of authority is structured by unconscious desires and childhood fantasies. To this extent, his account surely offers an important corrective to the Foucaultian ontology that I have developed so far. For instance, the insight that many individuals become emotionally invested in punishment brings out the point that subjects do not just repeat submissive acts out of habit, as Foucault's thesis on discipline seems to suggest, but enact power relations because they strongly wish to be punished in virtue of an unconscious desire for parental authority. Meanwhile, we have also seen that Freud's account of the Oedipal resolution appears to be at odds with the ideal of agonic democracy, that is, the aspiration to enact creative and experimental struggles in the face of power. Freud's idea of ethical agency centres on a strong, punitive identification with authority: in the face of loss, we blame ourselves for not living up to authoritative norms and, in the case of masochism, manifest our love of the status quo by seeking out, or even stimulating, dominating effects. But is this reification of authority the only way to overcome a violent release of omnipotent rage? Or are there other—more agonic—ways to mourn the loss of deeply held attachments? Put somewhat differently, how plausible is Freud's account of the Oedipus complex?

Freud himself was generally sombre about the possibilities civilisation possessed to weaken the Oedipal circle of self-blame. He incidentally suggested that cultural norms should allow for a limited release of instincts in order to mitigate the repetitive, reinforcing effects of the super-ego.[41] Still, he did not question the Oedipal resolution as such, but was convinced that this coping strategy was civilisation's most superior access to moral conduct and even attributed to it a universal ontological standing.[42] Foucault has warned us, however, that we should not take Freud's theory of familial arrangements for granted. For instance, in *History of Sexuality 1*, he points out that the central role of the father in Freud's account is in fact a deeply parochial norm indebted to the idealisation of patriarchal authority in the

[41] For instance, Freud suggested that flirting could mitigate the chances of infidelity.

[42] Importantly, Freud did not argue that the Oedipus complex was tantamount to an a-historical, transcendental limit but conceded that the Oedipal resolution was premised upon a distinctly social-historical custom, that is, the tendency of human beings to live together in a family: '*So long as the community assumes no other form than that of the family*, the conflict is bound to express itself in the Oedipus complex, to establish the conscience and to create the first sense of guilt.' (emphasis added). Yet, as we can see in his allusion to 'the' family, Freud did seem to suggest that the traditional nuclear family—consisting of a father, mother and their offspring—was an evident, universal custom for raising children that constituted the conditions of possibility of communal life. See, Freud (n 27) 79.

bourgeois family.[43] He also exposes some of the exclusionary effects of this local convention, showing how its marginalising tendencies reached much further than the bourgeois context in which this norm emerged. During the emergence and development of psychoanalysis, European states systematically started to displace children from poor families for fear of incest. It was believed that the miserable housing, and what were seen as primitive customs in the lower classes, would increase the chances of child abuse. Foucault points out that the Oedipal complex added credibility to this campaign: its assumption that incestuous desires are an ontological inclination of young children heightened the suspicions that child abuse would occur under unfit circumstances.

Foucault's historical critique of Freud's Oedipal resolution is well-made and, I should stress, has not lost its relevance today. Even now, some psychoanalytic thinkers are still committed to Freud's patriarchal idea of the family and mobilise this account to argue against dissenting practices, such as gay marriage.[44] I do not agree, however, with the implications that Foucault drew from his critique of Freud. For Foucault, Freud's tendency to universalise parochial claims about the family and its depoliticising effects were important reasons to reject psychoanalytic modes of inquiry altogether.[45] In my view, such a radical renunciation of the psychoanalytic tradition dismisses the critical developments that this tradition has made since Freud. For instance, various post-World War II psychoanalytic thinkers have come to reject the depiction of the Oedipal stage as the culmination of moral development. By identifying possibilities for individual empowerment in the pre-Oedipal relation between mother and child, they have displaced the privileged role of the father in Freud's account.[46] Moreover, rather

[43] Foucault, M, *The History of Sexuality, Volume 1: An Introduction* (New York, Random House, 1978) 129–30.

[44] For example, the influential French psychoanalyst Jacques-Alain Miller made extensive use of neo-Freudian psychoanalytic views on sexual difference in his arguments against gay marriage. Judith Butler discusses Miller's argument and other psychoanalytic objections against gay marriage in J Butler, E Laclau, S Zizek, *Contingencies, Hegemony, Universality: Contemporary Dialogues on the Left* (London, Verso, 2000) 144–47.

[45] For a good overview of Foucault's shifting positions with regard to Freud and a psychoanalytic and philosophical critique of his eventual rejection of Freud, see J Whitebrook, 'Freud, Foucault and "the Dialogue with Unreason"' (1999) 25 *Philosophy & Social Criticism* 29. Jacques Derrida offers an interesting reading of Foucault's ambiguity vis-a-vis Freud, comparing it to a ritualist peek-a-boo game that children play to master separation anxiety (J Derrida, '"To Do Justice to Freud": the History of Madness in the Age of Psychoanalysis' (1994) 20 *Critical Inquiry* 227).

[46] For instance, the feminist psychoanalyst Jessica Benjamin has highlighted how much the Oedipal resolution is premised upon a classic patriarchal distinction between the 'worldly realism' of men vis-a-vis the 'naive imagination' of women (J Benjamin, *The Bonds of Love: Psychoanalysis, Feminism, and the Problem of Domination* (New York, Pantheon, 1988) 147). Benjamin substantiates Freud's indebtedness to this hierarchy by alerting us to his insistence on the need for fatherly intervention to become morally autonomous. In Freud's view, it is only

than seeing the capacity (or desire) for self-punishment as the primary psychic condition of possibility for individual autonomy, neo-Freudian analysts have increasingly attended to the capacity for creative experiments as a key element in giving up fantasies of omnipotence. This shift, I contend, offers fruitful insights that can be made useful for an agonic theory of democratic resilience. The work of Donald Winnicott is a case in point.

D. Winnicott's Agonic Coping Strategy in the Face of Loss

Winnicott's contributions to psychoanalytic thought originate from a very different social world than do Freud's reflections. Whereas the latter offers a traditional bourgeois upper-middle class view of the world, the first bears the imprint of the progressive, more non-conformist spirit of the post-World War II era. Unlike Freud, Winnicott does not claim that we have to surrender our illusions and conform to social authority, but emphasises that we can make creative use of illusions that can help us to resist social authority. For sure, Winnicott agrees with Freud that the struggle with omnipotent fantasies is an ongoing task for human beings. His approach also emphasises that the confrontation with reality goes hand in hand with strong destructive impulses. But, in opposition to Freud, Winnicott does not argue that such hostility can only be pacified through an idealisation of authority or the desire for self-punishment. For Winnicott, narcissistic rage can be mitigated by a joyful discovery of creative agency, including the possibility of transforming current social authority and its predominant rules.

At the heart of Winnicott's ontology is the idea that human existence is animated by spontaneous, impulsive forces or 'primary aggression' that stem from an innate bodily propensity to motility.[47] In opposition to the desire to merge with the other (which is satisfied by the symbiosis with the caretaker), primary aggression searches for opposition: it looks for an object 'to push against.'[48] This ontology of spontaneous bodily forces bears some resemblance to the Nietzschean life-affirming energies that constitute Foucault's account of the subject. And, like Foucault, Winnicott underlines

when the child succeeds to internalise the prohibition of the *father* that he becomes capable of giving up omnipotent fantasies and becomes autonomous. He could not envision an important role for the mother in teaching the child to accept the difference between our desires and the external world. In fact, Freud tended to depict the pre-Oedipal bond between mother and child as primarily narcissist: a relation that amounted to an undifferentiated 'oceanic feeling', an experience that Freud admitted he had much 'difficulty' relating to.

[47] What Winnicott initially called 'primary aggression', he later referred to as 'aggressive impulse' or 'life force'.

[48] D Winnicott, 'Aggression in Relation to Emotional Development' in *Through Paediatrics to Psycho-Analysis* (London, The Hogarth Press and the Institute of Psycho-Analysis, 1975) 212.

that human beings need social practices to make constructive use of this impulse. That is, although aggression emerges spontaneously, Winnicott assumes that its manner of operation is crucially dependent upon cognitive abilities (such as consciousness, reason and the imagination) as well as social contexts. From birth onwards, aggression interacts with the 'psyche': the capacity to imagine the aliveness of the body and its relation with the environment.[49] While the psyche initially only allows for omnipotent fantasies and awareness of satisfaction or need, it gradually becomes capable of reasoning and developing interpretations about one's aggressive impulses. In turn, the interplay between psyche and aggression is crucially shaped by the 'holding environment': a social context that, at first, is constituted by parental care and, later on, extended by other social-cultural settings such as groups and politics.[50] If the environmental conditions are right, Winnicott suggests, the aggressive impulses can be cultivated on behalf of play, that is, the experimental revision of reality in light of a dream of fantasy.

Winnicott understands play as an 'intermediate area of experiencing' where fantasy and reality are linked but not conflated.[51] In play, the subject is capable of distinguishing between fantasy and reality and realises that the environment does not fulfil her wish for complete (omnipotent) control. The playing subject does not, however, comply with the current terms and manifestations of reality but tries to appropriate these worldly conditions in light of her fantasies. Play is thus situated in between subjectivity and objectivity, internal and external, fantasy and reality, yearnings for complete control over the world and acquiescing with the actual possibilities of this world.

The subject develops a capacity for play during the first months of early childhood when, after the initial symbiotic state, the infant gradually separates from the caretaker. Winnicott envisions the symbiotic state as essentially creative: the infant hallucinates that the breast which feeds her is her own creation and available at will. This stage of 'primary creativity' is not similar to play, however, because the infant cannot yet acknowledge that reality (the breast of the caretaker) is distinct from herself. The transition from 'primary creativity' to play takes place through an agonistic confrontation between the infant's aggression and the caretaker. At this point of development, the infant's aggression is inherently ruthless: it bites and squeezes the caretaker without concern for the results of its actions. The caretaker needs to 'survive' these destructive attacks:[52] she should neither retaliate

[49] D Winnicott, 'Mind and Its Relation to the Psyche-Soma' in *Through Paediatrics to Psycho-Analysis*, ibid 244.

[50] D Winnicott, 'The Theory of the Parent-Infant Relationship' in *The Maturational Processes and the Facilitating Environment* (London, Karnac Books, 1990) 47.

[51] D Winnicott, 'Transitional Objects and Transitional Phenomena' in *Playing and Reality* (London, Routledge, 2005) 3.

[52] D Winnicott, 'The Use of an Object and Relating through Identifications' in *Playing and Reality*, ibid 120.

the aggression with rejection or punishment nor smother the infant with so much comfort that the infant can no longer feel the 'zest for life' that the aggressive search for opposition provides.[53] When the caretaker succeeds in this task, the infant begins to experience reality as something that is not identical or susceptible to the control of her destructive behaviour.

From here on, the infant learns to distinguish fantasy and reality and begins to manage the anxiety that arises from being separate yet dependent upon the caretaker. To this end, it develops cognitive abilities, such as the potential to interpret the changes in the environment as dangerous or benign and the capacity to form beliefs about the reliability of the caretaker. But along with intellectualising her environment, the infant also soothes herself by actively seeking to transform the environment through playful acts. At first, play emerges through attachments to a 'transitional object': a doll or blanket that is experimentally altered (squeezed, bitten) in the light of fantasies. This embryonic form of play develops into more constructive forms of play during the 'stage of concern': a stage wherein the infant's affective life is enriched but also complicated by an ambivalent mixture of feelings. On the one hand, she begins to feel grief and guilt for the ruthless effects of her aggression upon the caretaker and this allows her to take responsibility for aggression.[54] But, on the other, she also starts to experience more reactive forms of aggression, such as anger and hatred. As in the earlier stage, the caretaker needs to remain resilient when confronted with the infant's outbursts so that the infant learns that the turmoil of her inner world need not lead to the collapse of the outer world. Meanwhile, the caretaker needs also to nourish the infant's joy in play. By receiving the infant's attempts to repair the (imaginatively) broken social ties, the infant develops 'a personal urge to give and to construct and to mend.'[55] At this point the infant also develops the capacity to use words. This allows the caretaker to expand the holding environment (that so far primarily consisted of bodily care such as feeding and physical holding) with verbal techniques such as exchanging interpretations about feelings. Eventually, these achievements evolve into the ability to participate in more mature forms of play: the 'transitional phenomena',[56]

[53] For instance, the infant might lose the 'zest for life' when the caretaker offers food before receiving the infant's signal. In such a case, the infant cannot sufficiently discharge aggression in the feeding process. D Winnicott, 'The Depressive Position in Normal Emotional Development' in *Through Paediatrics to Psycho-Analysis* (n 48) 268.

[54] Winnicott locates the development of a capacity for guilt prior to Freud's Oedipal stage, that is, in the second half of the first year. Like Freud, Winnicott links the capacity for guilt to the possibility of internalising existing social roles (such as pretending to nurse a baby or cooking a meal). But, in comparison to Freud, Winnicott puts more emphasis on the joy of contributing to social ties rather than the fear of punishment (Winnicott (n 48) 207).

[55] ibid, 206.

[56] D Winnicott, 'The Concept of a Healthy Individual' in *Home Is Where We Start From* (London, Penguin Books, 1990) 36.

such as art, religion, humour, philosophy, groups and political participation (the 'maintaining and rebuilding of the political structure').[57]

Winnicott is thus in agreement with Freud that the child's confrontation with reality is in need of parental supervision. Winnicott's caretaker, however, is much less punitive and fear-provoking than the intimidating father-figure in Freud's account. For instance, Winnicott highlights the role of parents in enabling the infant to experience her encounter with external reality as an opportunity for joyful play. Moreover, Winnicott puts more emphasis than Freud does on the need for individuals to remain in touch with their aggressive impulses in the face of social authority. For Winnicott, individual freedom, or 'free-hearted living', demands that we learn to keep stock of aggression rather than to succumb to the fear of punishment or, for that matter, to anticipate immediate satisfaction. In short, seen from the perspective of agonic democracy, Winnicott offers a much more fruitful strategy for coping with loss than Freud does. He suggests that coping with loss entails possibilities for a creative rather than a prima facie compliant attitude vis-a-vis social norms. Along with the capacity to conform to social norms, individuals can also, from an early age on, be taught to cultivate their aggressive potential on behalf of a playful transformation of social pressure.

E. Winnicott and Democratic Resilience

How might Winnicott's account be made useful for a theory of democratic resilience? What resources does Winnicott provide to think of ways that may enhance the potential of disempowered individuals facing civic loss? For Winnicott, the achievement of play, and the management of aggression that supports it, is an ongoing accomplishment that is 'never fully established.'[58] Throughout adult life, the subject is confronted with the challenge of relating the imagination to external reality: accepting, on the one hand, that there exists a gap between one's fantasies and current norms, demands or possibilities and, on the other hand, bridging this tension through play. This challenge implies that the subject has to cope with circumstances that hamper one's playful activities. When environments fail to accommodate or adequately hold playful interventions the subject needs to be able to search for or, better perhaps, *create* alternative conditions favourable to play. For my purpose of developing a theory of democratic resilience, I reconstruct three capacities that are central in the Winnicottian quest for play in the

[57] D Winnicott, 'Cure' in *Home Is Where We Start From*, ibid 119.

[58] D Winnicott, 'The Capacity for Concern' in *The Maturational Processes and the Facilitating Environment* (n 50) 74.

face of adversity and cite examples from democratic life to show how these capacities resonate with features of struggles of disempowered citizens

i. Mourning

For a start, the subject needs to develop a capacity for mourning to rearrange his primary aggression after loss. When a playful appropriation of reality is unsuccessful, primary aggression searches for another, more feasible, object. This search is characterised by a stage of mourning or a depressed mood that evokes feelings of sadness and self-loathing which, like a 'fog over the city', deaden one's sense of aliveness.[59] Although the ending of a depression cannot be enforced, Winnicott argues that an adequate holding environment can mitigate these painful feelings. Such an environment offers the support of 'memories of good experiences and of loved objects' which help the subject to lessen the hatred he feels toward the lost object.[60] Also, it might make available 'an external bad phenomenon' upon which the subject can project some of the self-loathing in order to relieve inner tension. And, finally, it could enact possibilities for play to cope with the strains of mourning:

> For instance, one is at a music hall and on to the stage come the dancers, trained to liveliness ... Might it not be that the main point of the performance is a denial of deadness, a defense against depressive 'death inside' ideas ...?[61]

The exercise of playful acts is thus not only an end-state of the mourning process but also an important technique that facilitates mourning: by engaging in play, the mourning subject cultivates a sense of aliveness that can mitigate the painful feeling of internal emptiness typical for the mourning stage. One way in which Winnicott's account of mourning can be extended for thinking about the resilience of disempowered citizens is suggested by David Eng and Shinhee Han's work on mourning patterns among Asian Americans.[62] Drawing on Winnicott, among others, Eng and Han see in Asian American studies programmes a promising holding environment for Asian Americans that could displace the pathological mourning habits cultivated in the mainstream practice of 'psychic citizenship' for Asian Americans. The hegemonic model of citizenship typically represents Asian Americans as such an economically successful and self-reliant 'model minority' that it leaves little room for Asian Americans to address and mourn their structural exclusions in cultural and political life. Negative feelings resulting from inequalities

[59] D Winnicott, 'The Value of Depression' in *Home Is Where We Start From* (n 56) 75.
[60] Winnicott (n 53) 275.
[61] D Winnicott, 'The Manic Defense' in *Through Paediatrics to Psycho-Analysis* (n 48) 131.
[62] D Eng and S Han, 'A Dialogue on Racial Melancholia' in D Eng and D Kazanjian (eds), *Loss: The Politics of Mourning* (Berkeley, University of California Press, 2003) 343–71.

are thus dealt with intrasubjectively and attributed to a failure of the individual self rather than worked through in concert with others and related to exclusions in mainstream society. These pathological mourning habits, Eng and Han argue, might be one of the reasons why depression and suicide have been rising so rapidly among Asian American students. In contrast, the recent establishment of Asian American studies programmes helps to establish communities for Asian American students wherein sadness and hatred about structural inequalities can be acknowledged and worked through collectively. Moreover, by allowing for 'the creation of new representations of Asian Americans',[63] the programmes offer possibilities for play that alleviate the suffering resulting from structural exclusions while also establishing a healthier object for putting to use primary aggression than the homogeneous representations in mainstream culture. Eng and Shan thus offer a compelling example of how Winnicott's account of mourning can be put to use for the resilience of disempowered citizens.[64] Without an adequate holding environment, disempowered citizens could remain enclosed in grief, focusing on their own inferiority rather than attempting to create new possibilities for politicising exclusions. The enactment of an alternative mourning environment which opens up possibilities for support, play and opportunities for releasing depressive feelings is a powerful strategy to break this circle and might help to build up the capacity for democratic resilience in the face of an unresponsive society.

ii. Dissidence

Winnicott's approach also highlights that resilience is dependent on a capacity for dissidence. Winnicott treats some degree of conformism to reality—or, as he puts it, 'the ability to compromise'—as a sign of emotional maturity. For instance, adjusting to predominant codes of civility is often central to gaining a place in the social practice to which the subject seeks to contribute. However, when such a compromise is no longer favourable to play, the subject needs to be able to change course and resist pressures to conform: 'In health, the compromise ceases to become allowable when the issues become crucial'.[65]

The capacity for dissent can be developed by holding on to anger. When experiencing anger, the subject feels she has become 'filled' up by

[63] ibid, 367.

[64] This section focuses on the analogies between Winnicott's theory of resilience and the case study of Eng and Han. Yet, as I point out in the next section, their case study (and the other examples that I cite) also challenges some core assumptions in Winnicott's account.

[65] D Winnicott, 'Ego Distortion in Terms of True and False Self' in *The Maturational Process and the Facilitating Environment* (n 50) 150.

unpleasant bodily sensations and disturbing ideas about being invaded.[66] Winnicott suggests that accumulating some of these negative tensions can energise the subject on behalf of a defence against intrusive forces: 'In health, the individual can store badness within for use in an attack on external forces that seem to threaten what is felt to be worth preserving.'[67] Holding on to anger can only serve as a healthy defence mechanism, however, when the subject is not entirely controlled or 'possessed' by fantasies and bodily tensions but remains open for feedback from the external world. In this way, angry energy will be spent on threats that actually exist so that 'the enemy can be met with economy of effort.'[68] In contrast, those who have lost touch with the world might usher angry attacks even when the environment no longer puts the subject at risk. In such a case, holding on to anger has become a compulsive habit rather than a potential resource for efficacious forms of dissent.

This connection between holding on to anger and remaining in touch with the external world is perhaps also the reason why Winnicott does not treat holding on to anger as a *necessary* condition for dissent. Rather than prescribing one particular strategy as a solution for all circumstances, Winnicott generally advocates flexibility or 'elbow room' in the usage of defence mechanisms and argues that attachments to these mechanisms should not become 'rigid'.[69] Although Winnicott does not specify what his plea for flexibility entails for anger, his argument likely implies that the attachment to a particular defence strategy, such as holding on to the anger, should not become overly strict but that one needs to be capable of adjusting or even letting go of the strategy in light of the characteristics of the environment in which the struggle for play is carried out. In this sense, we might say that holding on to anger functions like a transitional object: it can contribute to resilience when it sustains the capacity to transform reality, but when its task is done or when specific circumstances make holding on to anger corrosive of the quest for play, it is time to let anger go.

So although holding on to anger might not be essential for every democratic struggle, a democratic regime could, like the over-comforting caretaker, rob citizens of their vitality by asking them to give up their anger. In her study about an AIDS activist movement the sociologist Deborah Gould

[66] Winnicott (n 48) 207. Winnicott does not specify how anger is experienced in the body, but I assume we might think of sensations, such as a tightening of the chest or a clenching of the fists and jaw.

[67] ibid, 209.

[68] ibid.

[69] D Winnicott, 'Freedom' in *Home Is Where We Start From* (n 56) 231.

shows that holding on to anger can indeed help to invigorate democratic struggles. As one of the participants in this group puts it:

> We helped perpetuate that anger in the discussions that we had around the actions so that you [were] a bottle of emotions with a great sense of purpose. When you were at the demonstrations you sustained yourself on an adrenaline rush because you were chanting the whole time ... Physically maintaining that energy level does incredible things to you. You walk away from the demonstration feeling elated, really elated and purposeful.[70]

When majorities are unresponsive the democratic resilience of dissenting citizens could thus greatly benefit from social forms that cultivate anger on behalf of struggles against exclusions.

iii. Invention of New Techniques for Interaction

In addition to capacities for mourning and dissent, Winnicott's perspective suggests that resilience calls for a capacity to invent new forms of interaction. Winnicott emphasises this capacity in light of the dangers that the exchange of interpretations poses for playful agency. For instance, he notes that interpretations can inhibit play by intruding upon fantasy life: they call the subject to make experiences intelligible while play is dependent upon the possibility of dwelling in fantasies without having to make (immediate) sense. Furthermore, interpretations always to some extent compel the subject to make herself known in words that are never entirely her own and thereby harbour the risk of compliance. In view of these threats Winnicott's asserts that individuals are in need of a so-called 'right not to communicate.'[71] On the one hand, this right seeks to provide for a resting place, that is, to allow the subject to withdraw temporarily from the pressure to make her fantasies intelligible through verbal exchange and to offer a shelter against the dangers of compliance inherent in dialogue. But, on the other hand, this right may also make room for the creation of new forms of interaction that playfully transform predominant forms of communication. When the current modes of communication in a particular setting hamper the quest for play, a retreat from the norms and customs from that setting could help to put aggression to use for 'the establishment of a personal technique for communicating with does not lead to violation of the central self.'[72]

[70] Cited in D Gould, 'Passionate Political Processes' in J Goodwin and J Jasper (eds), *Rethinking Social Movements: Structure, Meaning, and Emotion* (Lanham MD, Rowman & Littlefield Publishers Inc, 2004) 172.

[71] D Winnicott, 'Communicating and Not Communicating Leading to a Study of Certain Opposites' in *The Maturational Processes and the Facilitating Environment* (n 50) 179–92.

[72] ibid, 190.

Winnicott's innovations of psychoanalytic practice exemplify how Winnicott himself tried to develop a new technique of interaction. In opposition to orthodox Freudian therapy—that encouraged patients to verbalise all their associations—Winnicott insisted upon the right of the analysand to remain silent. When the analysand was suspended from the pressure of talking out loud, Winnicott expected that the analysand would feel more free to sojourn in his fantasies and to put these in use for creating his own interpretations about his condition. In this way, therapeutic interaction would help the analysand to develop confidence in his capacity for play: instead of waiting for the analyst to deliver an authorative interpretation about the analysand's associations (as in the traditional Freudian 'talking cure'), the analysand could initiate the interpretative exchange. In other words, Winnicott believed that implementing a new technique of interaction was central in revising the traditional power relations between analyst and analysand and, in doing so, could make the analysand more resilient in his struggle for play.[73]

While Winnicott does not explain how the retreat from hegemonic forms of communication may benefit subjects who are engaged in action in concert, such as democratic struggles, his account acknowledges that collective transitional phenomena can offer the subject a 'resting-place' during the ongoing challenge of relating fantasy and reality.[74] Moreover, seeking out the solidarity of others who are engaged in similar quests for play can greatly benefit creative action and may thus serve as an important holding environment for the invention of new interaction techniques:

> We can share a respect for illusionary experience, and if we wish we may collect together and form a group on the basis of the similarity of our illusionary experiences. This is the natural root of grouping among human beings.[75]

These thoughts, taken together, suggest that disempowered citizens may build up resilience by collectively retreating from mainstream fora of democratic interaction. Such a withdrawal allows citizens to put their aggression to use for the creation of new strategies for interaction that are more favourable to a particular democratic struggle. So if the current power relations governing the interaction with majorities do not allow for politicisation, or fail to establish a more responsive form of civic engagement, citizens should not hesitate to put these dialogues to a halt and create alternative techniques of interaction that unsettle the power relations in those dialogues.

[73] Winnicott's idiosyncratic prose provides another example of Winnicott's own struggle to develop new techniques of interaction. By using self-created words rather than the technical terms characteristic for post-Freudian psychoanalytic writing and by infusing his writing with digressions, Winnicott tried to preserve a sense of individual playfulness that the hegemonic psychoanalytic style in his view tended to undermine.

[74] Winnicott (n 51) 3; Winnicott (n 56) 35.

[75] Winnicott (n 51) 4.

To illustrate how a retreat from mainstream dialogical settings can support the invention of new techniques of interaction and thereby build up the resilience of disempowered citizens who come together as a group, it is useful to turn to the Industrial Areas Foundation (IAF), a network of US grassroots organisations that was established by Saul Alinsky in 1940. A central tactic in contemporary IAF politics is the formation of so-called 'accountability sessions': political meetings where public officials and candidates are invited to buildings situated at the heart of the local communities that take part in IAF.[76] The withdrawal from mainstream political fora, such as government buildings, to spaces like churches and cafeterias that are frequented and controlled by the participants in IAF allows the movement to create forms of interaction that challenge the power relations in established political settings. For example, in being confronted with the numerous people that support IAF, the politicians come to see the potential power of the organisation and this, as Jeffrey Stout puts it, helps to 'put officials in a position of needing to negotiate with it.'[77] Furthermore, by taking charge of the meetings, IAF can put topics on the agenda that are much more difficult to address in established fora. During accountability meetings, the politicians are thus less capable of dismissing claims by IAF and, not unlike the Winnicottian analyst, called upon to wait for and respond to the interpretations of those who are normally situated in an inferior position. In doing so, IAF significantly enhances the resilience of its members. When citizens who are normally marginalised in official political arenas are enabled to alter the mode of interaction that structures political meetings, they learn that the confrontation with adversity might harbour possibilities for creative renewal and that they need not have to comply with norms and customs that inhibit their struggles for play.

F. Politicising Winnicott

So far I have argued that Winnicott's theory about play and aggression offers a highly instructive starting point for our thinking about democratic resilience. His perspective suggests that capacities for mourning, dissidence

[76] Several studies about IAF discuss the role of accountability sessions in empowering marginalised citizens. See, for instance, J Stout, *Blessed Are the Organized: Grassroots Democracy in America* (New Jersey, Princeton University Press, 2010); R Coles, 'Moving Democracy: Industrial Areas Foundation Social Movements and the Political Arts of Listening, Traveling, and Tabling' (2004) 5 *Political Theory* 32 678. Alinsky had also underscored the need for his organisation to devise 'new tactics and a new arena' when mainstream political settings for communicating with the powerful blocked the struggles of his movement (see S Alinsky, *Rules for Radicals: A Practical Primer for Realistic Radicals* (New York, Vintage Books, 1972) 142).

[77] Stout, ibid 109.

and the creation of interaction techniques are central in sustaining playful agency in the face of adversity, and I offered various examples in order to show that his view resonates with important elements of building up resilience in everyday democratic life. Yet, when putting Winnicott's theory to use for my perspective of agonic democracy, it is important to bear in mind Foucault's point that the analysis of power is a 'task inherent in all social existence'.[78] This implies, among other things, that the analysis of the conditions of democratic resilience should not be located in the axis of parental supervision and therapeutic interventions alone, but that it should also take into account how other social-historical power relations affect the capacity to withstand civic loss. We have seen that Winnicott acknowledges that the cultivation of resilience is dependent upon environmental conditions other than good enough parental care. The various transitional phenomena—arts, groups, u, politics—that exemplify adult forms of play offer the subject possibilities for retreat and building up creative agency when facing adversity. Yet, despite this emphasis on the contribution of social-cultural practices to developing resilience, Winnicott underrates the distinct transformative effect of these practices upon the capacities for mourning, dissent and the invention of interaction techniques that sustain the struggle for play. In his account, the influence of transitional phenomena upon affective life appears as an aggregation of the potential for play that was acquired during early childhood: he argues that the transitional experiences provided by social-cultural practices are '*in direct continuity* with the play area of the small child who is "lost" in play'[79] and claims that 'cultural influences can ... be studied as an overlap of innumerable personal patterns.'[80] And, throughout his work, the family is privileged as the most crucial site for realising this 'play area' and 'personal patterns.' For example, Winnicott treats the family as the most important environmental condition for constituting democratic agency: '*ordinary good homes* provide the only setting in which the innate democratic factor can be created.'[81] But social-cultural practices shape democratic agency in ways that exceed the family environment and often remould the capacities that were shaped in childhood. Consider, for instance, the alternative mourning environment offered by Asian American studies programmes that I referred to earlier. Eng and Han emphasise that

[78] See ch 3 text to n 100.

[79] Winnicott (n 51) 18 (emphasis added).

[80] D Winnicott, 'Psycho-Analysis and The Sense of Guilt' in *The Maturational Process and the Facilitating Environment* (n 50) 15.

[81] D Winnicott, 'Some Thoughts on The Meaning of the Word "Democracy"' in *Home Is Where We Start From* (n 56) 247. Winnicott makes a similar claim with respect to the personal identity needed for political participation, arguing that it '*can only become fact in each individual case because of good-enough mothering* and environmental provision of the holding variety at the stages of immaturity.' Winnicott (n 57) 119.

many of the Asian American students who might benefit from this holding environment often acquired their pathological mourning habits during their own upbringing. That is, since many Asian American families internalised the stereotype of the self-reliant Asian American minority prevalent in mainstream society, Asian Americans who do not conform to this model are not only barred from possibilities to mourn by the wider culture but often also rejected by their very own families.[82] This suggests that rather than singling out the family as the privileged site for cultivating democratic resilience, we should investigate more closely how the capacity to endure adversity is shaped and altered by the various transitional experiences in which citizens participate in later life. In other words, what could be relevant here might be the second homes of political collectivity rather than our first homes.

The work of the sociologist Arlie Hochschild offers crucial conceptual resources to analyse the emotional power relations that are transmitted by such political movements. In her seminal article on the social construction of emotions, Hochschild develops an important amendment to the psychoanalytical tradition.[83] She agrees with (neo-) Freudian theory that love and aggression provide the energetic building blocks for the emotional development of individuals. But she rightly points out that the psychoanalytic model has paid insufficient attention to the effect of social-historical norms on emotional experience. We can only acquire a good understanding of emotional processes when we take into account how this process is structured by so-called 'feeling rules': social-historical norms that tell us which emotions are appropriate in a particular situation and which are not.[84] For instance, at a funeral we do not only experience sadness because we have lost a loved one; this emotion also occurs because we are socially expected to feel sadness at such an event. Although Hochschild does not engage with Foucault's work, her analysis of feeling rules converges crucially with Foucault's ontology of power relations. Like Foucault, Hochschild emphasises that hierarchical norms, such as feeling rules, are implemented by social-historical techniques that individuals transmit to one another and apply to themselves. That is to say, feeling rules are put into practice by 'emotion work': various skills that individuals use in order to cultivate particular emotional responses. These techniques engage cognition (for example, we persuade ourselves that we should be friendly to someone), the body (such as breathing more slowly to calm down when angry), and include expressive

[82] Eng and Han (n 62) 352. As the anonymous reviewers reminded me, Gould and Stout also connect the cultivation of democratic resilience with the participation in a political collectivity rather than the relationships in early childhood that Winnicott sees as most crucial.

[83] A Hochschild, 'Emotion Work, Feeling Rules, and Social Structure' (1979) 85 *The American Journal of Sociology* 551.

[84] ibid, 563.

skills (we cry to release anger). Also, just as Foucault does in his analysis of power, Hochschild stresses that emotional power relations both produce and constrain certain effects:

> We can speak, then, of two broad types of emotion work: *evocation*, in which the cognitive focus is on a desired feeling which is initially absent, and *suppression*, in which the cognitive focus is on an undesired feeling which is initially present.[85]

Finally, Hochschild's account dovetails with Foucault in her emphasis on the possibility to resist power/knowledge relations: individuals can challenge feeling rules in processes of democratic opinion-formation as well as playfully contest the norms and techniques that structure their emotional life in a more informal manner.

In short, Hochschild's work links the psychoanalytic focus on affect with a much wider web of social-historical power relations than the family or therapy alone. Her account, one might say, brings out the affective dimension of the power/knowledge relations that structure social life and thereby offer a bridge between, on the one hand, Winnicott's relative blindness to the effect of social-historical norms on affective life and, on the other, Foucault's silence about the affective dimension of power/knowledge relations. More specifically, her notion of feeling rules makes us attentive to the way in which emotional experience is transformed by various norms that are dispersed throughout social life and that pressure us into certain emotional reactions rather than others.

Along these lines, the sociologist Erika Effler has shown in her ethnography of an anti-death penalty movement and a Catholic welfare movement how much the employment of anger in social movements is dependent upon locally specific rules and techniques that radically transform the affective life of the participants.[86] The anti-death penalty activists tried to change capital punishment laws through acts of civil disobedience (such as disrupting law trials that called for the death penalty), by organising vigils at the office of the district attorney, and by getting media attention for their cause. After the attacks on the World Trade Center in 2001, however, the political climate made it increasingly difficult for this group to gain attention for their cause: the media and local politicians focused mainly on the war on terror.

[85] ibid, 561 (emphasis added). According to Hochschild, ideology consists of feeling rules and 'framing rules'. Framing rules refer to rules that help us confer meaning upon a situation and are somewhat akin to Foucault's understanding of knowledge relations; feeling rules teach how to experience and respond to particular situations emotionally. Hochschild underlines that feelings rules and emotion work need to be understood in relation to other types of hierarchical oppositions that shape social life, such as patriarchial distinctions between men and women, capitalist distinctions between the status of workers and bosses, and so on.

[86] E Effler, *Laughing Saints and Righteous Heroes: Emotional Rhythms in Social Movement Groups* (Chicago, University of Chicago Press, 2010).

To help the participants to confront and transform these unresponsive circumstances, the staff of the group cultivated anger to encourage the mourning of losses and the persistence in dissent.[87] For example, by narrating stories about past injustices and drawing attention to impending death penalties, the staff helped the group members to redirect feelings of inadequacy and desperation into 'feelings of righteous anger and power.'[88] Furthermore, the staff stimulated the participants to hold on their anger by organising protests that put the activists in face-to-face conflicts with their political opponents. Effler's account illustrates powerfully how these rules and techniques—that were so well suited to the group's militant style—over time radically altered the affective experiences of the participants. For instance, while participating in the pro-tests initially unsettled new participants, it eventually strengthened their appetite to assert their cause:

> Newcomers found the small, highly visible, and confrontational vigils threatening and exhausting ... Vigil regulars, on the other hand, tended to get pumped up by the jeers of passersby. Face-to-face conflicts with hecklers enabled regulars to experience intense feelings of convictions and camaraderie.[89]

The participants in the Catholic movement were also pressed into an affective conversion process that transformed the usage of anger. This group was committed to ideals such as universal hospitality and a radical change in the hegemonic attitude to the poor, and enacted these aims by living in voluntary poverty in a poor urban neighbourhood and by helping homeless people. Realising these ambitions was challenging however: homeless people would confront the group members with so many problems (stealing goods, drug abuse and aggression toward others) that they had to be kicked out. When thwarted in their attempt to deliver hospitality, the participants felt a painful sense of failure, disappointment and frustration. Moreover, the experience that some people abused their service often initiated a judgemental, angry response toward the homeless people. But because anger tends to increase consciousness about boundaries and can thereby diminish the willingness to deliver universal hospitality, the rules and techniques of this group encouraged the participants to let go of this feeling or, better perhaps, to transform anger into feelings that were more attuned to the group's distinct ideal. For example, by sharing their sense of inadequacy, telling tragic stories about 'the injuries of children working in the sugarcane fields and grandmothers and their children sleeping on benches in the cold' and highlighting the absurd aspects in the stories, the participants tried to convert

[87] Effler's case study illustrates nicely that techniques for building up the capacity for mourning, dissent and the invention of new techniques for interaction in practice tend to overlap.

[88] Effler (n 86) 117. Stout also discusses the role of leaders in focusing anger on injustices. Stout (n 76) 64–69.

[89] Effler (n 86) 65.

anger into grief, humility and a sense of humour.[90] In this way, the participants could not only accept their failures but also cultivated a more easy-going attitude towards the disorderly and bleak circumstances that shaped their daily work and thereby built up the capacity to persist in their dissenting way of life. For example, in the early stages of his involvement with the group, the Catholic worker Nick experienced profound anger and cynicism because of the frustrations of living and serving in the rough conditions of a poor neighbourhood. But eventually 'angry Nick' became 'unflappable Nick … smiling in the face of personal aggression, hopelessness and chaotic conditions.'[91]

Effler's case studies offer a detailed account of two groups which tried to enact a dissenting ideal in dire circumstances and were thus, in a Winnicottian sense, involved in a struggle for play. Her ethnography suggests that Winnicott is right in pointing out that holding on to anger can serve democratic resilience but that it is not a viable strategy in all circumstances: for the Catholic movement, sustaining their dissent from mainstream society was much better served by stimulating the participants to let go of anger. Yet, her analysis also unsettles Winnicott's suggestion that the potential for dissent in groups derives from the family environments of the participants involved. The specific feeling rules and techniques in the democratic struggles that Effler discusses gradually displaced the habits for anger that the participants had learned in previous environments and inculcated a 'new emotional rhythm' that was better attuned to the ideals that the groups were committed to.

Effler's case studies also suggest that Winnicott says too little about the way in which transitional phenomena might undermine the potential to confront adversity. Consider, for example, Winnicott's claim that one needs to remain flexible in the usage of strategies of resilience so that they can be revised in light of particular circumstances. His account of the environmental failures that produce a tendency for rigid attachments treats inadequate parenting in early childhood as 'the most significant' environmental condition.[92] This suggests that our analysis of what endangers flexibility in democratic politics would need to focus primarily on the care that individual citizens received as infants; conversely, it suggests that such flexibility might be adequately secured when citizens have received good enough parenting early in life.[93] But, surely, the feeling rules that shape attachments

[90] ibid, 116.

[91] ibid, 134.

[92] Winnicott (n 69) 237.

[93] Though Winnicott himself does not connect his reading of rigidity with democratic agency, I think it is warranted to derive these implications from his account in light of what I mentioned earlier above, namely, Winnicott's treatment of the family as the most significant breeding ground for developing democratic agency.

in later life can also significantly diminish the potential for flexibility. For instance, Effler's study reveals the crucial effect of social movements upon developing a predisposition for rigid attachments to strategies for resilience. Consider the cultivation of humour among the Catholic workers. While humour made the workers more laidback and thereby helped them to endure daily frustrations, it also had a cost: in becoming more easy-going, the workers developed a strong aversion to planning and this often put off financial donors that the group relied upon for its survival. Yet, the local history of the movement made it difficult for the participants to alter or let go of this feeling rule: because humour had been so successful for confronting setbacks in the group's past, the workers insisted upon telling each other funny stories when the conflicts with the financial donors intensified. This left little room for experimenting with alternative approaches to confronting the problems with the donors or, for that matter, for trying out a new approach to attract necessary funds. So, in other words, Effler's analysis offers a compelling illustration of Winnicott's point that resilience can be undermined when we become trapped in strategies. Yet, at the same time, it also diverges from Winnicott's account insofar as it derives a tendency for rigidity not primarily from childhood experiences but conceptualises it as a potential drawback effect of the local feeling rules of social movements. Overall, Effler's case study thus powerfully confirms Hochschild's point that rather than focusing primarily on the early childhood of individuals we need to probe deeper into the particular feeling rules, such as transmitted by political collectivities, when trying to understand the cultivation of democratic resilience.

IV. EMOTIONAL BOUNDARY-MARKING

So far I have shown that democratic struggles can open up new possibilities for facing adversity but that these struggles also harbour possible dangers for democratic resilience, such as a tendency to discourage the renewal of feeling rules and techniques.

To end, I want to consider to what extent political collectivities that breed a loss of flexibility might open up possibilities for undoing rigidity. The movements that Effler studied seemed incapable of circumventing their rigid tendencies: over time, the movements became in the grip of a stifling 'logic' that was increasingly limiting possible actions, 'damming up potential paths so that action is pulled towards the few remaining paths, which reduces the flexibility of the actor.'[94] And, on Effler's understanding, this 'logic' is not only characteristic of the particular groups that she studied but illustrative

[94] Effler (n 86) 190.

of patterns of group involvement more generally. But are groups really destined to inflexibility? Or might there also be a more Winnicottian way of addressing a loss of flexibility, such as engaging in playful experiments with feeling rules and techniques that call for renewal?

For a preliminary answer to that question, I want to take my cue from the notion of 'boundary markers'—a term coined by the sociologist Michael Farrel.[95] In his study on influential artistic and political innovation movements, Farrel highlights the point that the vitality of dissenting groups is dependent upon group members who experiment with the boundaries set by the group's rules and practices:

> Rather than being a target of ridicule, their ideas [of the boundary markers, IR] are taken seriously and openly discussed ... The presence of a questioning minority stimulates thinking in other members, and, confronted with the negative feedback, the group develops more creative and workable solutions to their problems.[96]

While Farrel concentrates his reading of the practice of boundary-marking on the circulation of dissenting views within groups rather than strategies for resilience, his case studies suggest that boundary-marking might also be mobilised for the account of democratic resilience that I am developing. Consider, for instance, his discussion about the rise and fall of the 'bloomer dress': a technique that was central to the resilience of the American nineteenth century suffragette movement Ultra. For several years, the members of Ultra wore a loose-fitting combination of trouser and a short skirt that was radically different from the tight corsets and crinolines fashionable at the time. The bloomer dress served both as a new technique for interaction with the wider society—expressing the group's critique of male-dominated society—and also built up the capacity for dissent by daily disciplining the women into the feeling of non-conformism. At the point, however, when the group shifted its focus from criticising gender inequality to proposing legal reform, the dress became somewhat of an obstacle for realising their goals. It was the dress rather than their proposals for legal reform that attracted the media attention, and the radical appearance of the Ultras was a barrier in building coalitions with more conservative women's groups. In light of these problems, one of the leaders of this group, Elizabeth Stanton, urged the other members of Ultra to take off the dress. Her plea initially confused the others, and some women refused to give up the dress: they had become attached to its comforts and saw it as a crucial exemplary practice for other women. But Stanton persisted in her appeal to change course and eventually the others too came to realise that the dress had become a hindrance

[95] M Farrel, *Collaborative Circles: Friendship Dynamics and Creative Work* (Chicago, Chicago University Press, 2001).
[96] ibid, 282.

to realising their quest for women's rights and, like a transitional object, let the dress go.

What Farrel's account of boundary-marking suggests to me is that it is indeed possible for dissenting groups to diminish rigidity by engaging in playful experiments with feeling rules and techniques that build up resilience. In fact, such Winnicottian experiments could be crucial to enhance the groups' potential to confront adversity. Enduring a certain amount of aggression, instability and conflict within the group could help it to creatively adapt to changing circumstances, even though many participants may initially experience this trial as an undermining of their democratic resilience.

Meanwhile, such practices of emotional boundary-marking can increase the resilience of transitional networks, but they do not, of course, guarantee it. All groups break up at some point: people leave groups to participate in mainstream culture or they start another one that does a better job in stimulating their dissenting aims and needs for democratic resilience. Also, members withdraw from democratic politics to spend time and energy on other commitments or, for that matter, to recover from the burdens of democratic life.[97] During such retreats some people may feel so exhausted by democratic politics that they consider not returning at all. We have seen that Serenus, drained by the burdens of civic life, pondered the possibility of staying at home and to devote his life to the tranquil pleasure of introspection. Stanton also came to resent the toll of civic engagement on her energy and time. The difficult challenge of combining family commitments with the work in Ultra and her dissatisfaction with an increasingly mainstream agenda of the movement eventually made her distance herself from the movement.[98] In her last speech to the women's movement, Stanton surprised her audience by invoking a deeply individualist ontology. Rather than defending the quest for gender equality within the more conventional terms of eighteenth century liberal ideologies of individual rights, Stanton's speech—'The Solitude of Self'—drew attention to the fundamental solitariness of human beings:

> The strongest reason for giving women all the opportunities for higher education, for the full development of her faculties ... for giving her the most enlarged freedom of thought and action ... is the solitude and personal responsibility of her individual life. ... Think for a moment of the immeasurable solitude of self.

[97] Farrel's study indicates that innovation movements typically last for about ten or fifteen years. Ultra, however, endured for more than 40 years. Farrel attributes this exceptional time span to the immense task of changing a patriarchal society and the high level of intimacy and mutual support among the Ultra members (ibid, 262).

[98] She came to regret the fact that the movement succeeded to build a coalition with conservatives and religious reformists, as this made it difficult for her to push for a more radical agenda that included critiques of the clergy.

> We come into the world alone, unlike all who have gone before us, we leave it alone, under circumstances peculiar to ourselves. … In youth our most bitter disappointments, our brightest hopes and ambitions, are known only to ourselves. Even our friendships and our love we never fully share with another.[99]

With this ontology, Stanton declared her loyalty to, and support for, the ongoing political struggle for gender equality but also tried to detach herself from Ultra. Not unlike a transitional object, her engagement with ontology helped her realise her independence from Ultra—a movement that could no longer advocate the radical kind of feminism that Stanton was committed to and whose intimate relationships had become too demanding and suffocating for her.

In this chapter, I have also turned to ontology to defend an account of agonic democratic politics that might increase opportunities for dissenting views and practices. Like Stanton, I affirm that individuals are to some extent solitary creatures because their desires, needs and suffering are never identical to the social surroundings that shape them. My ontology, however, is not as individualist as the one that Stanton presented to her public; I have tried to negotiate between, on the one hand, the agonic strains of sociability and, on the other, the need for social support that disempowered individuals need in the face of civic loss. That is, my account draws attention to the fact that social forms provide promising possibilities for companionship and emotional discipline that can strengthen the democratic resilience of disempowered individuals—even though they can never entirely fulfil the needs for emotional empowerment that participants might need to engage in democratic politics, and are therefore crucially in need of agonic provocations.

V. CONCLUSION

This chapter presented the last step in developing an ontology of democratic politics. I turned to the psychoanalytic tradition to diagnose and ameliorate the affective burdens of democratic loss for citizens. Drawing upon psychoanalytic insights, I introduced three capacities that build up democratic resilience: a capacity to mourn, a capacity for dissidence and a capacity for inventing new techniques for interaction. This chapter also investigated the benefits of a democratic politicisation of ontology. We have seen that the methodological tools of the democratic politicisation of ontology were highly relevant in arriving at my account of democratic resilience. By way of articulating psychoanalytic ontologies of subjectivity I could amend my Foucaultian ontology of agonic freedom with an account of the affective conditions of democratic agency. In turn, my ideal of agonic freedom and

[99] Farrel (n 95) 159–60.

Foucault's historical critique of the Freudian ontology helped me to discern some anti-agonic effects of Freud's account and to open up space for Winnicott's alternative, more agonic, account of subjectivity. Furthermore, I challenged Winnicott's tendency to reduce the formation of democratic subjectivity to the family by recalling Foucault's ontological insight regarding the ubiquity of power/knowledge relations and agonic freedom. Hochschild's work on feeling rules and Effler's case study offered crucial help to make these Foucaultian insights useful for understanding the emotional dimension of political collectivities. In sum, one might say that Foucault functioned as my emotional boundary-marker during my encounters with psychoanalytic ontology, encouraging me to remain vigilant and attentive to the exclusionary effects in the psychoanalytic figures of truth that I mobilised for this account of democratic resilience. But, obviously, I have also resisted Foucault's intimations: rather than complying with his overly harsh rejection of psychoanalytic notions, I have tried to transfigure psychoanalytic concepts in a more agonic fashion.

7

Conclusion

DEMOCRACY AND ONTOLOGY investigates the role of ontology in political thought and practice by putting political liberalism in critical conversation with Foucault and psychoanalysis. In the process, my argument has focused on three interrelated questions. The first scrutinises political liberalism's key claim that a consensus can be 'freestanding' of ontological controversies: how plausible is the political liberalist attempt to separate contentious ontological claims from an account of democratic politics? The second question investigates the outlines of an ontology as an alternative to the political liberalist ontology: which ontological conditions should we take into account when we seek to nourish democratic politics? Finally, the third question relates to the methodology of political liberalism. In contrast to the political liberalist critical strategy that avoids ontology as an object of critique, I have introduced an alternative critical methodology that aims for the democratic politicisation of ontology. Which of these two practices of critique is more plausible, in light of the aim to stimulate the politicisation of political philosophy, as well as of the goal to provide orientation on democratic politics?

I. POLITICISING THE POLITICAL LIBERALIST ONTOLOGY

Political liberalism assumes that the ontological ideas resident in its theory of justice are so general that they do not discriminate against ontological traditions nor affect the structure or content of a conception of justice. Yet my detailed, critical investigation of this assumption has shown that political liberalism does not succeed in developing an ontologically uncontroversial theory of democratic justice. Not only do political liberals draw upon various contentious ontological claims, these assumptions also have a significant impact upon the way that they orient us in democratic politics.

My engagement with Rawls has focused on the ontological partiality of two normative aspirations of political liberalism: political autonomy and a fair distribution of mutual respect. As I set out in chapter two, his account of autonomy departs from a controversial individualist ontology: it conceptualises moral freedom as a mental capacity rather than as an intersubjective, historical practice. In turn, Rawls' ontology has an important effect on the way that political liberalism construes justice: the basic outlines of Rawls' normative scheme give much more priority to individual rights than collective goals such as the realisation of contentious cultural ways of life. Rawls' principle of mutual respect is also ontologically partial. While it is less individualist than his defence of freedom, its lack of attention to the role of the body in realising practices of mutual respect renders it ontologically contentious. Rawls' normative account about the essential features of a fair distribution of mutual respect mirrors this controversial ontological view: it gives no normative weight to the body.

In chapter four, I have approached the ontological problems in the social theory of political liberalism by looking at Tomasi's political liberalist account of a just democratic regime. Tomasi claims that he can analyse the social implications of rights without taking part in ontological disputes. Yet, I have argued that this claim cannot be maintained, because Tomasi's social theory is permeated with two ontological controversies. First, Tomasi's theory of tradition neglects the presence of power and conflict in traditional practices. The disorienting consequence of this exclusionary effect is that Tomasi's ontology blinds us to the struggles of citizens who challenge hegemonic traditional narratives. Second, I have highlighted that Tomasi's voluntarist ontology of political liberalist public culture neglects the impact of hegemonic traditions upon the interpretation of rights, and that it is thereby orienting us away from the problems that citizens who struggle with powerful traditions encounter when they try to make use of individual rights.

From the Foucaultian perspective that I have reconstructed in chapters three and four, it comes as little surprise that the political liberalist ontologies were not able to secure a 'freestanding' consensus. Since ontologies are a product of social-historical power struggles, they usher in exclusionary effects. That is to say, they orient us in some normative aspirations and social consequences of democratic politics, but also draw our attention away from other possibilities and dimensions of democratic life. Ontologies cannot transcend this predicament: *pace* political liberalism, they are never so general that they can rise above political disputes, but remain an essential feature of political conflicts.

In light of their exclusionary effects, ontological assumptions merit the critical attention of the democratic public. I contend that political philosophers can contribute to the democratic politicisation of ontology by bringing into view the contestability and disorienting effects of ontological assumptions, and by laying out rules of discussion for democratic debate that might stimulate the democratic contestation of ontology. Such a critical posture vis-à-vis ontology does not imply, however, that political philosophers should refrain from developing their own ontology. A key aim of this book has been to show that ontological theory can also contribute to democracy by helping us to see new possibilities for democratic politics that remain invisible in hegemonic ontologies such as political liberalism. Put differently, I consider both the development and the critique of ontological assumptions as essential tasks for political philosophers.

II. AN ALTERNATIVE ONTOLOGY OF DEMOCRATIC POLITICS

My ontology of agonic democratic politics has drawn upon Foucault's ontological claims about power and freedom as well as ontological insights taken from Winnicott's psychoanalytic perspective. This ontology brings into view social consequences and normative possibilities of democratic politics that remain invisible within political liberalism.

My reading of Foucault in chapter three provides the starting point for developing an ontology of democratic politics. I explain that the individual subject is ontologically constituted by bodily forces and power relations. Subjectivity becomes possible in virtue of submission, that is, the capacities of human beings for consciousness and action are fundamentally dependent upon incessant attempts of social-historical power relations to subjugate the body by means of exclusionary, hierarchical norms and disciplinary techniques. This ontology does not, however, preclude the possibility of individual freedom. Human beings are capable of contesting, resisting and creatively reshaping the power relations that try to domesticate the body. This idea of *agonic freedom* understands autonomy as an inherently heteronomous struggle rather than the exercise of a mental capacity: critical thinking, resisting or experimenting with power remains situated in power-laden ethical practices that discipline individuals by means of ideals, techniques and critical analyses of power.

While the exercise of agonic freedom is a possibility of social relations, agonism should not be mistaken for the teleological outcome of human interaction: agonic freedom can be undermined by the complete consolidation of power (domination) as well as the violent paralysis of social interaction (antagonism). To sustain the possibility of agonic freedom individuals need to submit themselves to social forms that encourage agonic struggles, and exercise their possibility for contestation on a regular basis. An agonic democratic politics aspires to the enactment of practices that encourage and give form to the ontological possibilities for agonic freedom, while intending the weakening of opportunities for domination and antagonism.

I have argued that this ontology of agonic freedom makes visible a normative possibility for democracy that is entirely missing in political liberalism. In opposition to the political liberalist ontology, the ontology of agonic freedom shows that democratic regimes are in need of citizens who regularly expose themselves to social conflicts in order to train their capacity for contest and experiment. For instance, when schools are confronted with conflicts about bodily rituals, such as the handshake, an agonic ontology suggests that such a dispute could provide the participants with a promising opportunity to get acquainted with the contestation of, and experimentation with, power relations. Political liberalism, in contrast, does not account for the cultivation of contestatory skills and only identifies the cultivation of virtues that secure our allegiance to conceptions of justice as a normative aim of democracy and education. In this way, I have argued, political liberalism belies its commitment to a vibrant contest over the ruling conceptions of justice within a society. A democratic politics that aims for such critical practices is dependent upon a citizenry that has become habituated to contestation.

Foucault's ontology of power also helps us to get a better understanding of the social consequences of individual rights than political liberalism. Foucault's writings on governmentality make the ontology of power productive for the analysis of liberal statehood, suggesting that liberal states discipline the population by submitting citizens to various controversial exclusionary knowledge regimes. I contend that this focus on the entanglement between liberal state power and knowledge production offers a fruitful starting-point for investigating the social effects of individual rights. It helps us see that liberal legal cultures, including political liberalism, contain a structural bias against citizens who challenge established knowledge regimes—an exclusionary effect that Tomasi fails to see.

Furthermore, Foucault's ontology of agonic freedom opens up an alternative to the political liberalist ideal of democratic debate. The ubiquity of power suggests that Rawls' criterion of reciprocity for public reason is impossible: democratic debates cannot abolish the influence of power relations upon the exchange of arguments, but remain conditioned by disciplinary inequalities. In contrast to the political liberalist aim to extinguish power, Foucault's ontology shows that democratic debates could make productive use of disciplinary power by submitting the participants in democratic debates to power-laden ethical techniques that stimulate agonic experiments with power—the so-called 'game of reciprocal elucidation'. This game specifies several discussion rules that might support the enactment of agonic freedom, such as, among others, a duty to listen and to elucidate one's discourse when introducing a proposal or critique in democratic debate. Unlike political liberalist public reason, this game includes a critical, experimental exploration of 'settled' convictions within public culture, including ontological regimes. Such a critical learning-process cannot yield a stable consensus, but it could pave the way for unstable, temporary coalitions that might initiate concerted actions.

While Foucault's ontology offers promising insights about democratic politics, it obviously cannot escape its own predicament of issuing exclusionary effects. One problematic limitation of Foucault's ontology is that it says nothing about the affective challenges of participating in agonic contests. That is to say, it orients us in the indispensability of agonic struggles for democratic politics, but remains silent about the emotional effects of losing an agonic contest, such as a sense of failure or feelings of resentment that a democratic defeat might induce. This blind spot potentially creates a motivational deficit in my Foucaultian perspective of agonic democracy: a democratic regime can only remain vibrant if citizens are emotionally empowered enough to struggle for dissenting views or practices. Political liberalism, for that matter, is also vulnerable to this charge: although Rawls does not aim for as many democratic conflicts as Foucault does, he is committed to a lively democratic debate that makes some room for marginalised outlooks. Yet, like Foucault, Rawls does not explain how disempowered citizens might cope with losing a democratic dispute on an emotional level.

To address this lacuna, the second and final step in developing my ontology of democratic politics has explicated an ontology of the emotional challenges of democratic contest provides. In chapter six, I have shown that Winnicott's psychoanalytic ontology offers crucial insights into the emotional conditions of democratic resilience, and has helped me identify a new normative aspiration for democratic regimes: the need for capacities and experiments that build up resilience. We have seen that Winnicott's understanding of subjectivity bears crucial resemblances to Foucault's ontology of agonic freedom. Like Foucault, Winnicott sees the subject as a heteronomous achievement which is constituted by expanding bodily forces as well as social-historical practices, and is capable of creatively transforming itself and the world. However, in opposition to Foucault, Winnicott's ontology explains how social forms might cultivate an agonic response to loss. When facing a loss, such as a democratic defeat, human beings are confronted with the painful challenge of coping with narcissist injury: the awareness that the norms, demands or possibilities in the external world are not identical to one's wishes. I have shown that this painful experience opens up possibilities of realigning oneself to the world in an agonic manner, that is, by resisting, creatively transforming and experimenting with the social conditions that shape the self. Such a playful attitude is crucially dependent, however, upon a capacity to mourn, a capacity for dissidence and a capacity for inventing new techniques for interaction. Furthermore, to renew strategies for democratic resilience, I introduced the notion of 'emotional boundary-marking': playful experiments with the established feeling rules and techniques for facing adversity.

III. THE DEMOCRATIC POLITICISATION OF ONTOLOGY

Both my aims to politicise political liberalism and to develop another, more orienting, alternative ontology of democratic politics have been crucially dependent upon an ongoing critique of ontology. Throughout this book, I have confronted ontological assumptions with actual struggles taken from democratic politics, normative ideals and competing ontological traditions, and I have also taken my cue from Foucault's critique that traces ontology back to its contingent, exclusionary social-historical roots.

My attempt to explicate ontology as a site for democratic politicisation is deeply at odds with political liberalist practices of critique. Political liberalism structurally excludes ontological premises from critical scrutiny: neither Rawls nor Tomasi treats ontology as a site of democratic contest in their attempts to arrive at a reflective equilibrium about democratic politics. I have argued that the political liberalist strategy to exclude ontology from critical scrutiny hampers a much needed democratic politicisation of political liberalism. Since political liberalism has no critical tools with which to render available its ontological commitments for democratic contestation, it leaves the exclusionary, disorienting consequences of its ontology intact. In this way, political liberalism works against its commitment to a democratic politicisation of political philosophy and constrains its own potential for providing more orientation in democratic politics.

I contend that the democratic politicisation of ontology provides a better impetus to the democratic politicisation of political philosophy and the need for orientation than the political liberalist practice of critique. For instance, in chapter two, I have politicised the political liberalist ontology with the assistance of a communitarian ontology of self and the example of the Dutch handshake dispute. Such confrontations help us see the lack of attention for, respectively, culture and the body in the political liberalist ontology. Foucault's historicisation of the ontological underpinnings of the social contract tradition (chapter three) offers another significant contribution to this politicisation of political liberalism. I have set out that the mentalist-individualist conception of self in social contract theory structurally orients us away from the influence of bodily discipline upon liberal democracies, signalling the need for an ontology that offers more orientation in the relation between culture, bodily discipline and democratic politics. My critique of Tomasi's political liberalist ontology of rights has also employed critical strategies central to the democratic politicisation of ontology. The mobilisation of Foucault's ontology and the dispute about religious freedom in the United States have been important steps for bringing into view the disorienting effects of Tomasi's voluntarist depiction of political liberalist legalism.

Importantly, my development of Foucault's ontology has also benefited from the democratic politicisation of ontology. In chapter three, I read Foucault's initial account of an ontology of power and body through the lens of his implicit normative commitment to democracy. This confrontation between ontological and normative assumptions has highlighted the fact that Foucault originally underestimated the need for an ontology of critical agency and positive effects of self-discipline, and has revealed the need to turn to his later writings on agonic freedom.

My mobilisation of psychoanalysis for an ontology of democratic resilience has also been critically supported by the democratic politicisation of ontology. Both the normative aspiration for agonic freedom and Foucault's historicisation of Freud's ontology of mourning helped to challenge Freud's influential, but anti-agonic, account and paved the way for Winnicott's more agonic alternative. And further, the critical confrontation between Winnicott's ontology and Foucault's ontological thesis about the ubiquity of power opened up space to challenge the reduction of the formation of democratic resilience to the nuclear family.

The democratic politicisation of ontology does not only seek to encourage a critical engagement with ontology among political philosophers, but also aims for the critical contestation of ontology in democratic practice. Unlike Rawls' ideal of public reason, my agonic ethics of reciprocal elucidation opens up space for citizens to criticise ontological regimes and to introduce controversial ontological arguments. I have argued that this conception of democratic debate is more conducive to the democratic politicisation of political philosophy than political liberalist public reason. Provided that participants accept critique of their own ontological postulates, they can introduce their ontology to criticise hegemonic democratic ideals such as political liberalism, including its ontological commitments.

In short, a critical engagement with ontology provides an impetus to our understanding of democratic politics and stimulates the ongoing critique of democratic theory. Instead of seeking to dispel controversial ontological claims from democratic thought and fundamental democratic debates, as political liberalism urges us to do, I have argued that ontological investigations open up agonic possibilities for democratic life. Much more, of course, could and needs to be investigated in order to further evaluate the strengths and weaknesses of my perspective. For instance, the critical comparison between political liberalist public reason and my proposal for reciprocal elucidation of ontology could benefit from empirical research into the functioning of dissenting ontological arguments in historical or contemporary democratic struggles, such as those carried out by feminist or ecological movements or by groups that challenge neo-liberalism. Such studies might also look at the emotional dynamics within such groups, in order to critically investigate to a greater degree my ontological thesis about the dependence of democratic resilience upon emotional techniques. I hope that this book encourages such future research and opens up the possibility of new provocations to political liberalism as well as to the agonic perspective that I have presented here.

Bibliography

Books, Chapters and Journal Articles

Alinsky, S, *Rules for Radicals: A Practical Primer for Realistic Radicals* (New York, Vintage Books, 1972).

Asad, T, *Genealogies of Religion: Discipline and Reasons of Power in Christianity and Islam* (Baltimore, Johns Hopkins University Press, 1993).

Barber, B, *Strong Democracy: Participatory Politics for a New Age* (Berkeley, University of California Press, 1984).

Beck, H and Wiegers, G, *Moslims in een westerse samenleving: Islam en ethiek* (Zoetermeer, Meinema, 2008).

Beld, T van den, 'Background Theories and Religious Beliefs: Their Role and Relation in Reflective Equilibrium' in W van der Burg and T van Willigenburg (eds), *Reflective Equilibrium: Essays in Honour of Robert Heeger* (Dordrecht, Kluwer Academic Publishers, 1998) 73–88.

Benhabib, S, *Situating the Self: Gender, Community and Postmodernism in Contemporary Ethics* (Cambridge, Polity Press, 1992).

Benjamin, J, *The Bonds of Love: Psychoanalysis, Feminism, and the Problem of Domination* (New York, Pantheon, 1988).

Bennett, J, *The Enchantment of Modern Life: Attachments, Crossings, and Ethics* (New Jersey, Princeton University Press, 2001).

Bentley, R and Owen, D, 'Ethical Loyalties, Civic Virtue and the Circumstances of Politics' (2001) 4 *Philosophical Explorations: An International Journal for the Philosophy of Mind and Action: Special Issue Civic Virtue and Pluralism* 223.

Borchert, D (ed), *Encyclopedia of Philosophy*, 2nd edn, vol 7 (Detroit, Macmillan Reference USA, 2006).

Brink, B van den, 'Liberalism beyond Justice: Citizens, Society, and the Boundaries of Political Theory' (2002) 112 *Ethics* 872.

—— 'Liberalism without Agreement: Political Autonomy and Agonistic Citizenship' in J Christman and J Anderson (eds), *Autonomy and the Challenges to Liberalism* (Cambridge, Cambridge University Press, 2005) 245–71.

Brown, W, *Politics out of History* (New Jersey, Princeton University Press, 2001).

—— *Regulating Aversion: Tolerance in the Age of Identity and Empire* (New Jersey, Princeton University Press, 2006).

Butler, J, 'Foucault and the Paradox of Bodily Inscriptions' (1989) 86 *The Journal of Philosophy* 601.

—— *The Psychic Life of Power: Theories in Subjection* (Stanford, Stanford University Press, 1997).

Butler, J, Laclau, E and Zizek, S, *Contingencies, Hegemony, Universality: Contemporary Dialogues on the Left* (London, Verso, 2000).

Bråkenhielm, C, 'Reflective Equilibrium and Cosmological Claims' in W van der Burg and T van Willigenburg (eds), *Reflective Equilibrium: Essays in Honour of Robert Heeger* (Dordrecht, Kluwer Academic Publishers, 1998) 157–70.
Burg, W van der and Willigenburg, T van (eds), *Reflective Equilibrium: Essays in Honour of Robert Heeger* (Dordrecht, Kluwer Academic Publishers, 1998).
Burg, W van der, 'Dynamic Ethics' (2003) 37 *The Journal of Value Inquiry* 13.
Carens, J, *Culture, Citizenship, and Community: A Contextual Exploration of Justice as Evenhandedness* (Oxford, Oxford University Press, 2000).
Clewell, T, 'Mourning beyond Melancholia: Freud's Psychoanalysis of Loss' (2004) 52 *Journal of the American Psychoanalytic Association* 43.
Coles, R, 'Foucault's Dialogical Artistic Ethos' (1991) 8 *Theory, Culture & Society* 99.
—— 'Moving Democracy: Industrial Areas Foundation Social Movements and the Political Arts of Listening, Traveling, and Tabling' (2004) (32)5 *Political Theory* 678.
Connolly, W, *The Ethos of Pluralization* (Minneapolis, University of Minnesota Press, 1995).
—— *Why I am not a Secularist* (Minneapolis, University of Minnesota Press, 1999).
—— *Pluralism* (Durham, Duke University Press, 2005).
Dahl, R, *Democracy and its Critics* (New Haven, Yale University Press, 1989).
Deleuze, G, 'Foldings, or the Inside of Thought (Subjectivation)' in M Kelly (ed), *Critique and Power: Recasting the Foucault/Habermas Debate* (Cambridge, The MIT Press, 1994) 315–46.
Derrida, J, '"To Do Justice to Freud": the History of Madness in the Age of Psychoanalysis' (1994) 20 *Critical Inquiry* 227.
Dreyfus, HL, 'Being and Power: Heidegger and Foucault' (1996) 4 *International Journal of Philosophical Studies* 1.
Dworkin, R, *Sovereign Virtue: The Theory and Practice of Equality* (Cambridge, Harvard University Press, 2000).
Eng, D and Han, S, 'A Dialogue on Racial Melancholia' in D Eng and D Kazanjian (eds), *Loss: The Politics of Mourning* (Berkeley, University of California Press, 2003) 343–71.
Effler, E, *Laughing Saints and Righteous Heroes: Emotional Rhythms in Social Movement Groups* (Chicago, University of Chicago Press, 2010).
Farrel, M, *Collaborative Circles: Friendship Dynamics and Creative Work* (Chicago, Chicago University Press, 2001).
Foucault, M, *Discipline and Punish* (London, Penguin Books, 1977).
—— *The History of Sexuality, Volume 1: An Introduction* (New York, Random House, 1978).
—— 'Questions on Geography' in C Gordon (ed), *Power/Knowledge: Selected Interviews and other Writings 1972–1977* (London, The Harvester Press, 1980) 63–77.
—— 'Nietzsche, Genealogy, History' in P Rabinow (ed), *The Foucault Reader* (New York, Pantheon Books, 1984) 76–100.
—— 'Final Interview' (1985) 5 *Raritan* 1.
—— *The Care of The Self: The History of Sexuality, Volume 3* (London, Penguin Books, 1988).

—— 'The Art of Telling the Truth' in L Kritzman (ed), *Politics, Philosophy, Culture: Interviews and other Writings 1977–1984* (London, Routledge 1988) 86–95.
—— 'The Concern for Truth' in L Kritzman (ed), *Politics, Philosophy, Culture: Interviews and other Writings 1977–1984* (London, Routledge, 1988) 255–70.
—— *The Use of Pleasure: The History of Sexuality, Volume 2* (London, Penguin Books, 1992).
—— 'On the Genealogy of Ethics: An Overview of Work in Progress' in P Rabinow (ed), *Ethics: Subjectivity and Truth* (New York, The New Press, 1997) 253–81.
—— 'Polemics, Politics, and Problematizations' in P Rabinow (ed), *Ethics: Subjectivity and Truth* (New York, The New Press, 1997) 111–21.
—— 'Technologies of the Self' in P Rabinow (ed), *Ethics: Subjectivity and Truth* (New York, The New Press, 1997) 223–53.
—— 'The Birth of Biopolitics' in P Rabinow (ed), *Ethics: Subjectivity and Truth* (New York, The New Press, 1997) 73–79.
—— 'The Ethics of the Concern for Self as a Practice of Freedom' in P Rabinow (ed), *Ethics: Subjectivity and Truth* (New York, The New Press, 1997) 281–303.
—— 'The Masked Philosopher' in P Rabinow (ed), *Ethics: Subjectivity and Truth* (New York, The New Press 1997) 321–28.
—— 'The Social Triumph of the Sexual Will' in P Rabinow (ed), *Ethics: Subjectivity and Truth* (New York, The New Press, 1997) 157–62.
—— 'What is Enlightenment' in P Rabinow (ed), *Ethics: Subjectivity and Truth* (New York, The New Press, 1997) 303–21.
—— 'An Interview by Stephen Riggins' in P Rabinow (ed), *Ethics: Subjectivity and Truth* (New York, The New Press, 1997) 121–33.
—— 'Omnes et Singulatim': Toward a Critique of Political Reason' in J Faubion (ed), *Power* (New York, The New Press, 2000) 1–90.
—— 'Questions of Method' in J Faubion (ed), *Power* (New York, The New Press, 2000) 223–39.
—— 'So Is It Important to Think' in J Faubion (ed), *Power* (New York, The New Press, 2000) 454–59.
—— 'Space, Knowledge, and Power' in J Faubion (ed), *Power* (New York, The New Press, 2000) 349–65.
—— 'The Risks of Security' in J Faubion (ed), *Power* (New York, The New Press, 2000) 365–81.
—— 'The Subject and Power' in J Faubion (ed), *Power* (New York, The New Press, 2000) 326–49.
—— 'Truth and Power' in J Faubion (ed), *Power* (New York, The New Press, 2000) 111–34.
—— in J Pearson (ed), *Fearless Speech* (Los Angeles, Semiotext(e), 2001).
—— 'Entretien sur la prison: le livre et sa méthode' in D Defert and F Ewald (eds), *Dits et Ecrits II* (Paris, Gallimard, 2001) 740–53.
—— 'Des Traveaux' in D Defert and F Ewald (eds), *Dits et Ecrits IV* (Paris, Gallimard, 2001) 366–67.
—— 'Une Histoire Restée Muette' in D Defert and F Ewald (eds), *Dits et Ecrits I* (Paris, Gallimard, 2001) 545–49.
—— in M Bertani and A Fontana (eds), *"Society Must Be Defended": Lectures at the Collège de France, 1975–1976* (New York, Picador, 2003).

—— *Naissance de la Biopolitique: Cours au Collège de France, 1978–1979* (Paris, Seuil/Gallimard, 2004).
—— in F Gros (ed), *The Hermeneutics of the Subject: Lectures at the Collège de France 1981–1982* (New York, Palgrave, 2005).
—— in M Senellart (ed), *Security, Territory, Population: Lectures at the Collège de France 1977–1978* (New York, Picador, 2007).
Fraser, N, 'The Uses and Abuses of French Discourse Theories for Feminist Politics' (1990) 17(2) *Boundary* 82.
Freeman, S, *Rawls* (London, Routledge, 2007).
Freud, S, 'The Interpretation of Dreams' in J Strachey (ed), *The Standard Edition of the Complete Psychological Works of Sigmund Freud*, Volume 5 (London, Hogarth Press and the Institute of Psycho-Analysis, 1953) 339–628.
—— 'Group Psychology and the Analysis of the Ego' in J Strachey (ed), *The Standard Edition of the Complete Psychological Works of Sigmund Freud* (paperback) (New York, WW Norton & Company, 1959).
—— 'Civilization and Its Discontents' in J Strachey (ed), *The Standard Edition of the Complete Psychological Works of Sigmund Freud* (paperback) (New York, WW Norton & Company, 1961).
—— 'Mourning and Melancholia' in J Strachey (ed), *The Standard Edition of the Complete Psychological Works of Sigmund Freud*, Volume 14 (London, The Hogarth Press and the Institute of Psycho-Analysis, 1961) 237–302.
—— 'Narcissism: An Introduction' in J Strachey (ed), *The Standard Edition of the Complete Psychological Works of Sigmund Freud*, Volume 14 (London, The Hogarth Press and the Institute of Psycho-Analysis, 1961) 67–102.
—— 'A Child is Being Beaten': A Contribution to the Study of the Origin of Sexual Perversions' in P Rieff (ed), *Sexuality and the Psychology of Love* (New York, Collier Books, 1963) 123–34.
—— 'Economic Problem in Masochism' in J Strachey (ed), *The Standard Edition of the Complete Psychological Works of Sigmund Freud*, Volume 19 (London, The Hogarth Press and the Institute of Psycho-Analysis, 1974) 157–42.
—— 'The Ego and the Id' in J Strachey (ed), *The Standard Edition of the Complete Psychological Works of Sigmund Freud*, Volume 19 (London, The Hogarth Press and the Institute of Psycho-Analysis, 1974) 3–68.
Glendon, M, *Rights Talk: the Impoverishment of Political Discourse* (New York, Free Press, 1991).
Gordon, C, 'Governmental Rationality: An Introduction' in G Burchell, C Gordon and P Miller (eds), *The Foucault Effect: Studies in Governmentality with Two Lectures by and an Interview with Michel Foucault* (London, Harvester Wheatsheaf, 1991) 1–51.
Gould, D, 'Passionate Political Processes' in J Goodwin and J Jasper (eds), *Rethinking Social Movements: Structure, Meaning, and Emotion* (Lanham, Maryland, Rowman & Littlefield Publishers Inc, 2004) 155–75.
Greenawalt, K, *Religion and the Constitution, Volume 1: Free Exercise and Fairness* (New Jersey, Princeton University Press, 2006).
Gutmann, A, 'Democracy' in R Goodin and P Pettit (eds), *A Companion to Contemporary Political Philosophy* (Oxford, Blackwell Publishers, 1993) 411–21.

Gutmann, A and Thompson, D, *Democracy and Disagreement* (Cambridge, The Belknap Press of Harvard University Press, 1996).
Habermas, J, 'Discourse Ethics: Notes on a Program of Philosophical Justification' in *Moral Consciousness and Communicative Action* (Cambridge, Polity Press, 1990) 43–115.
—— 'Philosophy as Stand-In and Interpreter' in *Moral Consciousness and Communicative Action* (Cambridge, Polity Press, 1990) 1–20.
—— *Between Facts and Norms: Contributions to a Discourse Theory of Law and Democracy* (Cambridge, MIT Press, 1996).
—— 'Reconciliation through the Public Use of Reason' in C Cronin and P De Greiff (eds), *The Inclusion of the Other: Studies in Political Theory* (Cambridge, The MIT Press, 1998) 49–73.
—— 'The Critique of Reason, Unmasking the Human Sciences: Michel Foucault' in M Kelly (ed), *Critique and Power: Recasting the Foucault/Habermas Debate* (Cambridge, MIT Press, 1994) 47–77.
—— *Between Naturalism and Religion: Philosophical Essays* (Cambridge, Polity Press, 2008).
Han, B, *Foucault's Critical Project: Between the Transcendental and the Historical* (Stanford, Stanford University Press, 2002).
Hampton, J, 'Should Political Philosophy Be Done Without Metaphysics?' in H Richardson and P Weithman (eds), *The Philosophy of Rawls: A Collection of Essays*, Volume 5 (New York, Garland, 1999) 177–200.
Heidegger, M, *Sein und Zeit* (Tübingen, Max Niemeyer Verlag, 1993).
Hochschild, A, 'Emotion Work, Feeling Rules, and Social Structure' (1979) 85 *The American Journal of Sociology* 551.
Honig, B, *Political Theory and the Displacement of Politics* (Ithaca, Cornell University Press, 1993).
—— *Democracy and the Foreigner* (New Jersey, Princeton University Press, 2003).
Jessop, B, 'Political Ontology, Political Theory, Political Philosophy, and the Ironic Contingencies of Political Life' in R Schmidinger and C Sedmak (eds), *Der Mensch—ein Zoon Politikon: Gemeinschaft, Őffentlichkeit, Macht* (Darmstadt, Wissenschaftliche Buchgesellschaft, 2005) 189–208.
Kant, I, 'Beantwortung der Frage: Was ist Aufklärung?' (1784) 4 *Berlinische Monatschrift* 481.
—— 'What is Orientation in Thinking' in H Reiss (ed), *Kant: Political Writings*, 2nd edn (Cambridge, Cambridge University Press, 1991) 237–49.
—— 'An Answer to the Question: What is Enlightenment?' in J Schmidt (ed), *What is Enlightenment? Eighteenth-Century Answers and Twentieth-Century Questions* (Los Angeles, University of California Press, 1996) 58–64.
—— 'Groundwork of the Metaphysics of Morals' in *Immanuel Kant: Practical Philosophy* (Cambridge, Cambridge University Press, 1996) 37–108.
—— in M Gregor (ed), *Critique of Practical Reason* (Cambridge, Cambridge University Press, 1997).
—— in P Guyer and A Wood (eds), *Critique of Pure Reason* (Cambridge, Cambridge University Press, 1999).
—— in P Guyer and E Matthes (eds), *Critique of Judgment* (Cambridge, Cambridge University Press, 2000).

Kelly, M, *The Political Philosophy of Michel Foucault* (New York, Routledge, 2009).
Laden, A, 'The House that Jack Built: Thirty Years of Reading Rawls' (2003) 113 *Ethics* 367.
—— 'Taking the Distinction between Persons Seriously' (2004) 1 *Journal of Moral Philosophy* 277.
Laplanche, J and Pontalis, JB, *The Language of Psycho-Analysis* (New York, WW Norton & Company, Inc, 1973).
Lefort, C, *Democracy and Political Theory* (Cambridge, Polity Press, 1988).
Lemke, T, 'An Indigestible Meal? Foucault, Governmentality and State Theory' (2007) 8 *Distinktion: Scandinavian Journal of Social Theory* 43.
Lindahl, H, 'The Opening: Alegality and Political Agonism' in A Schaap (ed), *Law and Agonist Politics* (Surrey, Ashgate Publishing Limited, 2009) 57–70.
MacIntyre, A, *After Virtue: a Study in Moral Theory*, Second (corrected) edn (London, Duckworth, 1985).
Mahmood, S, *Politics of Piety: The Islamic Revival and the Feminist Subject* (New Jersey, Princeton University Press, 2004).
March, A, *Islam and Liberal Citizenship: the Search for an Overlapping Consensus* (Oxford, Oxford University Press, 2009).
Marchart, O, *Post-Foundational Political Thought: Political Difference in Nancy, Lefort, Badiou and Laclau* (Edinburgh, Edinburgh University Press, 2007).
Mayhew, D, 'Political Science and Political Philosophy: Ontological Not Normative' (2000) 33 *PS: Political Science and Politics* 192.
Menke, C, *Spiegelungen der Gleichheit: Politische Philosophie nach Adorno und Derrida* (Suhrkamp Verlag, Frankfurt am Main, 2004).
Moss, J, 'Foucault, Rawls and Public Reason' in J Moss (ed), *The Later Foucault: Politics and Philosophy* (London, SAGE Publications, 1998) 149–63.
Mouffe, C, *The Democratic Paradox* (London, Verso, 2000).
Nietzsche, F, *Beyond Good and Evil: Prelude to a Philosophy of the Future* (New York, Vintage Books, 1955).
—— 'Zur Genealogie der Moral' in G Colli and M Montinari (eds), *Kritischen Studienausgabe*, Volume 5 (München, Deutscher Taschenbuch Verlag, 1999) 247–412.
Nozick, R, *Anarchy, State and Utopia* (New York, Basic Books, 1974).
Nussbaum, M, *Women and Human Development: The Capabilities Approach* (Cambridge, Cambridge University Press, 2000).
—— *Liberty of Conscience: In Defense of America's Tradition of Religious Equality* (New York, Basic Books, 2008).
Owen, D, *Maturity and Modernity: Nietzsche, Weber, Foucault and the Ambivalence of Reason* (London, Routledge, 1994).
—— 'Wittgenstein and Genealogy' (2001) 2 *Nordic Journal of Philosophy* 5.
—— 'The Expressive Agon: On Political Agency in a Constitutional Democratic Polity' in A Schaap (ed), *Law and Agonist Politics* (Surrey, Ashgate Publishing Limited, 2009) 71–86.
Parekh, B, 'Superior People: The Narrowness of Liberalism from Mill to Rawls' (25 February 1994) *Times Literary Supplement* 11–13.
—— *Rethinking Multiculturalism: Cultural Diversity and Political Theory* (London, Palgrave, 2000).

Patton, P, 'Foucault's Subject of Power' in J Moss (ed), *The Later Foucault: Politics and Philosophy* (London, Sage Publications, 1998) 64–77.

Penalver, E, 'Note: The Concept of Religion' (1997) 107 *The Yale Law Journal* 791.

Pitkin, H, *Fortune is a Woman: Gender and Politics in the Thought of Niccolo Machiavelli* (Berkeley, University of California Press, 1984).

Quine, W, *Ontological Relativity and Other Essays* (New York, Columbia University Press, 1969).

Rabinow, P, 'Introduction' in P Rabinow (ed), *Ethics: Subjectivity and Truth* (New York, The New Press, 1997) xi–xlii.

Rawls, J, 'Justice as Fairness: Political not Metaphysical' (1985) 14 *Philosophy and Public Affairs* 223.

—— *Political Liberalism: With a New Introduction and the 'Reply to Habermas'* (New York, Columbia University Press, 1996).

—— *A Theory of Justice: Revised Edition* (Cambridge, The Belknap Press of Harvard University Press, 1999).

—— 'The Idea of Public Reason Revisited' in *The Law of Peoples with 'The Idea of Public Reason Revisited'* (Cambridge, Harvard University Press, 1999) 129–80.

—— *Justice as Fairness: A Restatement* (Cambridge, The Belknap Press of Harvard University Press, 2001).

—— 'Outline of a Decision Procedure for Ethics' in S Freeman (ed), *Collected Papers* (Cambridge, Harvard University Press, 2001) 1–19.

—— 'The Independence of Moral Theory' in S Freeman (ed), *Collected Papers* (Cambridge, Harvard University Press, 2001) 286–302.

—— in S Freeman (ed), *Lectures of the History of Political Philosophy* (Cambridge, The Belknap Press of Harvard University Press, 2007).

Richardson, H and Weithman, P (eds), *The Philosophy of Rawls: A Collection of Essays, Volume 1–5* (New York, Garland, 1999).

Rorty, R, 'Priority of Democracy to Philosophy' in H Richardson and P Weithman (eds), *The Philosophy of Rawls: A Collection of Essays, Volume 5* (New York, Garland, 1999) 201–22.

Rose, N and Miller, P, 'Political Power beyond the State: Problematics of Government' (1992) 43 *The British Journal of Sociology* 173.

Rosenthal, I, 'Dreadlocks, hanenkammen en de juridische constructie van een godsdienstig domein' in O Tans, W Veraart,B Wolthuis and J Zwart (eds), *De grenzen van het goede leven: rechtsgeleerde opstellen aangeboden aan Prof mr A Soeteman* (Nijmegen, Ars Aequi Libri, 2009) 63–72.

—— 'The Dutch Pastorate: Pluralism Without Pain?' in I ter Avest (ed), *Education in Conflict, Religious Diversity and Education in Europe*, Volume 9 (Muster, Waxmann, 2010) 59–82.

Sandel, M, *Liberalism and the Limits of Justice* (Cambridge, Cambridge University Press, 1982).

Schmidt, J (ed), *What is Enlightenment? Eighteenth-Century Answers and Twentieth-Century Questions* (Los Angeles, University of California Press, 1996).

Seneca, L, 'On Tranquility of Mind' in *Moral Essays*, Volume 2 (Cambridge, Harvard & Heineman, 1928) 202–85.

Smart, C, *Feminism and The Power of Law* (New York, Routledge, 1989).

Soeteman, A, 'De religieuze dwergwerper. Over de consequenties van een beroep op de grondrechten' (1992) 21 *Rechtsfilosofie & Rechtstheorie* 100.

Spencer, H, *The Principles of Sociology*, Volume II (Oxford, Williams and Norgate, 1902).

Stout, J, *Blessed Are the Organized: Grassroots Democracy in America* (New Jersey, Princeton University Press, 2010).

Sullivan, W, *Paying the Words Extra: Religious Discourse in the Supreme Court of the United States* (Cambridge, Harvard University Center for the Study of World Religions, 1994).

—— '"Competing Theories of Religion and Law in the Supreme Court of the United States: an Hasidic Case" in special volume entitled "Religion, Law and the Construction of Identities"' (1996) 43 *Numen* 184.

—— *The Impossibility of Religious Freedom* (New Jersey, Princeton University Press, 2005).

Taylor, C, *Human Agency and Language: Philosophical Papers I* (Cambridge, Cambridge University Press, 1985).

—— *Philosophy and the Human Sciences: Philosophical Papers 2* (Cambridge, Cambridge University Press, 1985).

—— *Sources of the Self: The Making of the Modern Identity* (Cambridge, Cambridge University Press, 1989).

—— *The Malaise of Modernity* (Toronto, House of Anansi Press, 1991).

—— 'The Politics of Recognition' in A Gutmann (ed), *Multiculturalism: Examining the Politics of Recognition* (New Jersey, Princeton University Press, 1994).

—— *Philosophical Arguments* (Cambridge, Harvard University Press, 1995).

Tomasi, J, *Liberalism beyond Justice: Citizens, Society, and the Boundaries of Political Theory* (New Jersey, Princeton University Press, 2001).

Tully, J, 'To Think and Act Differently: Foucault's Four Reciprocal Objections to Habermas' Theory' in S Ashenden and D Owen (eds), *Foucault contra Habermas: Recasting the Dialogue between Genealogy and Critical Theory* (London, Sage Publications, 1999) 90–142.

—— 'The Agonic Freedom of Citizens' (1999) 28 *Economy and Society* 161.

—— 'Political Philosophy as a Critical Activity,' (2002) 30 *Political Theory* 533.

Warner, M, *The Trouble with Normal: Sex, Politics, and the Ethics of Queer Life* (Cambridge, Harvard University Press, 1999).

Warren, M, 'What is Political Philosophy' (1989) 22 *PS: Political Science and Politics* 606.

White, S, *Sustaining Affirmation: The Strengths of Weak Ontology in Political Theory* (New Jersey, Princeton University Press, 2000).

Whitebrook, J, 'Freud, Foucault and "the Dialogue with Unreason"' (1999) 25 *Philosophy & Social Criticism 29.*

Winnicott, D, 'Aggression in Relation to Emotional Development' in *Through Paediatrics to Psycho-Analysis* (London, The Hogarth Press and the Institute of Psycho-Analysis, 1975) 204–18.

—— 'The Depressive Position in Normal Emotional Development' in *Through Paediatrics to Psycho-Analysis* (London, The Hogarth Press and the Institute of Psycho-Analysis, 1975) 262–75.

—— 'The Manic Defense' in *Through Paediatrics to Psycho-Analysis* (London, The Hogarth Press and the Institute of Psycho-Analysis, 1975) 129–144.

—— 'Mind and Its Relation to the Psyche-Soma' in *Through Paediatrics to Psycho-Analysis* (London, The Hogarth Press and the Institute of Psycho-Analysis, 1982) 243–54.
—— 'The Capacity for Concern' in *The Maturational Processes and the Facilitating Environment* (London, Karnac Books, 1990) 73–82.
—— 'Communicating and Not Communicating Leading to a Study of Certain Opposites' in *The Maturational Processes and the Facilitating Environment* (London, Karnac Books, 1990) 179–92.
—— 'Ego Distortion in Terms of True and False Self' in *The Maturational Process and the Facilitating Environment* (London, Karnac Books, 1990) 140–52.
—— 'Psycho-Analysis and The Sense of Guilt' in *The Maturational Process and the Facilitating Environment* (London, Karnac Books, 1990) 15–28.
—— 'The Theory of the Parent-Infant Relationship' in *The Maturational Processes and the Facilitating Environment* (London, Karnac Books, 1990) 37–55.
—— 'The Concept of a Healthy Individual' in *Home Is Where We Start From* (London, Penguin Books, 1990) 21–34.
—— 'Cure' in *Home Is Where We Start From* (London, Penguin Books, 1990) 112–22.
—— 'The Value of Depression' in *Home Is Where We Start From* (London, Penguin Books, 1990) 71–79.
—— 'Freedom' in *Home Is Where We Start From* (London, Penguin Books, 1990) 228–38.
—— 'Some Thoughts on the Meaning of the Word "Democracy"' in *Home Is Where We Start From* (London, Penguin Books, 1990) 239–59.
—— 'The Use of an Object and Relating through Identifications' in *Playing and Reality* (London, Routledge, 2005) 115–27.
—— 'Transitional Objects and Transitional Phenomena' in *Playing and Reality* (London, Routledge, 2005) 1–34.
Wittgenstein, L, *On Certainty* (Oxford, Blackwell Publishing, 1969).
Wolin, S, *Politics and Vision: Continuity and Innovation in Western Political Thought* (London, George Allen & Unwin Ltd, 1961).

Internet Resources

Expertvillage, How to Prepare for a Job Interview: The Importance of the Handshake in a Job Interview: http://www.youtube.com/watch?v=KwOskMOqGL4.
Marwijk, F van, 'Groeten bij komen en gaan': http://www.lichaamstaal.nl/groet.html.
Rutte, M, 'Lees hier de Brief van Mark': https://vvd.nl/nieuws/lees-hier-de-brief-van-mark/.

News Items

Buijs, G, 'De Christelijke Traditie Wijst de Weg naar een Nieuw Samenlevingsideaal' (2007) *NRC Handelsblad*, 13 January 15.
Mees, H, 'Moslimemancipatie' (2007) *NRC Handelsblad*, 26 January 7.
Peters, B, 'Cohen heeft gelijk, handen schudden hoeft niet' (2008) *Elsevier* 22 February.

US Jurisprudence

Davis v Beacon, 133 US 333 (1890).
Torasco v Watkins, 367 US 488 (1961).
United States v Seeger, 380 US 163 (1965).
Wisconsin v Yoder, 406 US 205 (1972).
Africa v Commonwealth of Pennsylvania, 662 F.2d 1025 (3rd Circuit 1981).

Dutch Jurisprudence

Centrale Raad van Beroep, May 7, 2009 (LJN: BI2440).
Commissie Gelijke Behandeling, November 7, 2006 (2006-220).
Gerechtshof 's-Gravenhage, April 10, 2012 (ECLI:NL:GHSGR:2012:BW1270).

Index

www.ingramcontent.com/pod-product-compliance
Lightning Source LLC
Chambersburg PA
CBHW071257180926
51613CB00001B/59
9781509912216